SPITFIRE
A Complete Fighting History

SPITFIRE

A Complete Fighting History

Alfred Price

Contents

A fine close-up of Supermarine's Senior Test Pilot Jeffrey Quill at the controls of the six-hundreth production Spitfire, serial P 9450, during her test flight in April 1940. This aircraft went to No 64 Squadron and later took part in the Battle of Britain.

This book is dedicated to the men and women who transposed the Spitfire — a mere fabrication of aluminium alloy, steel, rubber, perspex and a few other things — into the centre-piece of an epic without parallel in the history of aviation.

Foreword
Wing Commander R. R. Stanford-Tuck, DSO DFC

When Alfred Price invited me to write a foreword to this book I was, of course, honoured; but I had the passing thought "Oh dear! Another air book to wade through".

My fears were quite unfounded. As soon as I had read the first few pages I was held by it and read on almost non-stop till I finished with Maffre's excellent 'Spitfire Swansong'.

I think the average member of the public during the war thought of Spitfire pilots as being gay, carefree, beer-swilling types, rather like the rugger club members one could see being very noisy in any pub on a Saturday night. Indeed, with a very few exceptions, nothing could have been further from the truth. Wartime flying and especially air combat in Spitfires was a very cold, calculating, 'cat and mouse' affair. Woe betide any fighter pilot who was casual or who day dreamed — he would very soon 'cop it up the back end', or one of his pals would. However, in spite of their deadly business, the Spitfire pilots had one great advantage — their aircraft — which they came to love in that strange way that men will love their cars or boats.

I got my hands on a Spitfire for the first time on a crisp morning in December 1938. It belonged to No 19 Squadron at Duxford. From the first moment I sat quietly in the cockpit, going through all the instruments, cockpit checks, take-off and landing procedures, etc, I thought "If it comes to a war, this is the girl for me." Later that day, after my first flight, I felt this even more and for the first time in any aircraft I felt I was really part of it.

Just over a year later the tremendous thrill of getting my first Me 109 over Dunkirk justified my high opinion of the handling and fighting qualities of the Spitfire. As the years went past she carried me through countless combats and difficult situations and gave of her utmost every time it was demanded. She was a true thoroughbred.

I was so enthralled reading this book and recalling the memories it brought back of the airmen I had known, the flying, and the wonderful spirit which existed in those years, that I was very tempted to write considerably more; but that is not my part in this book.

All I can say, with sincerity, is that this is a fine book about a fine aircraft and fine men and add my thanks to Alfred Price for asking me to write these few words.

January 1974
Sandwich, Kent.

Introduction to Part One

Few would dispute the contention that the Spitfire was the most famous aircraft ever to serve in the Royal Air Force. Yet why should the Spitfire have been placed on a pinnacle, so that she overshadows other aircraft whose achievements were scarcely less significant? The reasons are many, as I shall try to show on the pages which follow.

Without doubt, the Spitfire was good. Reginald Mitchell's original design was sound to the point of brilliance, with an outstanding and fundamental simplicity. After Mitchell's tragic and untimely death Joseph Smith took over the leadership of the Supermarine design team and set about exploiting the Spitfire's potential. It reflects the greatest credit on the engineering staff that the often far-reaching improvements were incorporated without disrupting the flow of production.

The resultant fighter remained in production for twelve years which bracketted the hardest-fought and technically most innovatory war in history. No other airframe design was ever so continuously, aggressively, thoroughly and successfully developed. And no less successful and thorough was the parallel development of the two Rolls Royce engines, the Merlin and the Griffon, which powered the Spitfire.

At the end of its development life the Spitfire carried an engine giving more than twice the power and weighing about three-quarters more than the original, had had its maximum take-off weight more than doubled, its fire-power increased by a factor of five, its maximum speed increased by a quarter and its rate of climb almost doubled. Except for one notable hiatus, when initially it came up against the Focke Wulf 190, the Spitfire remained unsurpassed as a short-range air-superiority fighter for almost the whole of the nine years following its first flight; moreover, it remained in front-line service in the Royal Air Force for nine years after that.

When production finally ended, in 1949, a total of more than twenty-two thousand Spitfires and Seafires had been built. It served in more than thirty air forces on six continents; more than a thousand were delivered to the Soviet Air Force and a similar number went to the US Army Force.

When appraising the historical significance of a combat aircraft, the Spitfire cannot be considered in isolation; it must be compared as fully as possible with equivalent enemy aircraft. For this reason I have included verbatim accounts from the reports on wartime comparative trials between various marks of the Spitfire and captured examples of the Messerschmitt 109 and the Focke Wulf 190 and between the Seafire and the Japanese Zeke. Generally, though not invariably, the Spitfires and Seafires could hold their own with their contemporaries. To show that technology marches on, however, I have also included an account of the battle trial between a ^pitfire and a Mach 2 Lightning; as is to ɒe expected, the former was outclassed.

So far I have spoken only of the measurable ingredients of the Spitfire's greatness. More subjective, but equally important, are the memories of those who flew her. Those I have spoken to relate that she was a sheer delight to fly, and without exception speak of their association with the Spitfire with pride and infectious enthusiasm. No form of active warfare is clean; but surely one of the least dirty is that of the fighter pilot, who sallies out into the sky to defend his homeland and loved ones.

The war itself provided further leavening for the Spitfire's lustrous reputation. How many other fighters has the Royal Air Force possessed which, for a time at least, had a performance superior to those in any other air force? But because there was no war they came and went almost un-noticed by the man in the street. Had there been no Second World War, it is almost certain that the Spitfire would have remained just one more of those pretty little fighters whose aerobatics delighted the crowds at air displays. The Spitfire achieved prominence not only because of what she could do, but because it was available at a time when Britain's needs — both defensive and morale — were greatest.

Yet there were other aircraft about which many of these things could have been said, but which never possessed the glamour of the Spitfire. In truth, the Spitfire achieved fame in such gigantic measure because she touched the very heart of the nation. She became the symbol of defiance during the grim days of the war and those who flew her were acclaimed as the valorous champions of their time. One rather unfortunate result was that the Spitfire came to overshadow much around her particularly, during the Battle of Britain, its comrade-in-arms the Hurricane. Despite the fact that the Hurricane was present in far greater numbers, saw much more of the action and shot down somewhat more enemy aircraft during the battle, a surprisingly large number of people still believe that the Spitfire almost alone won the great fight for survival in 1940.

When thinking of the Spitfire one's mind automatically turns to the well-known aces who flew her, men like 'Johnnie' Johnson, Douglas Bader, Robert Stanford-Tuck and Al Deere. These men have already told their stories in books which have, rightly, come to be numbered amongst the classic works on aerial warfare; but I am sure that they would agree that, even collectively, their own experiences represent only a minute fraction of those on the Spitfire which are worthy of recollection. To prevent repetition, therefore, in this book I have made use of accounts of those who, though less-well-known, also played important parts in the Spitfire story and who, in some cases, can judge her from viewpoints rather different from those of the fighter ace. I should like to take this opportunity to express my deep gratitude to those whose accounts appear in this book: Air Commodore Cozens, Colonel von Reisen, Group Captain Oxspring, Warrant Officer Tandy, Mr Alex Henshaw, Mr Ervin Miller, Mr Frank Hercliffe, Captain Law, Wing Commander Costain, Mr Raymond Baxter, Sir Morien Morgan, Wing Commander Middlebrook, Mr Eric Newton and Air Vice Marshal Nicholls. The words are theirs, I merely wrote them down. I am also grateful to Mr Ronnie Mogg for permission to use a verse from 'Fighters at Dawn'.

In choosing photographs for this book my primary aims have been to pick a selection which will give the broadest view of the Spitfire and the sort of war in which she fought and also to do full justice to her beauty. In respect of the last I believe that Charles Brown's pictures are without equal. I make no apology for using some of his photographs which have been published before; they are the work of a true artist and I cannot believe that their appearance here will give other than pleasure. For the other photographs, I have been extremely fortunate in having many good friends who generously lent me unpublished material from their collections. In particular I should like to tender my thanks to Jim Oughton, Derek Wood, Chris Shores, John Taylor, Mike Garbett, Brian Goulding, Charles Cain, Chaz Bowyer, Roger Freeman, 'Jackson' Dymond, Alex Lumsden, Bob Jones and Bruce Rigglesford. Most of all I should like to thank Ted Hooton, for his welcome encouragement and sound advice, for his painstaking checking of my manuscript and captions and for the rescue operation he mounted one cold, dark night. Credit is also due to Mike Brooke, who produced the line drawings.

Finally, I should like to thank my dear wife Jane for creating the domestic conditions which make authorship possible.

ALFRED PRICE

11

1
A Fighter is Born

Below: Reginald Mitchell, the Chief Designer at the Supermarine Company, led the team which created the Spitfire. Dogged by ill-health throughout his time on the project, he died in June 1937 at the age of 42 having seen only one example of the fighter completed, but with the knowledge that more than 300 were on order for the RAF.

Right, Below right: On March 22nd 1937 the prototype was undergoing high 'G' turns and looping trials from Martlesham Heath, to test the effectiveness of modified elevator gearing to overcome previous elevator buffeting. Suddenly the oil pressure fell to zero on the gauge and the engine began to run rough; the pilot cut the engine, and skilfully belly-landed the precious new aircraft on heath land beside the Woodbridge-Bawdsey road. The aircraft suffered only superficial damage and was easily repaired. Examination of the engine revealed that several connecting rods and big-ends had failed and the former had punched large holes through the crankcase. The cause of the trouble was oil starvation due to the application of 'G' and as a result the oil system of subsequent Merlins was modified. Note the changes in detail made to the prototype, since her first flight: the reduced size of the rudder horn balance, the new exhaust manifolds, the fitting of a castoring tail wheel instead of the skid, and the installation of the armament of eight machine guns (the muzzle flash eliminators of two of the Brownings can be seen protruding through the leading edge of the starboard wing). Note also the two raised panels above the trailing edge of the wing, to indicate to the pilot that the flaps were down; later Spitfires would have only a single panel on each wing for this purpose.

14

Left, Below left: The prototype Spitfire seen in her original form, pictured at the airfield at Eastleigh near Southampton probably just before her first flight on March 5th 1936. At this time the aircraft was unpainted and lacked fairings for the undercarriage legs; the gunports were empty, except for the port outer which housed the pitot tube.

Below: One of the most beautiful ever taken of the Spitfire, this photograph by Charles Brown depicts the prototype in the autumn of 1937 after she had been fully modified to Mark I standard; note the distinctive triple exhaust manifolds, a feature of the early marks of this aircraft. Like all the Charles

Brown photographs in this book, this one was taken with a Zeis Palmos plate camera with a maximum shooting rate of about one per minute. Amongst his friends this cumbersome piece of equipment was something of a joke, but few people laughed at the results he achieved with it.

2
Into Service
Air Commodore Henry Iliffe Cozens, CB AFC

Henry Cozens leading six of
his brand new Spitfires in
formation, for the benefit of
an official photographer in a
Blenheim, on October 31st
1938. The squadron number
on the tails was painted on
shortly before this flight and
was removed soon afterwards.

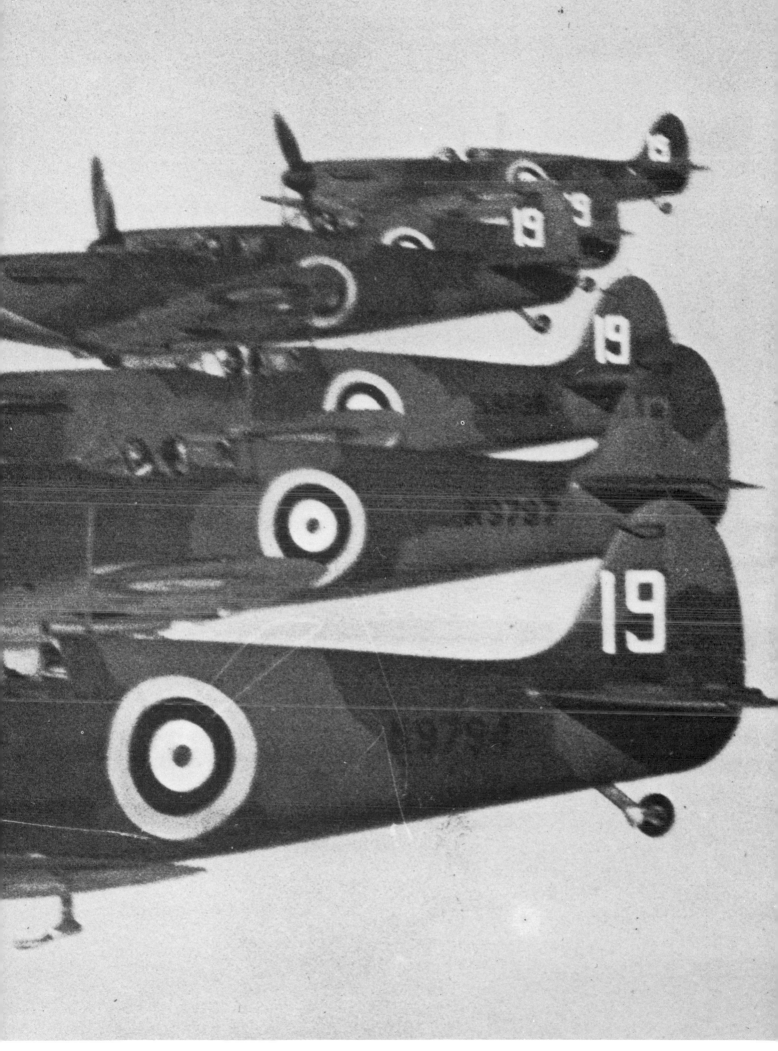

Right: K9789, the first Spitfire to be delivered to No 19 Squadron, arrived on August 4th 1938. She was to remain in front-line service until 1941, when she was sent to No 61 Operational Training Unit; early in 1943 she was relegated to service at a technical training school, before finally being scrapped in 1945.

Above: Henry Cozens pictured as a Flight Lieutenant, in the Royal Air Force officers' full-dress uniform of the 1930s; note the small busby. His career as a fighter pilot began on Sopwith Snipes in 1923 and before he retired he had flown Meteors and Vampires.

During the summer of 1938 the first Spitfires were issued to an RAF squadron, No 19 at Duxford. Henry Cozens commanded the Squadron then and his account of the introduction of the new high-performance monoplane into service conveys well the mood in the RAF — the finest flying club in the world — at that time.

In December 1937 I was promoted to Squadron Leader and posted to take command of No 19 Squadron based at Duxford near Cambridge. At that time we flew the Gloster Gauntlet, a biplane with an unimpressive performance compared with the sort of opposition we were likely to meet if it did come to a war with Germany. I heard a buzz that the first of the new Spitfire fighters were to be issued to a squadron based at Catterick in Yorkshire. I thought it might be possible to change this, so I got in touch with one of my friends at Fighter Command headquarters and asked him whether he thought the idea of sending the first of these new fighters so far north was sound. There was bound to be a lot of Air Ministry interest in the aircraft and Catterick was rather a long way from London; and besides, it was a notoriously small airfield. Might not Duxford, a larger airfield much closer to London, be more suitable? My questions must have prompted the correct line of thought because a few weeks later I heard that my own squadron, and No 66 which shared Duxford with us, would be the first to receive Spitfires.

On August 4th 1938, amid much excitement, we received the first of the new aircraft: Spitfire K 9789. I made my first flight in her on the 11th. At that time there were no pilots' notes on the Spitfire, no conversion courses and, of course, no dual control aircraft. I was shown round the cockpit, given a cheerful reminder to remember to extend the undercarriage before I landed, wished 'Good Luck', and off I went.

After flying the Gauntlet, my first impression of the Spitfire was that her acceleration seemed rather slow and the controls were a lot heavier than I had expected. Thinking about it afterwards, I realised why: the Gauntlet took off at about 70mph and was flat-out at about 220mph; the Spitfire took off at about the same speed but could do well over 350mph — in other words the speed range was much greater, and although the acceleration was in fact greater it took somewhat longer to reach its maximum speed. Moreover, as she neared the top end of her speed range, the Spitfire's controls became beautifully light.

On August 16th I collected the second of the Spitfires for Duxford, K 9792. Nos 19 and 66 Squadrons were ordered to carry out the intensive flying trials using these two aircraft; our instructions were to fly them both to 400 hours as rapidly as possible and report our findings. The two squadrons set about the task with enthusiasm and the two aircraft were airborne almost continuously from dawn to dusk; alone, I amassed 24 flying hours in the Spitfire before the end of August. We had a few adventures. I remember one fine afternoon seeing a Spitfire taxying in and, as usual, the groundcrew were all out watching her. Suddenly one of the undercarriage legs started to fold. In no time people were running towards the aircraft from all directions and they grabbed the wing and managed to hold it up until the propeller stopped. The precious fighter escaped damage.

During these intensive flying trials Air Chief Marshal Sir Hugh Dowding, the C in C Fighter Command, visited us at Duxford. I showed him over the Spitfire and then we went to my office. When we were alone together he told me the position regarding this aircraft, it came to a war. He said that the Hurricane was a great success and it could take on the Junkers 88 and the other German aircraft; but the Messerschmitt 109 was more than a match. So his question was: could the Spitfire take on the 109? If it could, then Fighter Command was prepared for war. If it could not, then we should have to think again.

As the intensive flying trial progressed I became convinced that the Spitfire could indeed take on the Messerschmitt 109 — and any other fighter then in existence. But that was not to say that she was perfect. For one thing the engines of these first Spitfires were difficult to start: the low-geared electric starter rotated the propeller blades so slowly that when a cylinder fired there was usually insufficient push to flick the engine round to fire the next; there would be a 'puff' noise, then the propeller would resume turning on the starter. Also, the early Merlin engines leaked oil terribly; it would run from the engine, down the fuselage and finally got blown away somewhere near the tail wheel. Yet another problem was what we called 'Spitfire Knuckle': when pumping up the undercarriage it was all too easy to rasp our knuckles on the side of the cockpit. There was a further problem for the taller pilots, who were always hitting their heads on the inside of the low cockpit canopy.

When we were about half way through the 400 hour trial I had a chat with Squadron Leader Fuller-Good who commanded 66 and we agreed that we had learned just about all we could from the exercise. I felt that if the First World War was anything to go by, no fighter was likely to last in action for anything like 400 hours. All we were now going

to find out was how to wear out two perfectly good Spitfires. So together we wrote an interim report on the new fighter and off it went. That set the wheels in motion and a few weeks later we received a high-powered deputation from the Air Ministry, Fighter Command Headquarters, Supermarine, Rolls Royce and Goodness knows where. We discussed the shortcomings at length and they promised to do what they could to overcome them. I remember that my own bandaged 'Spitfire Knuckle' made a particularly strong impression on the Supermarine team. The improvements we asked for were all incorporated in our own or later marks of the Spitfire. The simpler things like the bulged cockpit canopy to make life easier for the taller pilots and the faster starter motor, we received quite quickly. The improved oil seals for the Merlin took a little longer and leaking oil did remain

Top: First Spitfire write-off: on November 3rd 1938, with a total flying time of just over forty-one hours, K9792 ended her career at the close of Pilot Officer G. Sinclair's first flight in the type. The cause of the accident was a faulty axle stub which sheared during the landing. Sinclair was unhurt.

Above: Six of the original Spitfire pilots on No 19 Squadron: from left to right, Flying Officers Pace, Robinson, Clouston, Banham, Ball and, in the chair, Thomas.

Right: In an effort to reduce exhaust glare during night flying, Spitfire K9787 was tested with a new set of streamlined exhausts; although they were slightly better than the standard type, the improvement was not great enough to warrant production.

Far right: Press Day at Duxford, May 4th 1939 and for the first time No 19 Squadron was able to show off its new fighters on the the ground. By this time the squadron number on the fin has given way to the code-letters WZ on the fuselage and the white and yellow portions of the fuselage and above-wing roundels had been painted over in red and blue respectively. Other points of interest show up on this exceptionally clear Charles Brown photograph: the bead foresight for the guns, on the engine cowling mid-way between the pilot and the propeller; the protruding flash eliminators of the Browning guns; the bulged canopy hood on the third aircraft in line, contrasting with the flat early hood of the aircraft in front of it (this modification was not as some accounts have said to improve rearward visibility, but merely to allow greater headroom for the taller pilots); the undercarriage down indicator bar protruding from the top of the wing of the nearest aircraft; and the early type unarmoured windscreens and thin supporting masts for the radio aerials.

something of a problem throughout the Spitfire's service life. The later Mark I Spitfires had an engine-driven hydraulic system to raise and lower the undercarriage, which did away with the need to pump and resultant 'Spitfire Knuckle'.

During the early days we tried several different types of airscrew on the Spitfire. The original two-bladed fixed-pitch wooden propeller was designed to give its best performance at the high end of the performance envelope, but this produced serious disadvantages at the lower speeds; for example, during take-off it was almost stalled. We tried to get over this at first with a three-bladed propeller with a finer pitch, then with a three-bladed two-pitch propeller with one setting for take-off and another for high speed. I did not like the two-pitch propeller at all. It was far too easy to leave it in coarse pitch for take-off and that could give rise to a dangerous situation. There was no half-way house: the answer was the constant speed propeller, which automatically gave the correct pitch settings for all airspeeds. Early in 1939 I flew a trial with one of these and I remember being much impressed with the improvement in acceleration and general handling at low speeds. Fortunately, by the opening of the Battle of Britain, the operational Spitfires all had constant speed propellers.

Throughout the late summer and autumn of 1938 we received Spitfires at the rate of about one per week and the

Right: Spitfire I, Layout of cockpit.

Far right: The cockpit detail of one of the early production Mark I Spitfires; key:
1. Fixed Ring Gunsight.
2. Airspeed Indicator.
3. Artificial Horizon.
4. Rate of Climb and Descent Indicator.
5. Engine RPM Gauge.
6. Boost Gauge.
7. Fuel Pressure Gauge.
8. Oil Pressure Gauge.
9. Oil Temperature Gauge.
10. Radiator Temperature Gauge.
11. Directional Gyro.
12. Turn and Bank Indicator.
13 and 14. Fuel Contents Gauges.
15. 'Ki-gass' Fuel Priming Pump.
16. Priming Pump Selector Cock.
17. Fuel Cocks.
18. Gun Firing Button.
19. Tray for Magnetic Compass (compass not fitted to aircraft in photograph).
20. Hydraulic Handpump.
21. Undercarriage Position Selector.
22. Signalling Switch Box.
23. Control Column.
24. Rudder Pedals.

year was almost over before we were at our full strength of sixteen aircraft. Until we were up to strength and fully operational with Spitfires, we held on to our earlier Gauntlets and still flew them from time to time.

Jeffrey Quill, the Senior Test Pilot at Supermarine, was a frequent visitor to Duxford to see how we were getting on. One of the points he was a little anxious about was the size of the flaps on the Spitfire. Did we think they were too large for so light an aircraft? I agreed that they were a bit fierce, but I told him "Sooner or later people are going to hang things on this aircraft. I don't know what they will be, but I am certain that it will happen. And with the performance improvements planned by Supermarine the Spitfire is not going to get any *lighter,* is she?" He agreed that

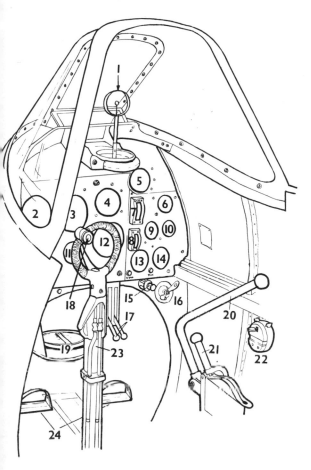

she would not, so we thought it better to leave the flaps alone and see what happened. As everybody now knows, the Spitfire more than doubled in weight during her development life; and to the very end the flaps were the same as they were in 1938.

When the Spitfires first arrived at Duxford they had lacked guns, but during the months that followed guns were fitted. I had my first experience of firing on November 3rd, at the range at Sutton Bridge; as it happened, it was a night sortie. I had expected a few sparks from each gun, but I was in no way prepared for the Brock's Benefit which came from each wing: the long tongues of flame lept out about ten feet in front of each gun. And the recoil of the eight fast-firing Brownings, after the two Vickers guns I had been used to in the Gauntlet, was unexpectedly severe; it slowed down the aircraft as though one had put the brakes on.

In January 1940 I left Duxford to take up a staff appointment. By then the Royal Air Force had more than a dozen squadrons fully equipped with the Spitfire, and several others were about to receive it. We on Nos 19 and 66 Squadrons had introduced the type into service and, I am proud to say, we did it without losing a man.

Below: Three new Spitfires pictured taking off from Eastleigh, at about the time of the outbreak of the Second World War. Up to September 3rd 1939 the Royal Air Force had accepted delivery of a total of 306 Spitfires, of which 187 formed the full equipment of ten squadrons (Nos 19, 41, 54, 65, 66, 72, 74, 602, 603 and 611) and part of the equipment of one more (No 609). A further 83 Spitfires were distributed as follows: at maintenance units, either in storage of for the fitting of operational equipment, 71; employed on trials at the makers or the various service test establishments, 11; and one had been allocated to a training unit. The remaining 36 Spitfires had been previously written-off in accidents.

3
First Encounter
Colonel Horst von Riesen

Spitfires of No 603 Squadron, the first unit to achieve a kill with the new fighter.

Above: Although the Spitfire pilots identified the enemy aircraft they engaged on October 16th 1939 as Heinkel 111s, they were in fact Junkers 88s like the one depicted here; during the action two of these bombers were shot down and others, including von Riesen's, suffered damage.

Right: Horst von Riesen who, as a young Leutnant, found himself confronted by Spitfires on the first day the new British fighter engaged the enemy: October 16th 1939.

On October 16th 1939 Spitfires of Nos 602 and 603 Squadrons took off to intercept a small force of German bombers attacking shipping in the Firth of Forth. For the first time, the new RAF fighter was to go into action against the enemy. Two of the German bombers were shot down, one of them being credited to Squadron Leader E. Stevens, the commander of No 603 Squadron. During the same engagement Pilot Officers Morton and Robertson, also of No 603 Squadron, reported intercepting an enemy aircraft 'thought to be an He111' over Rosyth and pursuing it out to sea at very low level. When they finally broke off their attacks the bomber's starboard engine was observed 'not running'. In fact the German bombers involved in the day's

attack on the Firth of Forth were not Heinkel 111s, as was widely reported in British accounts of the action, but Junkers 88s. And Horst von Riesen should know — because he was one of those on the receiving end!

In the autumn of 1939 I was a young Leutnant serving with the First *Gruppe* of *Kampfgeschwader 30,* based at Westerland on the island of Sylt. At that time we were the only unit in the *Luftwaffe* to be equipped with our fast new long range dive-bomber — the Junkers 88.

Initially our activities had kept us well clear of the British defences. But on the morning of October 16th one of our reconnaissance aircraft spotted the battlecruiser *HMS Hood* entering the Firth of Forth. We received orders to attack her, if we could catch her in open water; but at that stage of the war both sides tried hard to avoid causing civilian casualties and we had the strictest orders that if she was in harbour we were either to attack other warships outside, or else return with our bombs.

Nine of our aircraft were bombed-up and took off, but when we arrived over Rosyth we found Hood safely in dock — where we were not allowed to harm her. Just to the east of the Forth Bridge there were some small warships, however, and

I decided to attack one of these. I selected one and carried out a diving attack, but scored only a near-miss.

Then, as I was climbing away, my radio operator suddenly shouted over the intercom that there were several fighters about two kilometres away, diving on us. I looked in the direction he was pointing and as soon as I saw them I knew that I would need all the speed I could possibly squeeze out of my Junkers if we were to escape. I pushed down the nose and, throttles wide open, dived for the sea. But it was no good. The Spitfires, as we soon recognized them to be, had had the advantage of speed and height from the start and they soon caught up with us. As I sped down the Firth of Forth just a few metres above the surface, I could see clearly the splashes from the shells from the shore batteries, as they too joined in the unequal battle.

Now I thought I was finished. Guns were firing at me from all sides, and the Spitfires behind seemed to be taking turns at attacking. But I think my speed gave them all a bit of a surprise — I was doing more than 400 kilometres per hour (250mph), which must have been somewhat faster than any other bomber they had trained against at low level — and of course I jinked from side to side to make their aim as difficult as possible. At one stage in the pursuit I remember looking down and seeing what looked like rain drops hitting the water. It was all very strange. Then I realised what it was: those splashes marked the impact of bullets being aimed at me from above!

I had only one ally: time. Every minute longer the Junkers kept going meant another seven kilometres further out to sea and further from the Spitfires' base; and I had far more fuel to play with than they did. Finally, however, the inevitable happened: after a chase of more than twenty minutes there was a sudden 'phooff' and my starboard motor suddenly disappeared from view in a cloud of steam. One of the enemy bullets had pierced the radiator, releasing the vital coolant and without it the motor was finished. There was no alternative but to shut it down before it burst into flames.

My speed sagged to 180kph (112mph) — almost on the stall when flying asymmetric — and we were only a few metres above the waves. Now the Junkers was a lame duck. But when I looked round, expecting to see the Spitfires curving in to finish us off, there was no sign of them. They had turned round and gone home.

Even so, we were in a difficult position. With that airspeed there lay

Below: Spitfire Is of No 74 Squadron, pictured at Hornchurch early in 1940. The second Spitfire in the line would appear to be a new arrival, because her squadron letters had not yet been painted on.

ahead of us a flight of nearly four hours, if we were to get back to Westerland. During our training we had been told that a Ju 88 would not maintain height on one engine — and we were only barely doing so. Should we ditch there and then? I thought no; it was getting dark, nobody would pick us up and we would certainly drown or die of exposure. An alternative was to turn round and go back to Scotland, and crash land there. One of my crew suggested this but one of the others — I don't know who — shouted over the intercom 'No, no, never! If we go back there the Spitfires will certainly get us!' He was right. The thought of going back into that hornets' nest horrified us. So we decided to carry on as we were and see what happened. We prefered to risk death from drowing or the cold, rather than have to face those Spitfires again.

Gradually, as we burnt our fuel and the aircraft became lighter, I was able to coax the Junkers a little higher. The remaining motor, though pressed to the limit, continued running and finally we did get back to Westerland.

So it was that I survived my first encounter with Spitfires. I would meet them again during the Battle of Britain, over the Mediterranean and during the Battle of Sicily. It was not a pleasant experience.

Above, Right: With friends like that who needs enemies? Flight Lieutenant Wilfred Clouston of No 19 Squadron standing beside his aircraft as she lay on Newmarket racecourse, following an adventurous flight on March 4th 1940. He had been leading his section in a line astern formation when his No 2 collided with his tail and the propeller slashed away most of his tail control surfaces; skilfully he belly-landed the Spitfire, without incurring further major damage. Clouston displayed similar flying ability during the Battle of Britain, in which he was credited with twelve victories.

Right: An historic photograph: taken at Le Bourget airport, Paris, on May 16th 1940, it shows the Flamingo airliner which took Mr Churchill to discuss with the French premier the provision of the Royal Air Force fighters for the Battle of France. In the background may be seen the Spitfires of Blue Section of No 92 Squadron, which provided the escort.

28

Aces to be: Blue Section of No 92 Squadron, pictured in May 1940; from left to right, Pilot Officer Bob Holland (later credited with 13 victories), Flying Officer Robert Stanford-Tuck (later 29 victories) and Pilot Officer Alan Wright (later 10 victories). All three opened their scores while covering the Dunkirk evacuation. Beneath the open hood of the Spitfire in the background, it is just possible to make out the GR code letters carried by No 92 Squadron's aircraft for a short period early in the war.

GENERAL COMBAT REPORT   May 25th 1940

No 92 Squadron while on patrol Boulogne—Calais—Dunkirk from 1720 to 1920 hours sighted a large formation of enemy aircarft over Calais at 8-10,000ft. About 30 enemy aircraft, mostly ME 110s, were ahead and behind them a further group of 15-20 aircaraft of types not identified, but including Ju 87s and Ju 88s. Some aircraft started dive-bombing attacks on Boulogne harbour, with others circling in the vicinity. No 92 Squadron at 4,000ft climbed to engage and a series of dog fights ensued, mainly with Me 110s. Blue 1 states that he saw some Hurricanes already engaging the enemy, but as the sky was so full of aircraft a clear statement of the situation is impossible. As a result of the dogfight 7 Me 110s were definitely shot down, 5 Me 110s and 2 Ju 88s probably shot down. Most of our aircraft were hit many times.

Pilots state that the Me 110 evasive tactics are a steep turn towards the Spitfire's tail, to enable the rear gunner to open fire.

About 20 Me 110s were seen flying in line astern in a right circle round the bombers, which was very difficult to attack. The Me 110 is not so fast as the Spitfire on the level, but very good in a fast turn and a steep dive, though the Spitfire can hold it on a turn. They appear to use the stall turn a great deal.

Enemy camouflage standard.

During the first two minutes of the combat, a continuous transmission in German was heard on the R/T.

The following is an assessment of the aircraft shot down by the pilots:

	Certain	Possible
F/Lt Tuck	1 Me 110	1 Me 110
P/O Holland	2 Me 110	1 Ju 88
P/O Wright	1 Me 110	—
P/O Williams	1 Me 110	1 Me 110
Sgt Havercroft	—	1 Me 110
P/O Edwards	—	1 Ju 88
Sgt Barraclough	—	1 Me 110
P/O Bartley	2 Me 110	—

Sqn Ldr Bushell, F/Lt Gillies and Sgt Klipsche are missing (one Spitfire was seen to crash to the ground). F/Lt Green landed at Hawkinge with a bullet wound in his leg.

An Even Match

During the early war period, from September 1939 to May 1940, the Spitfire squadrons all remained in Britain and had no opportunity to go into action against their opposite numbers in the *Luftwaffe*. The lull in the west came to an abrupt halt on May 10th, however, when the Germans launched their great offensive into Holland, Belgium and France. Soon there was no need for the Spitfire squadrons to go overseas to new bases in order to meet the enemy; instead, the land battle was being fought on territory within even their limited radius of action from airfields in south-eastern England. From May 12th, when No 66 Squadron's Spitfires mounted a patrol over The Hague, the new fighter was committed to action in steadily greater numbers. At last the Spitfire was to come face-to-face with its *Luftwaffe* equivalent — the Messerschmitt 109E.

The initial encounters between these two adversaries were usually inconclusive, though they did demonstrate that they were obviously closely comparable in performance. Also during May 1940, however, in the still-peaceful skies over the Royal Aircraft Establishment at Farnborough, a Spitfire I and a captured Messerschmitt 109E fought a series of mock combats as part of a trial intended to determine the strengths and weaknesses of each compared with the other.

To provide a fair picture of the capability of each aircraft, they were flown in pre-planned tactical exercises. In the first of these, flown at 6,000 feet, the Messerschmitt was positioned ahead of the Spitfire and its pilot attempted to shake off his pursuer by means of a horizontal speed run, three of four tight turns in each direction, a dive, then a steep climb; afterwards the two aircraft changed positions and repeated the procedure, then engaged in a short free-play fight.

In level flight, the maximum speeds of the two aircraft were about equal. During the turns, flown at speeds between 90 and 220mph, the Spitfire had little difficulty in keeping behind; nor did the dive present the pursuer with any great problem. When the Messerschmitt was pulled out of the dive and into a steep climb at low airspeed, however, the Spitfire — whose optimum climb rate was achieved at a flatter angle but a higher airspeed — had difficulty in following; and even when she could follow, the pilots found it almost impossible to hold their gunsight on the target.

When the Spitfire was in front, it was clear that in a turning match at medium altitude and in the middle of her speed range, she was easily the better aircraft; also, with her superior rate of roll, she could shake off her pursuer by means of a flick half-roll and quick pull out of the

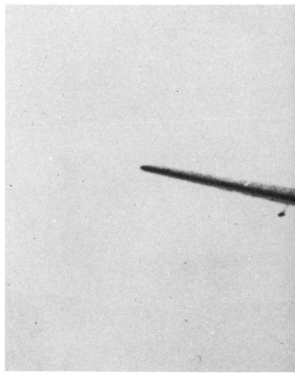

subsequent dive. The Messerschmitt pilot found the latter particularly difficult to counter, because when he rolled after the Spitfires his speed built up rapidly in the steep dive and his elevator became so heavy that a quick pull out was impossible. Of course, these advantages could be exploited only if the Spitfire was flown to her limits; during subsequent trial flights there were several occasions when the Messerschmitt succeeded in remaining on the tail of the Spitfire merely because the latter's pilot lacked experience and failed to tighten his turn sufficiently, for fear of stalling and spinning.

Manoeuverability at medium speeds is only one of many factors which can be turned to advantage in an air combat, however, and two points emerged from the trial whose significance was to be confirmed again and again during the great air battles soon to follow. The first was that if the Messerschmitt pilot pushed his aircraft into a sudden bunt and the Spitfire tried to follow, the latter's engine would splutter and stop because the normal float-type carburettor fitted to the Merlin ceased to deliver fuel; the Messerschmitt's Daimler Benz engine had direct fuel injection and did not suffer from this failing (later, Spitfire pilots learned to half-roll and pull down when following bunting Messerschmitt 109s, using an aileron turn to get back upright when they were established in the dive. It was not an ideal solution, but it did enable a good pilot to maintain the pursuit). The second point was that during diving manoeuvers at high speeds the controls, and particularly the ailerons, of both aircraft became progressively heavier; at 400mph the Spitfire's rate of roll was about the same as that of the Messerschmitt 109, with both pilots having to pull as hard as they could on the stick to get one-fifth aileron movement and both aircraft requiring about four seconds to roll through 45 degrees. Under these conditions the Spitfire ceased to have any clear advantage in manoeuverability and, as German fighter pilots soon discovered in combat, so long as they kept their speed up and evaded the Spitfire pilot would find it hard to bring his guns to bear.

One important lesson failed to emerge from the Farnborough trial: the general superiority of the German fighter at altitudes above 20,000 feet. Before the war, and during its early stages, many experts in Britain considered high altitude dogfighting to be so unlikely as not to warrant a trial; they would shortly learn otherwise.

Overall, however, the Spitfire I and the Messerschmitt 109E matched each other fairly evenly. If they fought, victory would almost invariably go to the side which was the more alert, which held the initiative, which understood the strengths and weaknesses of its opponents aircraft, which showed the better team work and which, in the last resort, could shoot the more accurately.

Below: The Messerschmitt 109E, which equipped virtually the whole of the German single-engined fighter force throughout 1940.

4
Battle of Britain

This Spitfire of No 92
Squadron crash-landed at
Biggin Hill in September
1940. Note the wheel and
undercarriage leg lying on
the grass just behind the
aircraft.

Left: Pilots of No 92 Squadron at readiness at Bibury, during the Battle of Britain. On the left is Flight Lieutenant Charles Kingcombe, one of the unit's top scorers, who during the battle was credited with three enemy aircraft destroyed, four probably destroyed and eight damaged. The pilot with his back to the camera is wearing a captured German life jacket, a trophy with few advantages over its British counterpart.

Left: Illustrating the mixed origins of the men who fought in the Battle of Britain are these four officers of No 19 Squadron pictured at Fowlmere: from left to right, Pilot Officer W. 'Jock' Cunningham, from Glasgow; Sub Lieutenant 'Admiral' Blake, a Fleet Air Arm pilot on loan to the RAF; Flight Lieutenant F. Dolezal, a Czech who had been in his own country's air force before the Germans took over, who had escaped and joined the French Air Force, escaped again and was now with the RAF; Flying Officer F. Brinsden, a New Zealander. Blake was killed in action right at the end of the battle, on October 29th, when his Spitfire was shot down by a Messerschmitt 109.

Above: Flying Officer 'Uncle Sam' Leckrone, an American volunteer, fought during the Battle with Nos 616 and 19 Squadrons; he later became a founder member of No 71, the first 'Eagle' Squadron.

Left: Groundcrewmen clustered round a Spitfire of No 92 Squadron during a rapid turn round, probably at Biggin Hill in September 1940.

Right: During a fight with Messerschmitt 109s on August 9th, Sergeant H. Mann of No 64 Squadron had a cannon shell jam his control column; he managed to land his Spitfire, albeit heavily, at Kenley.

Top: **Pilot Officer Alan Wright of No 92 Squadron** suffered hits to his aircraft during a fight with Messerschmitts on September 9th; one 7.9mm bullet fired from behind passed through his perspex hood, nicked the windscreen frame near the top, bounced off the toughened glass windscreen and smashed his reflector sight; Wright himself escaped injury.

Above: During a head-on confrontation with a Messerschmitt in September, Pilot Officer C. Bodie of No 66 Squadron had his toughened glass windscreen put to the test.

Right: Throughout the battle, gas attack on the Fighter Command airfields was an ever-present threat. Accordingly the ground crews always kept their gas masks and anti-gas capes close at hand—though rarely as close as this posed photograph might suggest. In the cockpit is Flight Lieutenant K. M. Gillies, the commander of 'A' Flight of No 66 Squadron; he was killed in action on October 4th.

Left: Members of the Luftwaffe examining a Spitfire of No 234 Squadron which had landed near near Cherbourg on August 15th, after suffering damage during an air battle over mid-Channel. Examination of other German photographs of the hole to the rear of the cockpit reveals that the plating had been blown outwards, almost certainly by the explosion of the destructor charge carried to demolish the secret IFF equipment. Note also the holed canopy, and the half-completed Luftwaffe cross on the fuselage.

Below: This picture of a burning Spitfire rolling past an He 111 appeared in a German aviation periodical shortly after the Battle of Britain.

Bob Oxspring was one of the few who fought in Fighter Command for control of the skies over Britain, during the fatefull summer of 1940. In this section he describes the action he is least likely to forget.

October 25th 1940; the Battle of Britain was in its closing stages, though at the time we had no way of knowing that this was the case. I was a very new Flight Lieutenant on No 66 Squadron, then based at Gravesend. Soon after breakfast we were scrambled and I was ordered to take my Flight of six Spitfires to patrol over Maidstone at 30,000 feet; the Germans were putting in the occasional fighter sweep and fighter-bomber attack and it was one of these we were after. When we arrived over Maidstone there was nothing to be seen, however; from the ground we received further orders to orbit overhead and wait.

It was nearly half an hour later that the 'bandits' did show up: six Messerschmitt 109s. For once we had a perfect set-up: we were up-sun, we had a 2,000 foot drop on them and the numbers were exactly equal. It did not often turn out like that during the Battle of Britain. I told my pilots to take one each and down we went. But the Germans were wide awake and I watched my man, the leader, suddenly barrel round and pull his fighter into a steep dive. I had been half expecting it and I tore down after him almost vertically, gaining slowly but surely. I had him cold. It never occured to me to watch my own tail — after all, we had covered all six of the Messerschmitts. Well, confidence is that nice warm feeling you have just before you slide over the banana skin. I was in range and just about to open fire when, suddenly, my Spitfire shuddered under the impact of a series of explosions. In fact those six Messerschmitts had been covering a seventh, a decoy aircraft a couple of thousand feet beneath them; their idea had been to bounce any of our fighters

5
A Day to Remember
Group Captain Bob Oxspring, DFC and two bars, AFC

having a go at it. And the German leader had taken me right in front of the decoy, who got in a good squirt at me as I went past.

He must have hit my elevator controls, because the next thing I knew my Spitfire was pulling uncontrollably up into a tight loop; a loop so tight that the 'G' forces squeezed me hard into my seat and blacked me out. As I went down the other side of the loop the aircraft straightened out and I could see again, but as the speed built up the jammed elevators took effect and up we went into a second loop. Obviously the time had come for me to part company with that Spitfire. But first I had to get the hood open and that was not proving easy: the only time I could reach up and see to do it was when the 'G' was off; but then we were screaming downhill fast and the hood would not budge. I thought my time had come and I remember thinking of the injustice of it all: hit just as I was about to blow that Messerschmitt out of the sky!

I have no idea how many loops the Spitfire did before I was finally able to slide back the hood. But it was not a moment too soon, because by then the oil tank was on fire and the flames were spreading back from the engine. I threw off my seat harness and stood up, but found I could go no further because I still had my helmet on and it was attached firmly to the aircraft. By now I was getting pretty desperate and I wrenched the helmet off with all my strength. Afterwards I found the helmet in the wreckage and saw that I had actually torn it across the leather; I was amazed at the force I must have summoned to do that.

The next thing I knew I was falling clear of my aircraft, head-down and on my back, at an angle of about forty-five degrees. I had no idea how high I was, so I pulled the D-ring right away. I knew it was a mistake, as soon as I did it.

When the parachute began to deploy, I was in just about the worst possible position. I remember watching, an interested spectator, as the canopy and the rigging lines came streaming out from between my legs. One of the lines coiled itself round my leg and when the canopy developed I found myself hanging upside down. I had never parachuted before, but from my sketchy previous instruction I was fairly certain that head-first was not the position to be in when I hit the ground! So I grabbed a handful of slack rigging lines on the opposite side to my entangled leg and started to climb up hand over hand. After a lot of kicking and pulling I managed to get my leg free; with a sigh of relief I sank back into my harness, right way up.

Now I had time to think about what was happening around me. The first thing that struck me was the quietness; the only sounds were the spasmodic bursts of cannon and machine-gun fire and the howls of the engines, coming from the battle still in progress high above: it seemed an age since I had been part of it. But my own troubles were not over yet.

Gradually it began to dawn on me that the straps leading up from my harness, instead of being comfortably clear of my head on either side, were tangled together and chafing my ears and face. And higher up the rigging lines were also tangled, preventing the canopy from developing to its fullest extent. That meant that I was falling much faster than I should have been; and

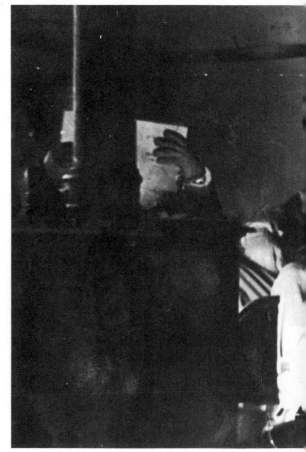

struggle as I might, I could not get the lines untangled. I went down past a cloud and it seemed to whizz by: it was not going to be a very pleasant landing. The only time I had ever needed a parachute and this had to happen!

Gradually I got lower, and I could make out trees and farm houses and curious faces raised skywards. At about 500 feet the wind carried me across some high tension cables and even though I was hundreds of feet above the wires I could not resist the instinct to lift my feet up. Still I was coming down much too fast. The one thing I needed most of all was a nice soft tree, to break my fall. And there in my line of drift, in answer to my prayer, was a wood full of them.

Just before I hit I covered my face with my arms and came to rest amid the crack of breaking twigs. When the noise stopped I cautiously lowered my arms and looked around. My parachute canopy was draped across a couple of trees and I was bouncing up and down between the trunks like a yo-yo. I was about twenty feet up, suspended above an asphalt road.

At about my level, just out of reach, was a small branch. By doing a sort of Tarzan stunt, swinging back and forth from side to side, I was able to get closer and closer until in the end I was able to grab hold of it. Gingerly I pulled myself

up and on to a thicker bough, before letting go of my harness. By this time quite a crowd had begun to collect underneath the tree; at first there seemed to be some doubt about my nationality but the vehemence of my Anglo-Saxon demands for help soon satisfied everyone that I was, in fact, British. Some Home Guard men made a human ladder by sitting on each others' shoulders and with their aid I managed to clamber down to mother earth. It had indeed been a memorable day.

Above: Bob Oxspring, pictured earlier in the war prior to a high altitude patrol, wearing the fleece-lined leather flying jacket and trousers issued to pilots. The jackets were popular; but the trousers were too cumbersome and restricted movement and were rarely worn by Spitfire pilots going into action.

Right: Fred Tandy, pictured in 1940 when he served on No 616 Squadron.

Below: Armourers at Duxford re-arming a Spitfire of No 19 Squadron in September 1940. Note that the fabric patches covering the gun ports have been blown off, indicating that the guns had been fired. The armourers under the near wing have just removed two of the used ammunition boxes and are in the process of removing the other two.

6
Feeding the Guns
Warrant Officer Fred Tandy, BEM

through the breech of the gun; this was important, because it meant that we could now re-arm the Spitfire without having to remove the top covers from the gun bays. As a result of continual practice, and with twelve covers to remove instead of the original twenty, we cut the original twenty-minute re-arming time down by more than half.

By the time of the Battle of Britain, re-arming had become a slick operation. As the Spitfire taxied in after its sortie, we armourers would be watching the canvas strips doped over the gun ports: if these had been blown off it meant the guns had been fired and re-arming was necessary. If this was the case and the aircraft was required to fly again immediately, the team of armourers would be waiting at the dispersal. Each man carried one ammunition box loaded with 300 rounds of .303" ammunition under each arm. During

Nobody who worked on the Spitfire's guns will ever forget the knuckle-rasping hand-slashing experience of having to feel one's way round the cramped gun bays with their sharp edges and numerous pieces of locking wire.

Top: A .303″ Browning installation from behind and above, with the upper panel removed. The rear stirrup with the screw for left-right harmonisation can be seen holding the rear of the gun.

Above: The installation from behind and below; to the left of the gun may be seen the harmonisation locking quadrant for raising or lowering the barrel; the braided cable running underneath the gun carried high pressure air to fire the weapon.

To operate effectively, those who fly are utterly dependant upon the skill, determination and enthusiasm of those who prepare and repair their aircraft. Representing those men who played such an essential part in winning the Battle of Britain, yet who never left the ground, is Fred Tandy. An armourer, his task during the battle was to ensure that when a pilot had the enemy in his sights and pressed the firing button, the battery of guns performed the final act in the long chain of events between the order to take-off and the destruction of an enemy. In this section he recounts the re-arming of the Spitfire's eight Browning guns.

I joined No 616 Squadron with Spitfire Is at Leconfield in January 1940, as an AC 1 armourer straight out of training. We were young and very keen and whenever there was an aircraft available we used to practice re-arming again and again to try to reduce the time needed. Initially it took a team of four armourers about twenty minutes to carry out this task. Then somebody worked out a way of using a canvas loop to pull the first round of the new ammunition belt

the Battle it was usual to load two of the guns with armour-piercing ammunition, two with incendiary and four guns with ball ammunition; four out of the last 25 rounds in each box of ball ammunition were tracer, to give the pilot an indication that he was nearly out.

Even before the propellor had stopped there would be two armourers under each wing, busily undoing the scores of half-turn Dzus fasteners securing the gun panels and the ammunition box covers. Once these covers were off, the next step was to have a quick look into the breech mechanism of each gun, to check that there had been no stoppage and that the gun was serviceable: if the breech block was stopped in the rear position, it meant that the pilot had ceased fire; if it was stopped in the forward position, it meant that he had run out of ammunition; if there had been a stoppage the breech would usually be in

the forward position, with a live round 'up the spout'.

Unless the gun was unserviceable, the breech mechanism would be pulled to the rear position if it was not there already; then the belts from the used ammunition boxes could be pulled clear, and the boxes themselves could be removed and placed on the ground out of the way. Now the guns were safe and one armourer on each side would start to swab out the gun barrels from the front, to clean away the crumbs of burnt cordite; for this he would use a cleaning rod, with first a piece of oily and then a piece of clean 'four-by-two' flannel. Meanwhile the second armourer in the pair would be clicking the full ammunition boxes into place from underneath the wing, and threading the canvas straps round the first round in each one through the feed ways. With a firm pull on each one in turn, he would bring the first round in each new box up

Below: Cartridge cases and belt links spewing out of the underwing chutes of a Spitfire, probably one belonging to No 602 Squadron, during the simultaneous firing of all eight Brownings at the butts. Almost certainly this firing was set up specially for the benefit of press cameramen, for it formed no part of the normal Spitfire checking procedure. If the serviceability of a gun was suspect, it was removed and fired individually. An interesting point to note on this photograph, however, is the horizontal strake running along the upper fuselage just in front of the cockpit; it was a local modification to enable a light alloy screen to be fitted to shield the pilot's eyes from the glare of the exhaust flames during night flying.

Right: Heinkel 111s under fire, during the Battle of Britain. Again and again German twin-engined bombers proved that they could absorb a tremendous amount of punishment from rifle-calibre machine guns. There were several occasions when bombers flew home with more than two hundred holes from .303 inch bullets —which would indicate a series of attacks from short range which probably exhausted almost the entire ammunition supply of more than one British fighter. Two important factors played an important part in the survival of these bombers: their armour protection and their self-sealing fuel tanks. The Heinkel 111, for example, carried some 600 pounds of steel plating well distributed to protect its crew. The self-sealing fuel tanks greatly reduced the chances of small bullet holes allowing the highly-inflammable petrol to stream out and be ignited by incendiary rounds; the bullets passed clean through the tanks but as the petrol began to run out it reacted with the covering of unvulcanised rubber, which swelled and sealed off the holes. Clearly, a heavier calibre weapon than the .303 inch Browning was needed for British fighters.

against the feed stops. Then he would cock the gun using either the special wire cocking tool or, more usually, his forage cap. Cocking brought the first round out of the belt on to the face of the breech block and at the same time released the canvas loop which could then be pulled clear. The armourer would look up into the gun from underneath to check that the round had actually fed on to the face of the breech block, then press the manual release to bring the block forwards to feed the round into the chamber; the rear-sear-retainer-keeper would hold the firing pin clear of the round, so there was no risk of the gun going off at this stage. But I would point out that it was considered very bad manners if you carried out this stage of the re-arming process, while the other fellow was still working on the gun barrel from the front!

Now, the only essential task remaining was to re-fit the gun and ammunition box covers to the underside of the wing. If there was time before the next take-off we would dope pieces of fabric over the firing ports, to keep the heat in and prevent the guns freezing up at high altitude; to save time during the Battle of Britain, we sometimes used ordinary medical sticking plaster for this purpose. If the grass was wet the Spitfire was notorious for throwing up mud and water on to the undersides of the wings during the take-off run; to prevent this moisture getting into the gun bays via the link and cartridge case ejector slots, we would dope pieces of newspaper over them.

At the end of a day's fighting we would take the recoils out of the guns and clean them properly; or, if the Spitfire had been stood down from immediate readiness to, say, 30 minutes, we would remove one recoil mechanism at a time for cleaning.

On the Spitfire our responsibilities as armourers did not end with the guns. Each morning we had to change the 'colours of the day' in the Plessey six-barrelled signal cartridge discharger. And each time the guns were fired we had to fit a new film magazine into the

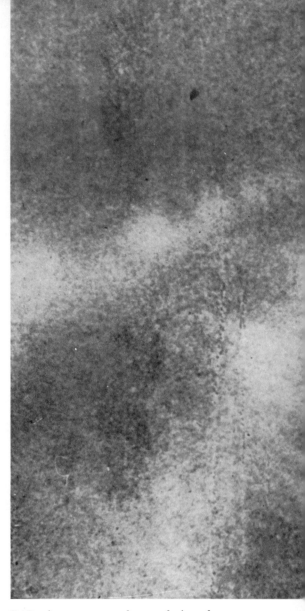

G42 cine-camera located in the port wing root. Finally we had to check for security the two 4 inch diameter parachute flares fitted in their long chutes just behind the cockpit; these were sometimes used during night flying.

In 1940 there was a tremendous sense of 'belonging' to one's fighter squadron. Three ground crewmen were allocated to each Spitfire: a fitter, a rigger and an armourer; and it was a matter of great distress if anything happened to 'their' pilot. Yet in spite of quite severe losses in pilots, morale was sky-high. At Kenley during the Battle of Britain we could see the combats being fought overhead; we could see the enemy aircraft being shot down and we knew that we on the ground had our own vital part to play in bringing this about. For a young lad of nineteen, they were stirring times.

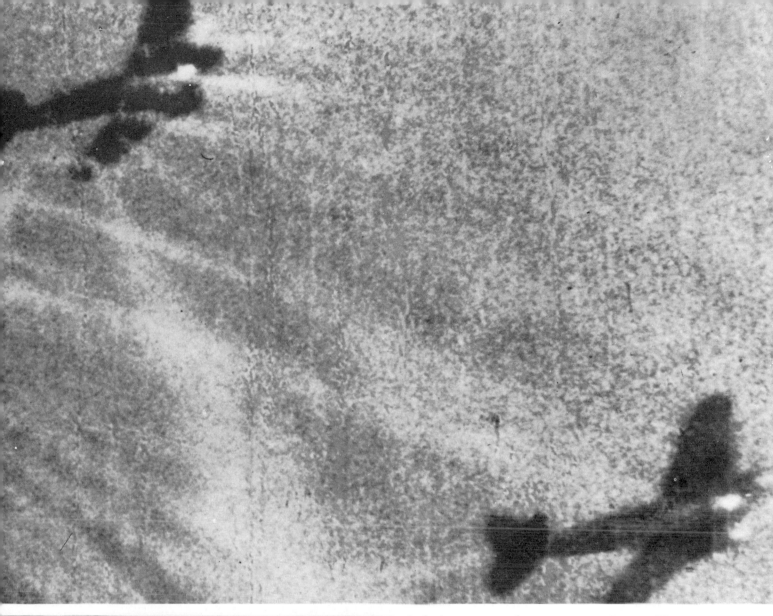

Left: An answer to the problem: the 20mm Hispano cannon. Seen here is the prototype installation of this weapon in a Spitfire I, serial L1007, in June 1939. During the early stages of the Battle of Britain No 19 Squadron flew cannon-armed Spitfires in action; but in its early form the 20mm Hispano installation proved unreliable and was the subject of frequent stoppages. The aircraft fitted with it had to be withdrawn from operations pending modifications. By the end of 1940 the bugs had been ironed out and the cannon armed Spitfire entered general service. Fired from short range the 20mm solid round could defeat the thickest armour carried by the German medium bombers; hits near the fuel tanks with the 20mm high explosive round stood a good chance of causing petrol leaks which the self sealing was quite unable to staunch.

Above: Enough to make the difference: the small amount of sweep-up shown, on the tail-plane trailing edge of Spitfire P7525, was sufficient to spoil the airflow over the rudder and elevators; this limited her diving speed to 320mph 1AS and produced an uncomfortable left yaw.

Sorting Out a Rogue

18th January 1941.
Aeroplane and Armament Experimental Establishment Boscombe Down.
Spitfire II P 7525 (66 Squadron): Handling and Diving Trials.

Small defects in an airframe, defects not readily apparent to the eye, can cause unusual handling characteristics in the air. When that happened to Spitfires and all the normal cures had been tried and had failed, the experts at Boscombe Down were called in to try to find out what was wrong. This report illustrates how they cured the poor handling characteristics found on Spitfire P 7525. The report was written early in 1941. Yet even before it began to be circulated it had ceased to be of relevant interest so far as P 7525 was concerned: almost immediately after the Spitfire had been put right and returned to No 66 Squadron, she was written off in a crash after running out of fuel in bad weather.

1.0 Introduction.

Complaints were made by No 66 Squadron that the handling qualities of this aeroplane, which was representative of others in the Squadron, were bad because in spite of full forward trim the aeroplane could not be dived to more than 320mph IAS. Also, it was very left wing low in the dive and there was insufficient rudder bias to prevent it from yawing to the left. There was a considerable amount of aileron snatch which was also a subject of complaint.

2.0 Tests carried out

2.1 The aeroplane was flown as received and the Squadron's criticisms confirmed. It was check weighed and the centre of gravity determined; also the range of trimmer movement was checked. These measurements confirmed that the aeroplane was a normal Spitfire II so far as these points were concerned. Examination of the fin and tail plane trailing edges showed that they were swept up sufficiently to spoil the flow over the rudder and elevator and the respective trimmers. The

48

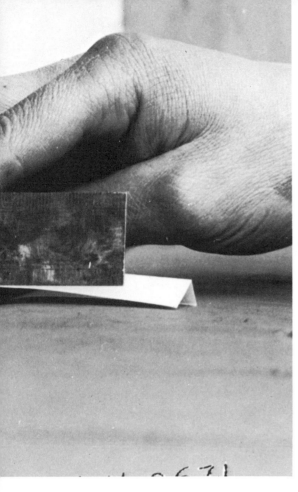

attached photograph shows this clearly. 2.2 The trailing edges of the fin and tail plane were dressed down until the sweep up was removed. In addition, the 8″ and 6″ lengths of under standard-size trimming cord doped to the upper port and lower starboard aileron trailing edges respectively were removed and a single 10″ length of full size cord was doped to the upper trailing edge of the port aileron*. A certain amount of the backlash present in the aileron circuit was absorbed by tightening the cables but the remainder could not be eliminated readily, because it was due to a little slackness in the hinge pins.

2.3 After these alterations the aeroplane was flown to check the handling and diving qualities. It was trimmed for full throttle level flight, the elevator trimmer indicator then being at the normal setting of 1½ to 1¼ divisions nose down and dived up to the limiting

---

*On the early Spitfires fitted with fabric-covered ailerons, lengths of cord were doped on the ailerons to trim the aircraft to fly 'hands off' in the rolling plane. On later aircraft with metal-covered ailerons, trim was achieved by bending them.

speed of 460mph IAS. No abnormal forward pressure was required on the control column and neither yaw nor wing dropping was experienced in the dive when the normal amount of starboard bias was used. The ailerons were found to be slightly overbalanced, until at about 440mph IAS the over-balancing and snatching became disconcerting. This snatching was very apparent in tight turns and to a lesser degree when pulling out of the dives.

3.0 Conclusions

3.1 The modifications carried out on the aeroplane restored its handling qualities to normal and made it representative of other Mark II Spitfires, with the exception of the aileron control.

3.2 The trailing edges of all fin and tailplane surfaces of Spitfire aeroplanes should be carefully inspected to ensure that the contours are not distorted.

3.3 Aileron hing pins should have just sufficient clearance to eliminate mechanical stiffness; the control cables should be kept taut.

Above: On finals for landing, after a curved approach to enable the pilot to keep the airfield in sight. Hood locked open . . . side door on half-cock position (to prevent any possibility of the hood slamming shut in the event of a mishap) . . . break-pressure checked . . . undercarriage down (below 160mph), two green lights and indicator bars out . . . mixture rich . . . pitch lever to fully fine . . . flaps down (below 140mph) . . . over the hedge at 85mph indicated . . . ease the stick gently back to hold her off the ground as the speed falls away . . . 64mph indicated and she stalls gently on to the ground.

Spitfire Vs of the second
Norwegian fighter squadron
to form in Britain, No 332,
pictured at Catterick.

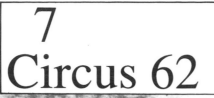

7
Circus 62

By the end of 1940 the Luftwaffe had had to cease its large scale daylight operatons over Britain, as the bulk of its combat units began moving eastwards for the planned invasion of Russia. Relieved of the need to defend Britain against massed air attacks the new C in C Fighter Command, Air Chief Marshal Sir Sholto Douglas, adopted a policy he termed 'leaning forward into France'.

From the beginning of 1941 Fighter Command flew offensive sweeps over the northern fringes of occupied Europe. The German invasion of Russia, in June, provided an added driving force for these operations: anything the British forces could now do, to divert German forces away from the eastern front, was of great importance.

The 'Circus' was the largest of the routine offensive air operations mounted over northern Europe during 1941. We shall now examine one of these in detail: No 62, which took place on Thursday, August 7th.

Above: "That's where you're going . . ." Squadron Leader 'Spy' de la Torre, the station Intelligence officer, points out the route of Circus 62 soon after it had been marked up in the briefing room at Biggin Hill on August 7th 1941. The concentration of parallel lines shows the route of the bombers and their escorting wings to and from Lille. The less distinct lines from the west show the planned routes of the Tangmere and Hornchurch Wings into the target area.

Right: The briefing board at Biggin Hill on August 7th 1941, being prepared for the briefing of pilots prior to Circus 62. The board shows the duties of each of the fighter wings taking part in the operation; when completed it will show each one's time to rendezvous with the bombers (if applicable) and the times for each wing to be at the English coast, the French coast and the target.

The object of the Circus operation was to use a small force of RAF bombers as bait, to lure up the German fighters which could then be engaged by the large covering force of RAF fighters. The ground target for Circus 62 was the power station at Lille and six Blenheim bombers of No 2 Group were to attack it. In its composition the Circus forces could be likened to a lot of froth but very little beer. The 'beer', the force of six bombers, was covered by a mass of 'froth': no fewer than eighteen squadrons of Spitfires and two squadrons of Hurricanes, to provide escort and support during the various phases of the action.

Late on the afternoon of the 7th the bombers joined up with their escorting fighters over Manston and headed south-eastwards towards their target. As the close-cover fighter squadrons slid into their briefed positions, this part of the force took on a recognisable shape. With the bombers at 12,000 feet flew the Spitfires of No 71 (US Eagle) Squadron; behind and 1,000 feet above them came those of No 111; and behind and a further 1,000 feet above came the Spitfires of No 222 Squadron. These three squadrons, all from North Weald, comprised the escort wing. Similarly

stepped up behind and above came three more Spitfire squadrons, Nos 452 (Australian), 485 (New Zealand) and 602 Squadrons from Kenley, making up the escort cover wing.

These six squadrons of fighters and one of bombers formed the hub of aerial activity, around which the supporting wings of fighters centred their activity. Planned in great detail, the Circus was indeed a far cry from the hasty defensive scrambles of the Battle of Britain just a few months earlier; now, holding the initiative, Fighter Command could assemble its forces at times of its own choosing and direct them for maximum effect.

Above left: Bader's Spitfire, carrying his initials on the rear fuselage.

Left: Wing Commander Douglas Bader, third from the left, led the Tangmere Wing in the Target Support role during Circus 62. He is seen here a week before the operation with, from the left, Flying Officer 'Johnnie' Johnson and Flight Lieutenant 'Cocky' Dundas. The officer on the far right was Lieutenant Llewellyn, an observer from the US Army Air Force (at that time the USA was still neutral).

At 27,000 feet, high above the bombers and their immediate escorts, flew the Spitfires of the Biggin Hill Wing (Nos 72, 92 and 609 Squadrons). These, with the Spitfires of the Hornchurch Wing (Nos 403 (Canadian), 603 and 611 Squadrons) and the Tangmere Wing (Nos 41, 610 and 616 Squadrons), comprised the target support force whose task was to establish air superiority in the general area of the target during the attack. Whilst the Biggin Hill Wing was to move in with the bombers, the other two were to cross the French coast at Le Touquet and, sweeping eastwards high over the German airfields, engage the enemy fighters as they came up.

The three Target Support Wings, comprising more than a hundred Spitfires, were out looking for trouble. But the small German fighter force remaining in the west, outnumbered and with orders to conserve its resources, refused to be drawn into a pitched battle. Instead the fighter *Gruppen,* enjoying the assistance of ground radar, concentrated on harrying the raiders and picking off stragglers. The subsequent report from the Tangmere Wing, commanded during this operation by Wing Commander Douglas Bader, illustrates well the sort of spasmodic action which resulted:

Wing met over base, crossed the English coast over Hastings at 23/24/25000 feet and made a landfall over Le Touquet at 23/24/27000 feet. A large orbit was made between Merville and Le Touquet. Proceeded towards the target area, encountering many Me 109s approximately 1,000 feet above. Enemy aircraft came down out of the sun on the starboard quarter; the Wing turned to attack and the enemy aircraft dived away refusing to engage, but dogfights ensued. These tactics ensued over the Hazebrouck, Merville and Lille areas and on the way back to the French coast, where the 109s broke away. The coast was recrossed by squadrons separately between Le Touquet and Boulogne; all the pilots and aircraft had returned by 18.55, with the exception of one from 41 Squadron.

The Biggin Hill and Hornchurch Wings fought similarly inconclusive engagements.

In the mean time the Blenheims were able to reach Lille unmolested by enemy fighters, only to find their target shrouded in cloud. Without bombing

Above: Spitfire Mk Vs of No 603 Squadron which, operating as part of the Hornchurch Wing, took part in Circus 62.

Right: Squadron Leader Rankin (without jacket, left) with Flight Lieutenant Charles Kingcombe, lighting cigarettes immediately after their return to Biggin Hill from an operation over northern France in the summer of 1941. During Circus 62 Rankin was credited with the destruction of one Messerschmitt 109 and with causing damage to a second.

they withdrew north-westwards along the planned route and attacked their alternative target: invasion barges moored in the canal at Gravelines.

Positioned to cover the initial phase of the withdrawal were two Polish-manned Spitfire squadrons from Northolt (Nos 306 and 308), which made up the Forward Support Wing. While the Blenheims were closing on Gravelines No 308 Squadron was the object of a particularly sharp attack during which an estimated eighteen Messerschmitts 'bounced' the Spitfires and, in the brisk action which followed, shot down two before the Poles could retaliate.

Covering the final phase of the withdrawal was the Rear Support Wing, comprising one Spitfire and two Hurricane Squadrons (respectively Nos 19, 257 and 401 (Canadian)) drawn from No 12 Group. This wing also came under attack and lost two Spitfires and a Hurricane.

From start to finish, the incursion over German-held France had lasted just over half an hour. During that time a force of more than two hundred RAF aircraft had drawn into battle a considerably smaller number of German fighters, claiming to have destroyed three of them and probably destroyed three more; this, at a cost of six British aircraft destroyed and their pilots killed or captured.

Truely, Circus No 62 cannot be considered as one of the more impressive feats of British arms. Yet it would be unwise to judge the value of such operations as a simple profit-and-loss account. In war a fighting force must be given the opportunity to fight, or its spirit will wither and die; by keeping Fighter Command in action in this way, even if the terms were unfavourable, Sir Sholto Douglas ensured that his pilots remained combat-hardened during the difficult period following the Battle of Britain.

Above: During 1941 the Spitfire squadrons of Fighter Command gradually re-equipped with the Mark V and this version bore the brunt of the offensive operations over northern France that summer. This particular aircraft, serial R6923, was one of the original cannon-armed Mark Is which fought during the early part of the Battle of Britain with No 19 Squadron. After her withdrawal from operations she was modified to Mark V standard by the fitting of a more-powerful Merlin 45 engine and, with a modified feed system to the Hispano cannon, was re-issued to No 92 Squadron early the following year. At the controls when this photograph was taken was Squadron Leader Jimmy Rankin, the commander of No 92 Squadron.

Above: A Messerschmitt 109F pictured going down in flames before the guns of a Spitfire; during Circus 62 RAF pilots reported shooting down three aircraft of this type and damaging three others. The 'F' model of the famous German fighter was a slightly re-designed and more powerful version of the 'E' which had fought during the Battle of Britain and was comparable in performance with the Mark V Spitfire.

Above: This Spitfire IIB, which belonged to the Polish No 306 Squadron, made an emergency landing at Biggin Hill in August 1941. She had suffered five hits from 20mm rounds, two of them explosive, and numerous hits from machine gun bullets. Note the effect of the two explosive shells, on the rudder and the port tailplane. The latter had blown away almost the entire lower surface and must have made control in pitch very difficult. (Unfortunately more details of the cause of the damage could not be found, in spite of an intensive search, because apparently some Polish units did not consider such 'minor' battle damage worthy of mention in their diaries).

Top right: A Mark V Spitfire undergoing a 30-hour inspection, probably at Hornchurch early in 1942. The fitters and riggers can be seen working through their long lists of items requiring checking. For example, the engine cowlings have been removed for examination to allow the oil filter to be removed and cleaned, and the engine to be checked for possible oil, fuel or coolant leaks; the propeller spinner has been removed to allow checking for possible damage, or leakage from the hydraulic pitch-change mechanism.

Below: A few days, but greatly differing circumstances, separate these two photographs. An RAF ground crewman points out that the victory tally on the Wing Commander Stanford-Tuck's Spitfire stands at twenty-nine, but the total was never to get any higher. On January 28th 1942, just over a month after his final kill, Stanford-Tuck's engine was hit by ground fire during a straffing attack. As he was gliding in for a crash landing a Flak emplacement opened up on him so Stanford-Tuck kicked his nose round and gave the gunners a quick 'squirt' before he hit the ground; he later learned that a chance round had gone right down the slim barrel of the German 20mm gun and split it open.

German gunners, doubtless impressed by Stanford-Tuck's markmanship, examine the mount of their fallen adversary. As commander of the Biggin Hill Wing, Robert Stanford-Tuck carried his initials on his aircraft.

Left: Each morning the Spitfires had to be run up to high revs on the ground to check the operation of the propeller constant speed unit and the two magnetos, with two or more ground crewmen serving as 'breathing ballast' holding down the tail. Pleasant enough on a warm sunny day, this task could be a miserable one on a bitterly cold winter's morning.

Below left: Squadron Leader P. Davies, who commanded No 19 Squadron during much of 1942, pictured in an early version of the 'K' Type dinghy issued to Spitfire pilots. On a smooth millpond like the one seen here, the greatest discomfort from riding in such a craft was likely to be a wet behind; in an open sea, without protection from the wind and spray, such a craft could be the lonliest and most dispiriting place on earth. Yet the necessity for the dinghy could not be argued; a Mae West lifejacket would prevent a man from drowning, but that was all it would do; if he wore normal flying kit his period of useful consciousness in the waters round Britain could be as little as two hours during the summer months, falling to about 45 minutes during the winter. Later versions of the 'K' Type dinghy carried a simple apron to provide the survivor with some protection from the elements. Probably the record for time adrift in a single-seat dinghy, as a survivor, is held by a Pole: Flight Lieutenant L. Kurylowicz of No 316 Squadron; he baled out of his Spitfire over mid-Channel in the autumn of 1943 and, following a gruelling battle for life during which he rode out a near-gale, was finally rescued after eighty-five hours in the water.

Right: A reconnaissance Spitfire pictured in her element, high above the earth. If possible when over enemy territory, reconnaissance pilots preferred to fly just underneath the thin layer of sky where condensation trails form; in that way they could expect a little extra warning of the approach of enemy aircraft trying to 'bounce' them from above.

8
Spitfire Spyplane

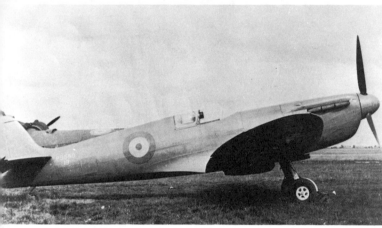

Above: These three Spitfires had originally been ordered as fighters, Mark Is; but prior to delivery were modified into the photographic reconnaissance Type C by the removal of all guns and armour and the installation of extra fuel tanks in and under the wings and two vertical cameras in the rear fuselage. Some aircraft were adapted to carry cameras in the underwing tanks.

During 1941 all three Spitfires were further modified to PR Type F standard by the addition of a 29 gallon fuel tank under the pilot's seat, a deeper nose cowling to house the larger oil tank necessary for the longer flights, additional oxygen bottles and a new canopy with side blisters. All three were Type F Spitfires when these photographs were taken. Top: X4492, showing clearly her port underwing fuel tank. Centre: X4498, pictured at the time in July 1941 when she belonged to No 3 Photographic Reconnaissance Unit at Oakington, with Squadron Leader R. Elliott at the controls. Above: P9550, one of the very early PR Spitfire conversions, had begun operations with A Flight of the original Photographic Reconnaissance Unit in July 1940, flying from Wick in northern Scotland; now modified to Type F standard, her bulged nose for the extra oil tank is clearly shown.

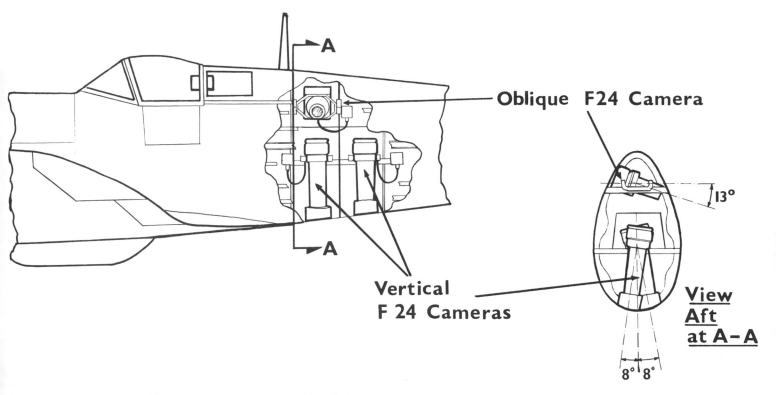

Oblique F24 Camera

Vertical F24 Cameras

View Aft at A-A

13°

8° 8°

Top left: A close-up of the fuselage of a PR Type F, showing the access hatch for the vertically mounted cameras; note also the bulge on the side of the canopy, to enable the pilot to see directly underneath the aircraft for vertical photography.

Above: Spitfire camera mountings for photographic reconnaissance. Basically there were two types of mounting: vertical or oblique, the latter for low-altitude photography. The drawing here shows both types of camera mountings with one oblique and two vertical although; so far as is known, no Spitfire in service ever carried cameras for both oblique and vertical photography at the same time because access to the lower cameras for servicing would have been very awkward. The vertical cameras shown here were two F24s and this was known as the X fitting; if two smaller F8 cameras were installed this was known as the W fitting and the majority of PR Spitfires used for medium-high altitude reconnaissance had one of these two fitments.

Some of the classic reconnaissance photographs of the Second World War were taken from Spitfires.

Centre left: Into the valley of the shadow of death . . . : a remarkably clear picture of the German heavy cruiser Hipper in dry dock, taken by Pilot Officer J. Chandler on January 26th 1941 as he flew low over the heavily defended port of Brest.

Far left Bottom: the famous photograph of the Wuerzburg radar set at the top of the cliffs at Bruneval, taken on December 5th 1941 by Flight Lieutenant Tony Hill, which led to a commando attack and its capture.

Left: a further 'scoop' by Hill: taken on May 2nd 1942 over the Dutch island of Walcheren, this picture was the first to reach Britain to show the details of the Giant Wuerzburg radar used to control Luftwaffe night fighters; the startled operator (bottom right) about to mount the steps later served as a human yardstick and made it possible for interpreters to measure the exact size of the reflector dish—and thus deduce the radar's operating characteristics.

Outclassed

War is no respector of reputations. If an opponent introduces greatly improved equipment, a position of air superiority can be translated into one of inferiority in a matter of weeks. That began to happen to RAF Fighter Command in the autumn of 1941, as the German fighter *Gruppen* in France gradually re-equipped with the Focke Wulf 190. In June 1942 the RAF secured an airworthy example of this new German fighter and within days of its capture it was undergoing hastily-arranged combat trials with each of the operational Allied fighters. Reproduced below is the report by the Air Fighting Development Unit on the trial of the Fw 190 against the Spitfire V, which illustrates in stark terms the measure of the inferiority of Fighter Command's equipment during most of the third year of the war.

The Fw 190 was compared with a Spitfire VB from an operational squadron for speed and all-round manoeuverability at heights up to 25,000 feet. The Fw 190 is superior in speed at all heights, and the approximate differences are listed as follows:-

At 1,000 ft the Fw 190 is 25-30mph faster than the Spitfire VB.
At 3,000 ft the Fw 190 is 30-35mph faster than the Spitfire VB.
At 5,000 ft the Fw 190 is 25mph faster than the Spitfire VB.
At 9,000 ft the Fw 190 is 25-30mph faster than the Spitfire VB (second blower in operation).
At 15,000 ft the Fw 190 is 20mph faster than the Spitfire VB.
At 18,000 ft the Fw 190 is 20mph faster than the Spitfire VB.
At 21,000 ft the Fw 190 is 25mph faster than the Spitfire VB.
At 25,000 ft the Fw 190 is 20-25mph faster than the Spitfire VB.

Climb The climb of the Fw 190 is superior to that of the Spitfire VB at all heights. The best speeds for climbing

are approximately the same, but the angle of the Fw 190 is considerably steeper. Under maximum continuous climbing conditions the climb of the Fw 190 is about 450ft/min better up to 25,000 feet.

With both aircraft flying at high cruising speed and then pulling up into a climb, the superior climb of the Fw 190 is even more marked. When both aircraft are pulled up into a climb from a dive, the Fw 190 draws away very rapidly and the pilot of the Spitfire has no hope of catching it.

Dive Comparative dives between the two aircraft have shown that the Fw 190 can leave the Spitfire with ease, particularly during the initial stages.

Manoeuverability The manoeuverability of the Fw 190 is better than that of the Spitfire VB except in turning circles, If on the other hand the Spitfire was flying at maximum continuous cruising and was 'bounced' under the same conditions, it had a reasonable chance of avoiding being caught by opening the

throttle and going into a *shallow* dive, provided the Fw 190 was seen in time. This forced the Fw 190 into a stern chase and although it eventually caught the Spitfire, it took some time and as a result was drawn a considerable distance away from its base. This is a particularly useful method of evasion for the Spitfire if it is 'bounced' when returning from a sweep. This manoeuvre has been carried out during recent operations and has been successful on several occasions.

If the Spitfire VB is 'bounced' it is thought unwise to evade by diving steeply, as the Fw 190 will have little difficulty in catching up owing to its superiority in the dive.

The above trials have shown that the Spitfire VB must cruise at high speed when in an area where enemy fighters can be expected. It will then, in addition to lessening the chances of being successfully 'bounced', have a better chance of catching the Fw 190, particularly if it has the advantage of surprise.

Above: After Circus 101, flown on September 21st 1941, returning pilots of the Polish No 315 Squadron reported engaging an '. . . unknown enemy aircraft with a radial engine.' The RAF would soon learn to know and respect the Focke Wulf 190 which, it soon became clear, almost completely outclassed the Spitfire Mark V—the best aircraft Fighter Command then had operational.

To See Was to Live

Left: With so much at stake, the cleaning of the canopy assumed an almost ritualistic importance prior to an operational sortie. A fragile material, perspex could be scratched unwittingly even by wiping it with a handkerchief; only the very softest of cloths could be used for cleaning it.

Above right: This is why fighter pilots demanded that their canopies and windscreens be absolutely clean and brightly transparent. Hold this photograph 18 inches away from your face, out to one side. Now, imagine that you are in a Spitfire over enemy territory, liable to be 'bounced' at any time. You begin your systematic search of the sky, beginning at the left and the rear. Your eyes move in a slow and deliberate up-and-down zig-zag movement, sweeping from high above to below the horizon and working round clockwise until you get to the right and the rear; then you search once more in the direction of the sun, glance into the cockpit to check that all is still well there and begin all over again. Your life depends upon the efficiency of your search: if an enemy fighter ever reaches a position where its size is that shown in the photograph it will be 600 yards away, with its pilot just about to open fire; if he gets any closer without your seeing him, the chances are that your epitaph will be a simple victory bar painted on his aircraft when he gets home. Whatever the romantics might have one believe, air fighting is a rough and nasty business with no quarter given; the 'sitting duck' usually ended up as a 'dead duck'.

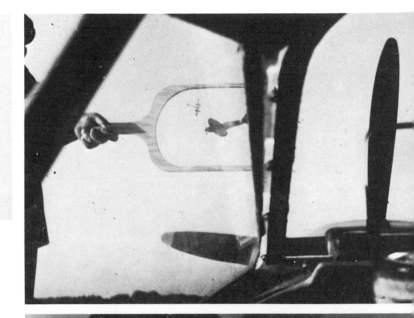

Although the side perspex might appear transparent when looking at objects down sun, Top right, a glance at the same objects into sun soon revealed the extent of light-scattering due to even the slightest scratching on the hood.

A problem, and a solution. Oil slinging was a common occurance from the constant-speed propellers fitted to Spitfires. In the photograph (Below) taken immediately after a fight, the left half of the windscreen had been cleaned while the right half had had the oil left on; note the deterioration in visibility caused by the oil. Some Spitfires, like this one (Below right) were fitted with a simple locally-made oil collector ring to prevent the oil from spraying on the windscreen.

9
Production Testing
Alex Henshaw, MBE

A brand-new Mark V pictured immediately after take-off from Castle Bromwich.

Those fortunate enough to have watched Alex Henshaw display a Spitfire still talk about the experience, for he is acknowledged to be a virtuoso in the art of aerobatics. During his six-year career as a production and development test pilot he came to know the Spitfire as few men can have done — which is hardly surprising, considering the fact that he personnally test flew more than one in ten of all of those built.

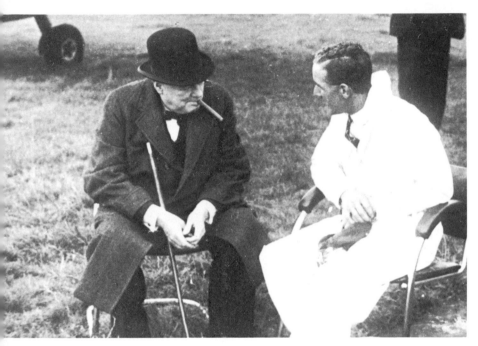

Above: Alex Henshaw discussing his work with Mr Churchill, when the latter paid a visit to the Castle Bromwich plant.

I learned to fly at my own expense at the age of twenty, and during the years that followed flying occupied most of my spare time. During the 1930s a skilful and resourceful pilot with money or suitable sponsors could make a name for himself in aviation. I became very enthusiastic about competition flying and enjoyed a run of successes culminating in the winning of the King's Cup in 1938. In the following year I took the records for the flight from London to Cape Town and return; for the solo flight, these records still stand in 1973.

When the war came I accepted a job with Vickers as a test pilot and after testing Wellingtons at Weybridge and Spitfires and Walruses at Southampton, in the summer of 1940 I became Chief Test Pilot at the new Spitfire factory at Castle Bromwich. During the years that

followed I became responsible, in addition, for flight testing the Spitfires built at Cosford and Desford, the Seafires at South Marsden and the repaired aircraft at Cowley. I remained at this work until 1946, by which time I had flown a total of 2,360 different Spitfires and Seafires — more than one in ten of all of those built.

As a production test pilot, one's task is really that of flight inspector; one has to satisfy oneself that everything works as it should and that the aircraft behaves as it was designed to. Unless there was some unforeseen snag, the flight test procedure for the Spitfire was straight-forward. The procedure differed somewhat from mark to mark, so in this description I shall confine myself to that for the Mark V.

After a thorough pre-flight check I would take off and, once at circuit height, I would trim the aircraft and try to get her to fly straight-and-level with hands off the stick. The Mark V lacked aileron trim tabs and most of the new ones had a tendency to fly with one wing low. When that happened I would land immediately and taxi to one corner of the airfield, where a mechanic would be waiting. He carried a special tool rather like a tuning fork, and on my instruction he would bend the trailing edge of the

aileron on his side once, twice or thrice, up or down. Then he would go round to the other side, and similarly bend the opposite aileron in the other direction. That done I would take off again and trim the aircraft to fly hands-off, to see whether the wing dropping had been cleared; usually it had, but if it had not the process was repeated until the trim was acceptable (sometimes, if bending alone was not sufficient, it was necessary to change the ailerons). It was a Heath Robinson system, but it did work.

Once the trim was satisfactory, I would take the Spitfire up in a full throttle climb at 2,850rpm to the rated altitude of the one or both supercharger blowers. Then I would make a careful check of the power output from the engine, calibrated for height and temperature. Many factors could give a false reading: a leaking boost gauge line, a high ambient temperature, a faultily calibrated rev-counter, or even an incorrectly set-up altimeter. If all appeared satisfactory, I would then put her into a dive at full power and 3,000rpm, and trim her to fly hands and feet off at 460 mph IAS. Unless this was all right, adjustments would be necessary to the elevator trim; or slight dressing down might be needed to the trailing edge of the tailplane.

Personally, I never cleared a Spitfire unless I had carried out a few aerobatic tests to determine how good or how bad she was; but the extent of this depended upon how tired or how rushed we were.

The production test was usually quite a brisk affair: the initial circuit lasted less than ten minutes and the main flight took between twenty and thirty minutes. Then the aircraft received a final once-over by our ground mechanics, any faults were rectified, and the Spitfire was ready for collection. Sometimes I would make more than twenty such test flights in a single day, necessary if previous bad weather had stopped flying and, with the production line going at full blast, the number of aircraft awaiting testing begain to mount.

As I have said, unless there was some unforeseen snag the flight test procedure was usually straightforward. But we did get the odd problem that gave us a lot of worry before we could get it sorted out. For example, there was one Spitfire which had been returned to us with a report that she behaved all right at normal speeds, but in high-speed dives she vibrated to such an extent that it seemed about to break up; a complete wing-change had been suggested. We at Castle Bromwich treated the report with some reserve; besides, a wing-change

During the Second World War men and women were drafted into the aircraft factories from all walks of life and, considering the sketchy training many of them received, the quality of the end product was remarkably high. These standards were the result of extreme specialisation by members of the work force, jigging for even the simplest of tasks, and rigorous inspection.

Below left: women putting together the port wing of a Spitfire.

Below: Seamstresses in the fabric shop, covering rudders.

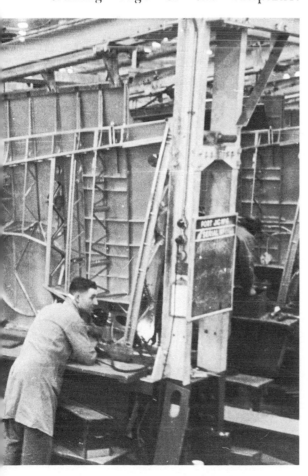

was a major job and we wanted to be sure that the fault could not be cleared by less drastic measures. However, when two of my experienced test pilots confirmed the seriousness of the vibration (one had even prepared to bail out), I knew we had to take the report seriously. I took the Spitfire up and, as everyone had said, at normal speeds every dial and gauge read correctly and her performance was average for the mark. I did some mild aerobatics and still everything seemed to be normal. So I stepped up the aerobatics, and as I dived preparatory to some vertical rolls there was a sudden bang like an explosion; there was a terrible row and the Spitfire seemed to vibrate so violently that I hastily prepared to bail out. I pulled out of the dive and then, as suddenly as it had began, the staccato noise and vibration ceased. It was all very mysterious. I flew

around for a while mulling over the matter, and finally decided to do a series of dives from high level and take down some figures; so far as I was able, I prepared myself for a possible break-up. At about 430mph in the first such dive the vibration set in again and I had to brace myself against the cockpit to take the figures I wanted. As I did so I found that I could read all the gauges quite easily; the readings were all normal. Gradually it dawned on me that while there was some vibration, the worst part of the problem was the staccato sound; and while the latter was certainly disturbing to the pilot, it appeared to be quite unharmful to the machine. Momentarily I took my hands off the controls and pressed them over the ear pads of my flying helmet to damp out the sound; to my surprise and intense relief, the Spitfire seemed to be behaving like

speed built up it would flap vigorously between the armour plating and the nearly empty fuel tank; and if that happened it would almost certainly give rise to the sort of kettle-drumming noise we had experienced. I immediately landed and had the tank top-cover removed; sure enough, the self-sealer had come adrift. With a new fuel tank fitted, she proved to be a perfectly ordinary Spitfire.

I loved the Spitfire, in every one of her many versions. But it has to be admitted that the later marks did not handle quite so nicely as the earlier ones had done. One test of manoeuverability was to throw her into a flick roll, and see how many times she rolled. With a Mark II or a Mark V one got two and a half flick rolls, but the later Mark IX was heavier and you got only one and a half; with the later and still heavier marks one got even less. Similarly with the earlier versions one could take off and go straight into a half loop and roll off the top, but the later Spitfires were much too heavy for that. The essence of aircraft design is compromise and an improvement at one end of the performance envelope is rarely obtained without a deterioration somewhere else.

Below: Spitfire EP 615 did not reach the RAF! On August 18th 1942, during a transit flight between Cosford and Castle Bromwich, Alex Henshaw suffered an engine failure. He tried to belly land between some houses near Willenhall but unfortunately an open camera flap caused one wing to stall first and drop, as he was committed to his final approach. The Spitfire struck a large tree which tore off the starboard wing, smashed into a nearby house, careered through the kitchen garden shedding pieces as she did so and finally came to rest in a field. Remarkably, in view of the damage to the aircraft, Henshaw escaped with only cuts, bruises and a severe shaking.

any other at that speed. I felt that I now had the key to the problem. But where was the noise coming from? I climbed the Spitfire again and took her into a third dive, and this time I felt all round the cockpit and thought I could feel a hard persistent hammering near the engine. I was however sure that the banging had nothing to do with the engine or the airscrew, for these had been changed earlier without curing the problem. It seemed to be coming from the engine bulkhead — or perhaps the main petrol tank. Then it came to me with such simplicity and suddenness that I couldn't resist shouting at myself for being such a bloody fool and not guessing the reason earlier. The top of the upper petrol tank had a thick outer covering of hard rubber self-sealer, and above it was a heavy piece of bullet-proof plating. If the self-sealer had become partially detatched, as the

The Balance Restored

Right: On August 19th 1942 Allied forces launched a large scale 'reconnaissance in force' on the French port of Dieppe, under a defensive umbrella provided by RAF Fighter Command. A total of forty-eight squadrons of Spitfires took part in the operation: forty-two with the Mark V, two with the Mark VI and four with the Mark IX. Throughout the day the fighters warded off repeated German attempts to attack the mass of shipping off the coast. In the photograph (top right) a Dornier 217 is seen under attack by a Spitfire; (bottom right), the same aircraft going down with its port engine belching smoke.

Below: Mark IX Spitfires of No 611 Squadron, one of the first units to receive the type.

The supremacy of the Focke Wulf 190 over the Spitfires lasted from September 1941 until July 1942, when No 64 Squadron received the first of the Mark IX Spitfires to enter service. With an airframe similar to that of the Mark V, the Mark IX was fitted with the new Merlin 61 engine which employed a two-stage supercharger using two centrifugal impellors in series. The new engine gave a substantial improvement in high altitude performance over the Merlin 46, which powered the Spitfire Mark V: at 30,000 feet the Merlin 46 developed 720 horse power whereas the Merlin 61 developed 1,020 — an improvement of more than forty per cent. This extra power was sufficient to close the gap in performance between the Spitfires and the Fw 190. Indeed, as this Air Fighting Development Unit report shows, the performance of these two fighters were now about as close as they could possibly be, considering the fact that they were quite different aircraft.

The Fw 190 was compared with a full operational Spitfire IX for speed and manoeuverability at heights up to 25,000 feet. The Spitfire IX at most heights is slightly superior in speed to the Fw 190 and the approximate differences in speeds at various heights are as follows:-

At 2,000ft the Fw 190 is 7-8mph faster than the Spitfire IX.
At 5,000ft the Fw 190 and the Spitfire IX are approximately the same
At 8,000ft the Spitfire IX is 8mph faster than the Fw 190.
At 15,000ft the Spitfire IX is 5mph faster than the Fw 190.
At 18,000ft the Fw 190 is 3mph faster than the Spitfire IX.
At 21,000ft the Fw 190 and the Spitfire IX are approximately the same.
At 25,000ft the Spitfire IX is 5-7mph faster than the Fw 190.

Climb During comparative climbs at various heights up to 23,000 feet, with both aircraft flying under maximum continuous climbing conditions, little difference was found between the two aircraft although on the whole the Spitfire IX was slightly better. Above 22,000 feet the climb of the Fw 190 is

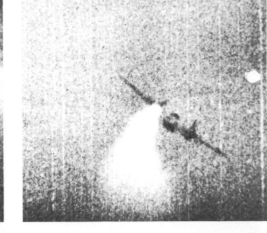

Below: As a measure to improve the performance of the Spitfire Mark V vis-a-vis the Fw 190, the wings of the former were 'clipped' by more than four feet. The modification increased the the rate of roll slightly, by reducing the inertia moment of the wing; it also increased the maximum speed by about 5mph up to 15,000 feet, though at the expense of both speed and rate of climb above 20,000 feet. Fitted with Merlins modified to give maximum power at low altitude, the clipped-winged version went into service designated the LF Mark V. She was not popular with those who flew her, however, and was referred to as the 'clipped, cropped and clapped Spitty'—referring to her shortened wings, the reduced size of the Merlin's supercharger blades and the fact that many of the aircraft had given their best during earlier service. This example belonged to No 315 (Polish) Squadron.

Below, right: High Endeavour. In 1940 the Luftwaffe took delivery of a small number of Junkers 86P high level reconnaissance aircraft and these began operations over the British Isles. Powered by two double supercharged two-stroke diesel engines, the Ju 86P could cruise at 36,000 feet; the later Ju 86R could cruise at 45,000 feet. The two-man crew was housed in a fully-pressurised cabin. These high-flying intruders and the ever-present possibility that the Germans might employ very-high-flying bombers in quantity, spurred the development of versions of the Spitfire for high altitude interception work. The Mark VI was the first specially-built variant of the Spitfire for high-altitude fighting and went into service in the spring of 1942. As well as a highly-supercharged version of the Merlin, the Mark VI was fitted with a pressure cabin and a longer-span wing; the latter was pointed, to reduce the strength (and therefore the drag) of the wing-tip vortices induced when flying at high angles of attack at high altitude. This example belonged to No 124 Squadron, one of the few units to receive the version.

Left: Squadron Leader Herbert Hallowes commanded No 165 Squadron during the Dieppe action and was credited with one Do 217 shot down and a further one damaged. He ended the war holding the rank of Wing Commander, credited with twenty-one victories.

falling off rapidly, whereas the climb of the Spitfire IX is increasing. When both aircraft were flying at high cruising speed and were pulled up into a climb from level flight, the Fw 190 had a slight advantage in the initial stages of the climb due to its better acceleration. This superiority was slightly increased when both aircraft were pulled up into the climb from a dive.

It must be appreciated that the differences between the two aircraft are only slight and that in actual combat the advantage in climb will be with the aircraft that has the initiative.

Dive The Fw 190 is faster than the Spitfire IX in a dive, particularly during the initial stage. This superiority is not as marked as with the Spitfire VB.

Manoeuverability The Fw 190 is more manoeuverable than the Spitfire IX except in turning circles, when it is out-turned without difficulty.

The superior rate of roll of the Fw 190 enabled it to avoid the Spitfire IX if attacked when in a turn, by flicking over into a diving turn in the opposite direction and, as with the Spitfire VB, the Spitfire IX had great difficulty in following this manoeuvre. It would have been easier for the Spitfire IX to follow the Fw 190 in the diving turn if its engine had been fitted with a negative 'G' carburettor, as this type of engine

with the ordinary carburettor cuts very easily.

The Spitfire IX's worst heights for fighting the Fw 190 were between 18,000 and 22,000 feet and below 3,000 feet. At these heights the Fw 190 is a little faster.

Both aircraft 'Bounced' one another in order to ascertain the best avasive tactics to adopt. The Spitfire IX could not be caught when 'bounced' if it was cruising at high speed and saw the Fw 190 when well out of range. When the Spitfire IX was cruising at low speed its inferiority in acceleration gave the Fw 190 a reasonable chance of catching it up and the same applied if the position was reversed and the Fw 190 was 'bounced' by the Spitfire IX, except that the overtaking took a little longer.

The initial acceleration of the Fw 190 is better than the Spitfire IX under all conditions of flight, except that in level flight at such altitudes where the Spitfire has a speed advantage and then, provided the Spitfire is cruising at high speed, there is little to choose between the acceleration of the two aircraft.

The general impression gained by the pilots taking part in the trials is that the Spitfire IX compares favourably with the Fw 190 and that provided the Spitfire has the initiative, it undoubtedly has a good chance of shooting down the Fw 190.

Below: Malta Spitfires. The first fighter (as distinct from reconnaissance) Spitfires to deploy for operations overseas were those flown off the deck of the aircraft carrier HMS Eagle to Malta in March 1942. During that operation and in the months that followed a total of 275 Spitfires were delivered to the beleaguered island, by by Eagle and the USS Wasp; these were sufficient to break the back of the German air attack on Malta. When this photograph of No 126 Squadron's aircraft was taken, at Luqa in the late summer, Spitfires at readiness could even be lined up in the open without undue risk.

10
Eagle Squadron, Eighth Air Force
Ervin Miller

Left: This Spitfire of No 121 'Eagle' Squadron was photographed in September 1942, a few days before the unit was handed over to the USAAF where it became No 335 Fighter Squadron.

About a thousand Spitfires of various Marks saw service in the US Army Air Force during the Second World War. An American citizen, Ervin Miller flew Spitfires with No 133 'Eagle' Squadron of the Royal Air Force, remained with the unit when it was transferred to the US Eighth Air Force and became the 336th Fighter Squadron in September 1942 and saw the Squadron's Spitfires replaced by Thunderbolts in the spring of the following year. In this section he recounts one American's very personnal memories of the most famous British fighter.

A citizen of the then-neutral USA, I volunteered for service as a pilot in the Royal Air Force in 1940. I was a young man who had fallen head-over-heels in love with flying and my job at the time, that of a US Government equipment inspector, served merely as a means of getting money to pay for my time airborne. By the middle of 1940 I had amassed about four hundred flying hours in light aircraft. In volunteering for the

RAF I must admit I had no noble motives like helping defeat Nazism, or defending freedom, or anything like that. All I wanted to do was get my hands on a really high-performance aircraft (at that time entry as a pilot into the US Army Air Corps was very restricted; if one did not have a degree — and I did not — it was almost impossible).

Initially things moved very slowly and it was mid-1941 before I began my advanced flying course (paid for by the British government) at a private flying school at Tulsa, Oklahoma. Towards the end of the year I received the King's Commision as a Pilot Officer in the RAF and came to Britain for further training which culminated at the Spitfire Operational Training Unit at Llandow in the spring of 1942.

The following May I joined No 133 'Eagle' Squadron at Biggin Hill, which was operating Spitfire Vs; the commander, Squadron Leader 'Tommy' Thomas, and the ground crewmen were British, the rest of the pilots were American. After a period of familiaris-

Below: Second Lieutenant Ervin Miller, pictured at Debden in 1942 soon after his transfer to the USAAF from the RAF.

ation I began flying on operations in June, but not until the end of July did I see (or rather, take part in) an air combat. On the 28th we were operating as one of the support wings for a sweep over France when Focke Wulfs and Messerschmitts 'bounced' us. I was flying as No 2 to Flight Lieutenant Don Blakeslee, my Flight Commander*, and before take-off he had said to me "If we get bounced, for Christ's sake don't lose me." Well, we were 'bounced' — and I didn't lose him. I just hung on like a leech and all I recall of my first dogfight was the sight of his tailwheel; I don't think I even noticed a Jerry!

I flew on a few more operations then, in August, the Squadron received some exciting news: we were to re-equip with the new Mark IX Spitfire. I made my first flight in one on the 26th; she was a beauty. While the old Mark V became 'mushy' above 20,000 feet as the engine power began to fall away, the Mark IX

*Blakeslee later rose to the rank of Colonel in the USAF, and ended the war credited with fifteen victories in aerial combat.

with her more-powerful Merlin and two-stage supercharger just seemed to go on and on up. Conversion presented no problems; as soon as we had sufficient Mark IXs we were declared operational on type.

In the mean time, even more fundamental changes were in the wind. It had been decided at high level that the three RAF 'Eagle' Squadrons, Nos 71, 121 and 133, were to transfer to the US Army Air Force where they would become respectively the 334th, 335th and 336th Squadrons of the 4th Fighter Group to be based at Debden. A few of the pilots elected to stay in the RAF but the rest, myself included, made the switch.

Just before the hand-over ceremony, however, disaster struck No 133 Squadron. On September 26th we were ordered to send twelve Spitfires, plus two spares, to the airfield at Bolt Head in Devonshire; the latter was to serve as forward operating base for a routine covering patrol for Fortresses attacking a German airfield near Brest. Only twelve

Below: The first USAAF fighter unit to see action in Europe, as distinct from the American-manned but RAF controlled 'Eagle' Squadrons, was the 31st Fighter Group which became operational in August 1942. In this photograph two Spitfire Vs of No 307 Squadron, part of the Group, are seen about to take off from Manston for a sweep over France shortly after the unit became operational.

of the Spitfires were required for the operation and as I was about to walk out with the others my Flight Commander, Flight Lieutenant Marion Jackson, called over "You stay behind this time, Dusty." The drop-out from the other Flight, Don Gentile*, and I had both been itching to have a go at the Focke Wulfs with our new Spitfires and we begged not be be left behind. But the Flight Commanders were adamant: we would stay at Bolt Head. Don and I did not realise it, but our respective guardian angels were watching over us that day.

The Squadron started up and took off, then formed up and disappeared into the layer of cloud. On the ground Don and I kicked our heels until their planned time of return, but there was no sign of them. Then the Spitfire Vs of a Canadian Squadron engaged in the same operation

*Don Gentile ended the war as a Major, credited with twenty-one victories in air combat.

Below: Second Lieutenant Don Gentile, pictured shortly after his transfer from the RAF to the USAAF, with his Spitfire 'Buckeye-Don'. Gentile ended the war credited with twenty-one victories in air combat, making him the top scorer of the ex-'Eagle' Squadron pilots.

returned, late, on the very last of their fuel. When our Squadron's Spitfires' limit of endurance time came and went, with still no sign of them, we knew that something dreadful had happened. Then we heard that one of our pilots, Bob Beaty, had crash landed a few miles up the coast; he had run out of fuel, but managed to glide back the last few miles and had reached land.

Later we were able to piece together the story of what had happened to the others. The Squadron had set out over 10/10th cloud cover which concealed the ground features and, unknown to them, at their altitude there was a north-easterly jet-stream with winds of over 100mph. The Spitfires were blown far into the Bay of Biscay before, on ETA and having sighted nothing the leader, Flight Lieutenant Dick Brettell, turned round for home. He called one of the ground direction-finding stations for a steer and the one he received placed him about where he expected to be (a single direction-finder could not, of course, provide range). Again on ETA the formation closed-up and let down through the layer of cloud. When they emerged out the bottom they found themselves over land, which they took to

Above: A clipped-wing Spitfire V of the 336th Fighter Squadron, seen at Debden following a landing accident which collapsed the port undercarriage leg.

be Cornwall. After a fruitless search for their airfield the eleven Spitfires found a large town, which they flew over at low level in an attempt to get a fix; by that time the aircraft were getting low on fuel. Suddenly all Hell broke loose: the town was the port of Brest, one of the most heavily defended German positions in France. Several of the Spitfires were shot down immediately by *Flak* or fighters; my good friend Gene Neville, who was occupying my usual position as No 2 to the Flight Commander, suffered a direct hit from *Flak* and was killed instantly. And those Spitfires which were not shot down simply ran out of fuel and crashed. Beaty had managed to get back only because his engine was running roughly and he had left the formation to return early. For him, Don Gentile and me, it had been a very narrow escape.

Following this incident the Spitfire IX, with which Fighter Command had hoped to take the Germans by surprise, came off the secret list. Afterwards there was a full court of inquiry. I understand that the existence of the strong tail wind had been known, but this vital information had not been passed to the fighter squadrons. I heard later that as a result some of the Sector controllers received hasty postings

to insalubrious destinations in the Far East.

The formal ceremony to hand the 'Eagle' Squadrons over to the USAAF took place at Debden on September 29th, three days after the Brest disaster, and it was a sadly depleted No 133 Squadron which took part. Moreover we had had to leave our shiny new Mark IX Spitfires at Biggin Hill and at Debden there were only the old Mark Vs. We were soon brought up to strength again with replacement pilots, however, and operations continued much as before.

From time to time we provided support for the daylight bomber attacks into occupied Europe; but the Spitfire was so restricted in range that we could not go where the action was. Of course the Germans knew this and again and again we saw them closing in on the bombers as shortage of fuel forced us to turn back.

One day in January 1943 General Hunter, the Commander of the VIIIth Fighter Command, came to visit us at Debden. He said he had a 'surprise' for us — we were soon to re-equip with the very latest American fighter, the P-47 Thunderbolt. As he spoke we heard an unusual engine note outside and one of

Spitfire Vs of the US 67th Tactical Reconnaissance Group which was based at Membury near Swindon from the autumn of 1942 until November 1943, as part of the Eighth Air Force. From time to time the unit's Spitfires took part in RAF fighter sweeps over northern France, though never in Group or Squadron strength.

the new fighters landed and taxied up beside one of our Spitfires. We went outside to look it over. It was huge: the wing tip of the P-47 came higher than the cockpit of the Spitfire. When we strapped into a Spitfire we felt snug and part of the aircraft; the Thunderbolt cockpit, on the other hand, was so large that we felt if we slipped off the Goddamned seat we would break a leg! We were horrified at the thought of going to war in such a machine: we had had enough trouble with the Focke Wulfs in our nimble Spitfire Vs; now this lumbering seven-ton monster seemed infinitely worse, a true 'air inferiority fighter'. Initial mock dog-fights between Thunderbolts and Spitfires seemed to confirm these feelings; we lost four Thunderbolt pilots in rapid succession, spinning in from low level while trying to match Spitfires in turns. In the end our headquarters issued an order banning mock dogfighting in Thunderbolts below 8,000 feet.

Gradually, however, we learnt how to fight in the Thunderbolt. At high altitude she was a 'hot ship' and very fast in the dive, the technique was not to 'mix it' with the enemy but to pounce on him from above, make one quick pass and get back up to altitude; if anyone tried to escape from a Thunderbolt by diving, we had him cold. Even more important, at last we had a fighter with the range to penetrate deeply into enemy territory — where the action was. So, reluctantly, we had to give up our beautiful little Spitfires and convert to the new juggernauts. The war was moving on and we had to move with it.

The change to the Thunderbolt might have been necessary militarily, but my heart remained with the Spitfire. Even now, thirty years after I flew them on operations, the mere sound or sight of a Spitfire brings me a deep feeling of nostalgia and many pleasant memories. She was such a gentle little aeroplane, without a trace of viciousness. She was a dream to handle in the air. I feel genuinely sorry for the modern fighter pilot who has never had the chance to get his hands on a Spitfire; he will never know what real flying was like.

11
Mediterranean Spits

Above: A Mark V, probably belonging to No 242 Group, pictured in Tunisia early in 1943. The aircraft was standing on the then-new Somerfield track used for the rapid construction of all-weather airfields; first the runway was rolled flat and covered with coir matting, then the operating surface of wire netting was laid on top.

Above right: Amongst the fighter units which went into Algeria and Morocco in November 1942 with the Allied invasion forces were two USAAF fighter Groups,

the 31st and the 52nd equipped with the Spitfire V. This example belonged to the 308th Fighter Squadron, part of the 31st Fighter Group.

Right: This Spitfire, pictured undergoing an engine run at an RAF maintenance unit in North Africa, has the fuselage marking of the 52nd Fighter Group. However the wings carry RAF roundels, in indicating that parts of more than one aircraft had been used to assemble this complete one.

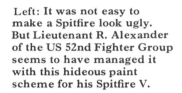

Left: It was not easy to make a Spitfire look ugly. But Lieutenant R. Alexander of the US 52nd Fighter Group seems to have managed it with this hideous paint scheme for his Spitfire V.

Bottom left, Below: No 145 Squadron had been the first unit in North Africa to become operational with Spitfires, in June 1942. It was also the first to transfer to Sicily and these photographs show its Spitfires at the newly-prepared airfield at Pachino on July 13th 1943, just three days after the invasion of the island. Spitfires were operating from the airstrip even before the army engineers had finished rolling out the taxi ways.

After the 'Junkers Party'. On the morning of July 25th 1943 Wing Commander Colin Gray was leading a sweep by thirty-three Spitfires of No 322 Wing over north-eastern Sicily, when he stumbled upon a large force of Junkers 52 transports about to land at Milazzo. During the ensuing 'party', twenty-one of the transports and four escorts were shot down. Gray (centre), who accounted for two of the Ju 52s, is pictured with other pilots from his Wing who were successful that day.

Seen wearing what passed for uniform during the Italian campaign are the senior officers of the Spitfire-equipped No 244 Wing. From left to right: Squadron Leader 'Stan' Turner, commanding No 417 Squadron RCAF; Squadron Leader 'Hunk' Humphreys, No 92 Squadron; Wing Commander Wilfred Duncan-Smith, the Wing Leader; Group Captain Charles Kingcombe, commanding officer of the Wing; Squadron Leader Lance Wade, an American who commanded No 145 Squadron; and Major 'Bennie' Osler, a South African who commanded No 601 Squadron.

Ordeal by mud. Ground-crewmen of No 92 Squadron endeavouring to shift a Mark VIII which had become bogged down, probably at Canne in central Italy.

Spitfires of No 43 Squadron, pictured at Capodichino near Naples during the winter of 1943; in the background is Mount Vesuvius.

Left: A Spitfire V of a USAAF unit in Italy, with General Doolittle at the controls; the General had asked to 'try his hand' at flying the nimble little fighter.

Right: A Mark IX Spitfire operated by the 309th Squadron of the 31st Fighter Group in Italy.

Below: Four-cannon Spitfire Vs of No 2 Squadron, South African Air Force, pictured in line-astern formation over the Adriatic.

Centre right: After the invasion of Italy in 1943 many Spitfires were used for ground attack work and, as was common in the area, local modifications were often made. Shown here is a Spitfire V of 126 squadron modified by the unit personnel to carry a 250lb bomb under each wing. On the one shown here, the arming wire attached to the front of the bomb prevented the small nose vane from turning which, after a certain number of revolutions, would set the fuse to "live". When the bomb was dropped normally, the wire remained with the aircraft; but if the pilot had to jettison his bombs over friendly territotry he was able to select a "safe" setting which caused an electrical solenoid to release the arming wire from the aircraft. This prevented the vane from turning after the bomb left the aircraft to ensure that no big bang ensued! This particular bomb was subsequently dropped "live" on a radar station in Albania.

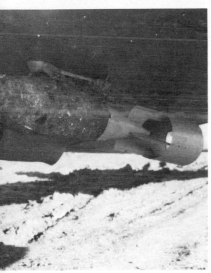

Below left: The makeshift arrangements for field maintenance are well illustrated here. Again, this is 126 squadron at Grottaglie in March 1944. There are many interesting points to note in the photograph: the battered oil-drum holding up the rear fuselage, and the two serviceable radiator units about to be fitted—an awkward job. Behind the ladder is the pilot's seat mounting; on the starboard wing is the long handle for the hydraulic hand-pump used for retraction tests, and also a cannon feed-drum for the starboard gun which has been removed. One of the most useful tools—a tommy-bar—is lying on the right-hand edge of the workbench and it is simply an old .303 Browning machine-gun barrel.

Below: Showing off her pointed wing-tips, this HF Mark VIII of No 417 Squadron RCAF is seen retracting her undercarriage immediately after take off from her base in Italy.

Defending Down Under

Left: Early in 1943 No 54 Squadron arrived in Darwin, Northern Australia, to take part in the defence of the area against Japanese attacks. In this photograph, one of the Squadron's Mark Vs is pictured just outside her camouflaged dispersal.

Bottom left: Early in 1944 No 54 Squadron re-equipped with Spitfire VIIIs. This interesting photograph, probably taken at Darwin, shows one of these aircraft with a four-cannon armament and pointed wing-tips for high altitude work.

Far left: Flight Lieutenant Tony Foster, left, was one of the more successful pilots of No 54 Squadron; credited with 3½ aircraft destroyed during the Battle of Britain, he opened the unit's score in the Far East on February 6th when he shot down a high-flying Japanese reconnaissance aircraft. He is seen here chatting to Flying Officer Tony Hughes.

Right: The overhead camouflage netting throws an interesting pattern of shadows on this Spitfire being readied at her dispersal at Darwin.

Left: The Spitfire flown by the commander of No 54 Squadron, Squadron Leader Eric Gibbs, being pushed into her dispersal.

Below: Taxying out for take-off.

12
An Aerodynamicists's View

Sir Morien Morgan, CB MA CEng FRAeS

From the time of her first flight, to well after the end of the Second World War, the Spitfire was continually modified to improve her fighting ability. In this section Sir Morien Morgan summarises these changes, and throws a new light on the basic reason for the Spitfire's long and successful service career.

In 1935 I joined the Aerodynamics Flight at the Royal Aircraft Establishment at Farnborough and from the start specialised in aircraft stability and handling. At that time there were several new monoplanes being built — including the Spitfire — which flew faster, climbed faster, and landed much faster than the biplanes that preceded them. I remember that there was a terrific rush to develop these new aeroplanes and learn their foibles, to telescope the whole business of background research design, pilot training and the rest of it; looking back, I am amazed that everyone did as well as they did — the designers, the research people and, of course, the pilots.

Let me give an example of the sort of mistaken ideas that got around early in the life of the Spitfire. We at Farnborough worked closely with the Aeroplane and Armament Experimental Establishment at Martlesham Heath, where they did the preliminary trials on the Spitfire and the other new military aircraft. I remember being there one day and talking to a very experienced RAF aerobatic pilot who had been involved with the tied-together formation aerobatic displays at Hendon. He had just landed after his first flight in the Spitfire prototype, utterly convinced that the days of close formation flying in fighters were numbered; he had handled his throttle in the same way as he did in a biplane and the much cleaner Spitfire had taken so long to lose speed that he thought close formation flying in such an aeroplane would be impossible. I was a young man at the time and what he said made a great impression on me: what effect would *this* have on future aerial combat? Later, when Martlesham had two or three Spitfires, they tried flying them in formation; and there was no real problem. I think the lesson here is that it is important for the pilots to get their hands on a new aircraft; when they do, it is surprising how fast they are able to adapt themselves to new conditions.

Looking back, I think that the greatest problem at the end of the 1930s was that it was extremely difficult to visualise what combat would be like in the new monoplane fighters; the only air fighting experts we had were from the First World War and that had been twenty years earlier. I think we all paid to much attention to the behaviour of an aeroplane flying on a calm sunny day and

Right: Pictured at Farnborough, this Spitfire IX carried modifications for the accurate measurement of airflow. On either side of the engine cowling she carried protruding lines of pitot heads, to measure the slip-stream from the three-bladed propeller—itself unusual on this mark of Spitfire; a further four pitot heads were mounted along the leading edge of the wing.

Below: Sir Morien Morgan.

harmonising the controls so that they could do nice aerobatic displays; we seemed to miss the importance of handling at speeds around the maximum permissable, in fast dives. Before the war, I remember, people thought that it was rather an academic exercise to scream downhill at one's maximum permissable speed.

The war soon brought us face to face with reality: once our fighter pilots started to mix it with the enemy they found that their main adversary, the Messerschmitt 109 which was less manoeuverable than the Spitfire, simply refused to dogfight in the manner expected; any German pilot who tried it did not live very long. Frequently the fight would develop into a diving race, either trying to 'bounce' the other fellow from out of the sun, or else trying to get away after being 'bounced'. And with the early Spitfires as one neared 400mph the ailerons became heavier and heavier, until at 430mph the pilot needed all the strength of both hands to get about one tenth aileron movement. In an air combat this was a crippling defect: if one was diving on an enemy the idea was to fire at him on the way down, and the poor aileron control made this very difficult. At the time there was a terrific flap about it and my Handling Research Team at Farnborough had the job of helping to track down the cause. Luckily

the reason was found quite quickly: at high speeds the fabric covering of the ailerons ballooned out, so that the trailing edge became much thicker. Now the amount of stick force required to move a control surface is critically dependant upon the sharpness of the angle of the trailing edge of the surface and just a small increase in the angle can make a considerable difference to the force needed. The answer was to replace the fabric on the ailerons with light alloy, which did not balloon at high speeds. Vickers hastily knocked out a set of metal-covered ailerons and when these were fitted to the Spitfire there was a dramatic improvement in its high speed handling characteristics. During 1941 there was a large-scale retrospective modification programme to fit all the Spitfires with the new ailerons.

In war nothing stands still; the Germans and the Japanese improved their aircraft and so did we. The key to higher performance was a more powerful engine and Rolls Royce began to get more and more power first out of the Merlin and then out of the Griffon. The Spitfire began to carry progressively larger propellers, with four and later five blades, to absorb this extra power. Aerodynamically, such a propellor produced an effect on stability similar to that one would expect from a large cruciform fin on the nose, while the

Below: This Spitfire Mark IV, the only one built, was the first to be fitted with the Griffon engine; the latter was developed from the Merlin and was only a little larger externally, but it had a cubic capacity greater by more than a third. At the time this photograph was taken the aircraft was being used to test the mock-up of the proposed six-cannon installation for the Spitfire, and modified flaps.

Bottom: The Spitfire XII was the first Griffon-engined version to enter service; only one hundred were built, and the Mark XII went into service with Nos 41 and 91 Squadrons early in 1943. The Griffon rotated the propeller in the opposite direction to the Merlin; thus, instead of the accustomed swing to the left during take-off, the Griffon Spitfires swung strongly to the right. On one occasion a pilot took off in one of the new Spitfires without receiving a briefing on this important difference. As he lined-up for take-off he wound on full right rudder trim and put on a boot-full of right rudder to catch the expected fierce torque from the engine when it took effect. He pushed open the throttle and, with everything set the wrong way, the Spitfire swung viciously to the right like an unleashed animal; she finally got airborne at ninety degrees to the intended direction of take-off, narrowly missing a hangar in her path. It was a chastened and extremely attentive young man who landed the Spitfire a few minutes later, to learn the mysteries of the new version!

slipstream rotation tried to screw the machine into a roll; the rotating propeller would twist the air behind it so that it hit the fin and tailplane at an angle. These factors combined to produce unpleasant handling characteristics during the climb at full power: a great deal of twist and airflow on the side of the fin, trying to make the aircraft roll and yaw simultaneously, at a time when there was insufficient airspeed over the rudder for it to 'bite' properly. These effects tended to become more and more serious as the Spitfire progressed through its various marks, and had to be corrected by adding more area to the fin and rudder. For the most part the story of the aerodynamic development of the Spitfire was one of piling on more and more power transmitted through larger and larger propellers and the airframe designer having to tailor the rear end to compensate for this. Some of the very late versions of the Spitfire were fitted with the contra-rotating propeller, which was the only real solution to the problem; but these did not go into service until well after the end of the war and then in only small numbers.

I have mentioned some of the problems we had with the Spitfire, but with her thin wing she was able to cope with the greater engine powers and the higher speeds better than any other fighter of her vintage. The thickness-

chord ratio at the wing root of the Spitfire was only about 13 per cent, compared with 14.8 per cent for the Messerschmitt 109 and 16 per cent for the Hurricane; even the later Mustang, hailed as a very clean aeroplane, had a 16 per cent wing. After the first year of war there was a steady pressure on designers to increase the maximum permissible diving speed of the new fighters entering service, because this was one of the things the pilots really wanted for combat. As a result we soon found ourselves on the brink of the subsonic region, with shock waves beginning to form on the wing. Now on a fattish wing the shock waves begin to form quite early, at about .7 Mach (roughly 500mph at 20,000 feet, depending on temperature). As the aircraft neared the speed of sound the shock waves got stronger and on those wartime aircraft they would begin to upset the airflow over the wing, effect fore and aft stability, and cause all sorts

of unpleasant effects. One way to postpone the Mach effects is to use a swept-back wing; but another is to have a thinner wing and that is why we at Farnborough selected the Spitfire as one of the aircraft for the exploratory work on high speed dives. This series of trials began in May 1943, and during its course Squadron Leader 'Marty' Martindale managed to get a Spitfire XI diving at about .9 Mach[*]. This was a most remarkable effort for an aircraft designed in 1935 and I think I am right in saying that this speed was not exceeded until the Americans began their trials with the rocket-powered Bell X-1 in

[*] It must be stressed that to achieve such a high Mach number the Spitfire had to be taken straight down in a 45 degree dive, from 40,000 feet to about 20,000 feet. Thus the ability to reach such a high Mach number was unlikely to occur during a fighter-versus-fighter combat, though reconnaissance Spitfires were sometimes to use high speed dives to escape from enemy jet fighters (see page 132).

1948; certainly the RAF had nothing able to out-dive the Spitfire until the swept-wing F-86 Sabre came into service in 1951. It was during one of these high speed dives, in April 1944, while he was coming down at more than 600mph, that 'Marty' suffered a loss of oil pressure to the airscrew constant speed unit; the propeller simply went round faster and faster, taking the protesting engine with it, until the blades fractured and the engine shook itself to pieces. In masterly fashion he regained control and after a glide of some 20 miles he landed safely at Farnborough in his strained aircraft. The following month he was flying a replacement Spitfire in a further trial in the series, and again at a high Mach number he suffered a burst super-charger. This time the weather was bad and he eventually crash landed in a wood not far from the airfield; he managed to scramble clear of his burning aircraft on the ground then, in spite of spinal

injuries, he returned to the wreck and retrieved the vital recording camera. For this he received a well-earned AFC.

Why was the Spitfire so good? I think it was because it had such a thin wing. Of course, Mitchell had been meticulous in his attention to detail in the design of the Spitfire; but basically the reason for her ability to remain in the forefront of the technological race for so long was the fact that she had a wing thinner than that of any of her contemporaries. Considering that he could have had little knowledge of Mach effects, Mitchell's decision to use such a thin wing was not only bold but in-spired. We now know that it was a close run thing: had he made the wing just a little thinner it would probably have been too weak, and aileron reversal would have been encountered lower down the speed scale. And if that had happened, the Spitfire would have been just one more of those aircraft that did not quite make the grade.

In a long war of attrition, repair was just as important as production.

Left: the large Spitfire salvage section at the overhaul and repair factory of Air Service Training at Hamble.

Top, Above: this seemingly ruined Mark XII, which had belonged to No 91 Squadron, was actually repaired at Hamble and put back in service.

Equal to the Very Best

The Mark XIV was the most potent version of the Spitfire to enter large-scale service before the end of the Second World War. In the spring of 1944 No 610 Squadron became operational with the Mark, eight years after the prototype Spitfire made her initial flight and five and a half years after the first Mark Is entered service. How did the Spitfire XIV stand in 1944, in comparison with other modern fighters in the Royal Air Force, the US Army Air Force and the *Luftwaffe?* Fortunately we know in some detail, for early in 1944 the Air Fighting Development Unit ran a trial to compare her with the Tempest V, the Mustang III (P-51B), the Focke Wulf 190A and the Messerschmitt 109G; had he lived to read the report, Reginald Mitchell would have had little reason to feel humble . . .

Brief Tactical Comparison with the Tempest V

Range and Endurance Rough comparisons have been made at the maximum cruising conditions of both aircraft. It is interesting that the indicated airspeed of each is about 280mph and the range of each is about identical; both with full fuel load (including long-range tanks) and without.

Maximum Speed From 0-10,000 feet the Tempest V is 20mph faster than the Spitfire XIV. There is then little to choose until 22,000 feet, when the Spitfire XIV becomes 30-40mph faster, the Tempest's operational ceiling being about 30,000 feet as opposed to the Spitfire XIV's 40,000 feet.

Maximum Climb The Tempest is not in the same class as the Spitfire XIV. The Tempest V, however, has a considerably better zoom climb, holding a higher

Below: A section of Spitfire XIVs of No 610 Squadron, the first unit to receive this version. The aircraft nearest the camera was piloted by the squadron commander, Squadron Leader R. Newbury.

speed throughout the manoeuvre. If the climb is prolonged until climbing speed is reached then, of course, the Spitfire XIV will begin to catch up and pull ahead.

Dive The Tempest V gains on the Spitfire XIV.

Turning Circle The Spitfire XIV easily out-turns the Tempest.

Rate of Roll The Spitfire XIV rolls faster at speeds below 300mph, but definitely more slowly at speeds greater than 350mph.

Conclusions The tactical attributes of the two aircraft being completely different, they require a separate handling technique in combat. For this reason, Typhoon squadrons should convert to Tempests, and Spitfire squadrons to Spitfire XIVs, and definitely never vice-versa, or each aircraft's particular advantages would not be appreciated. Regarding performance, if correctly handled, the Tempest is better below about 20,000 feet and the Spitfire XIV is better above that height.

Tactical Comparison with the Mustang III

Radius of Action Without a long-range tank, the Spitfire XIV has no endurance compared with the Mustang. With a 90 gallon long-range tank it has about half the range of the Mustang III fitted with two 62½ gallon long-range tanks.

Maximum Speed The maximum speeds are practically identical.

Maximum Climb The Spitfire XIV is very much better.

Dive The Mustang pulls away.

Turning Circle The Spitfire XIV is the better.

Rate of Roll. The advantage tends to be with the Spitfire XIV.

Conclusion With the exception of endurance, no conclusions should be drawn as these two aircraft should never be enemies. The choice is a matter of taste.

Combat Trial Against the Fw 190A

Maximum Speeds From 0-5,000ft and 15,000-20,000ft the Spitfire XIV is only

Below: The first Mark I Spitfires to be delivered carried no armour; but it was not long before steel plating to the rear of the pilot's seat, and a toughened glass windscreen, became standard. The armour fitted to the Spitfire Mark XIV was typical of that in a western fighter of the late war period; it was designed to protect the pilot against German Mauser 20mm armour-piercing rounds fired at medium ranges from the rear 20 degree cone and German 13mm rounds fired from the forward 20 degree cone (the former from attacking fighters, the latter from defending bombers). Although it suffered in the process, the engine also afforded the pilot considerable protection against rounds fired from ahead.

Light Alloy: 8 SWG – approx 4 mm 10 SWG – approx 3 mm

Armour Plate: 7mm 6mm 4mm

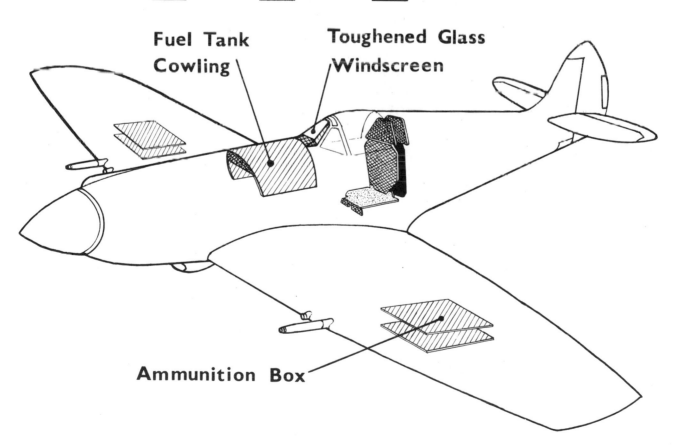

Fuel Tank Cowling

Toughened Glass Windscreen

Ammunition Box

20mph faster; at all other heights it is up to 60mph faster than the Fw 190A. It is estimated to have about the same maximum speed as the new Fw 190 (DB 603) at all heights*.

Maximum Climb The Spitfire XIV has a considerably greater rate of climb than the Fw 190A or (estimated) the new Fw 190 (DB 603) at all heights.

Dive After the initial part of the dive, during which the Fw 190 gains slightly, the Spitfire XIV has a slight advantage.

Turning Circle The Spitfire XIV can easily turn inside the Fw 190. Though in the case of a right-hand turn, this difference is not quite so pronounced.

Rate of Roll The Fw 190 is very much better.

Conclusions In defence, the Spitfire XIV should use its remarkable maximum climb and turning circle against any enemy aircraft. In the attack it can afford to 'mix it' but should beware the quick roll and dive. If this manoeuvre is used by an Fw 190 and the Spitfire XIV follows, it will probably not be able to close the range until the Fw 190 has pulled out of its dive.

Combat Trial Against the Me 109G

Maximum Speed The Spitfire XIV is 40mph faster at all heights except near 16,000ft, where it is only 10mph faster.

Maximum Climb. The same result: at 16,000ft the two aircraft are identical, otherwise the Spitfire XIV out-climbs the Me 109G. The zoom climb is practically identical when the climb is made without opening the throttle. Climbing at full throttle, the Spitfire XIV draws away from the Me 109G quite easily.

Dive During the initial part of the dive, the Me 109G pulls away slightly, but when a speed of 380mph is reached, the Spitfire XIV begins to gain on the Me 109G.

Turning Circle The Spitfire XIV easily out-turns the Me 109G in either direction.

Rate of Roll The Spitfire XIV rolls much more quickly.

Conclusion The Spitfire XIV is superior to the Me 109G in every respect.

Combat Performance with 90 Gallon Long-Range Tanks

As the Spitfire XIV has a very short range it has been assumed that when a long-range tank is to be carried, it is most likely to be the 90 gallon tank rather than the 30 gallon or 45 gallon. Pending further instructions, no drops or trials have been carried out with the 30 gallon or the 45 gallon tanks. The aircraft's performance with either can be estimated from the results given below of trials with the 90 gallon long-range tank.

Drops The aircraft was fitted with assistor springs as for the Spitfire IX. Two drops were made with empty tanks at 50ft and 25,000ft, 250mph IAS, with no real trouble. Cine photographs were taken and show the tank dropping quite clear of the aircraft. Further trials would be necessary to check these results thoroughly.

Speeds About 20mph is knocked off the maximum speed and correspondingly off the speed at intermediate throttle settings. The aircraft is then still faster than the Fw 190A and the Me 109G above 20,000 feet.

Climb Climb is most effected. With a half-full tank its maximum climb becomes identical with the Spitfire IX without the tank. Even with a full tank it can therefore climb as fast as the Fw 190A or the Me 109G. Its zoom climb is hardly effected.

Dive So long as the tank is more than one-third full, the dive acceleration is similar.

Turning Circle The Spitfire XIV now has a definitely wider turning circle than before, but it is still within those of the Fw 190A and the Me 109G.

Rate of Roll Similar to that when no tank is fitted.

Conclusions Even with a 90 gallon long-range tank, the Spitfire XIV can equal or outclass the Fw 190A and the Me 109G in every respect. Its main advantages remain the tight turn and the maximum climb.

*This is a reference to the 'D' version of the Fw 190, fitted with the more powerful Daimler Benz 603 motor, whose appearance had long been predicted by Allied air intelligence; in fact, the first Fw 190Ds were not encountered in combat until late in the summer of 1944.

The Second Greatest Thrill a Man Can Have
Frank Hercliffe

A Seafire with a trainee pilot about to touch down on the short deck of the escort carrier HMS Ravager Lieutenant Astin was on the bats, while Lieutenant Cunningham maintained a strong professional interest in the proceedings.

Right: As she approached to land on HMS Attacker this Seafire L.11c of 879 squadron went too low; note the raised arms of the batsman, behind the screen, telling the pilot he must go up.

Centre Right: The pilot applied power to clear the edge of the deck but overdid it, and began to increase his speed. He was now in the wrong attitude to take a wire and bounced over all of them . . .

Below right: . . . going full-tilt into the barrier . . .

Bottom right: . . . before finally coming to rest in the forward deck park after smashing the tail of a stationary Seafire.

Far right: The Seafire was judged a write-off and, after everything useful had been stripped from her, axes were used to smash the wings and fuselage to ensure that when dumped the wreckage would sink rapidly.

Below far right: Carefully the wreckage was lowered into the water, lest it should sink too quickly and foul the ship's screw or rudder.

The landing of any sort of fixed-winged aircraft on the deck of a ship requires flying skill of a high order. But to land a Seafire on the short flight deck of an escort carrier was particularly difficult, for there was little margin for error.

Having completed almost a hundred hours flying time in the Seafire and made scores of aerodrome dummy deck landings at the Naval Air Station at Henstridge in Somerset, as a young Sub-lieutenant I was judged to be ready for my first landing on a carrier at sea. Accordingly I took off from the Naval Air Station at Ayr one fine summer's day and made off north-eastwards at 3,000 feet towards the training carrier *HMS Ravager,* which was cruising off the Isle of Arran. A few minutes after take-off I caught sight of her — or rather her wake — as she pushed herself through the water at about 20 knots. From the air she looked ridiculously small. Could I *really* land on that?

Over the radio I received clearance to join the carrier's circuit; and once I was down at 500 feet she did look a little bigger — though still too small for my liking. Quickly I ran through my pre-landing checks: wheels, flaps and hook down, mixture rich and propeller in fine pitch. Then I pulled my harness

Above: When the remains were well clear the line was let slip, and another Seafire was consigned to 'the greatest dustbin in the world'.

Below: Flying accidents were not the sole hazard to aircraft, life and limb on an aircraft carrier. During the night of August 6th 1943 the escort carrier HMS Hunter, carying the Seafires of Nos 899 and 834 Squadrons, ran into a gale in the Bay of Biscay. One of the Seafires had not been lashed down securely enough and broke free. Defying all attempts by the ship's crew to secure her, she smashed into the next aircraft and cut her free also. The process continued and within a short time the hangar was filled with Seafires sliding up and down the deck as the ship rolled and pitched, bent on destroying themselves and all around them. This photograph, showing Hunter's hangar as it looked on August 7th, convey the scene of utter chaos and destruction. The Seafires were of the 11C version, which lacked provision for wing folding.

Seafires pictured with some of the more exotic naval loads: Top with the Mine 'A' Mark VIII, which weighed 500 pounds; Centre: with two 200 pound smoke floats; and Above with the 250 pound 'B' bomb. The 'B' (or buoyant) Bomb had a hollow nose section, and was designed to attack moving armoured warships from underneath. Released into the water ahead of the target ship, the bomb's momentum took it to a depth of about 50 feet before it up-ended and floated nose-first to the surface; on the way up it would (hopefully) be 'run-over' by the ship and explode against the thin bottom plating. Great things had been expected from this weapon prior to the war and it was issued to several RAF and Fleet Air Arm squadrons; but the problem of accurate aiming was never solved and the 'B' bomb was rarely and never successfully used on operations.

Right: A Seafire III, showing the method of wing folding introduced with this version.

tight, pulled down my goggles, and slid back the hood. The view over the nose of the Seafire was notoriously bad and the only way to put one down on the deck was to fly a curved approach to enable one to keep the carrier in sight throughout. I began my run in from a position about half a mile off *Ravager's* port quarter, with my head out the port side of the cockpit watching the antics of the batsman on the port side of the carrier.

During the final approach I knew I had to follow the batsman's instructions implicitly; since my own head was outside the cockpit I had no idea what my instruments were reading and I had to rely on him to bring me in. But the batsmen were all very experienced deck landing pilots themselves and they knew their business; merely by observing the attitude of the Seafire, they could judge her speed to within 2 or 3 knots. That final approach took well under a minute, but at the time it felt like a lifetime: nose well up, plenty of power on and the deck getting progressively larger and larger. The batsman's signals told me I was doing all right: down a bit . . . down a bit . . . OK . . . OK . . . Suddenly his left forearm went horizontally across his chest: cut! I yanked back the throttle and for an instant everything seemed to go quiet. Then the hook caught the No 2 wire, my Seafire was plucked from the sky and the wheels hit the deck with a thump. Firmly I was drawn to a halt and, thanks to my tightened straps, I had no feeling of violent deceleration. I was down!

Almost at once people seemed to emerge from holes all round the deck. The Deck Control Officer ran out to a position in front of my starboard wing, two seamen ran out clutching chocks and made for my wheels, and through the corner of my eye I could see others struggling to clear my hook from the wire and lock it in the 'up' position under the fuselage. The next thing I knew, the DCO was waving his flag above his head: the signal for me to rev. up the engine for an immediate take off. I was much too busy for any self-congratulations, which was probably just as well.

The take-off from a carrier was straight forward, though it did involve a bit of juggling immediately afterwards. Because of the risk of ditching we always launched with our canopies open and the door catches on half-cock so that we could get them open quickly if we had to make a hurried exit. For the actual take-off we held the stick in the right hand and the throttle in the left. Then, as soon as we were airborne, we had to change hands and take the stick in the left, so that we could retract the undercarriage with the lever on our right. That done we had to change hands again, controlling the Seafire with the right hand while closing fully the door with our left. Then we changed hands yet again, holding the stick in the left hand while sliding forward the canopy with our right. After that a final change of hands, to enable us to press the throttle-mounted transmit button and announce to the world that we were safely airborne. At the end of it all, I knew how the proverbial one-armed paper-hanger must have felt!

That first day I did eight landings, with a break for coffee in the middle; my third was a bit hairey, when I took No 7 out of the eight wires — had I taken the 8th, I should also have hit the barrier. So it was that I had my initiation into the realities of landing a Seafire on the deck of an escort carrier — the second greatest thrill a man can have.

13
Gunfire Spotter
Captain Dick Law, CBE DSC RN (Retired)

Versatility was one of the most important assets possessed by the Spitfire, and during the Second World War she was employed on a range of tasks which probably went far beyond Reginald Mitchell's wildest dreams for his beautiful little fighter. One such was that of spotting for the heavy naval guns which played such an important part during the invasion of Normandy.

In March 1944 I was a Lieutenant serving as the Senior Pilot of No 886 Squadron, equipped with the Seafire L III. It was then that we learned that our role in the forthcoming invasion was to be that of gunfire spotters for the bombarding battleships, cruisers and monitors. Our targets were to be the German coastal batteries, with their large calibre guns set in massive concrete emplacements, positioned to cover all possible landing areas along the northern coast of France.

The importance of our spotting role was drilled into us from the beginning and there was no feeling that we, as fighter pilots, were to be missemployed during the great invasion. Only heavy naval gunfire, corrected from the air and sustained for a period of days if need be, could neutralise these powerful defensive positions during the critical period while our troops fought their way ashore: low level bombing would have been too costly, high level bombing would have been too inaccurate and neither type of bombing could have brought speedy retaliation against the new batteries the Germans were almost certain to bring up.

Gradually we learnt the mechanics of bringing heavy gunfire to bear on a target; first on a sand table, then with a

Lieutenant Dick Law bringing his Seafire close alongside the photographic aircraft. The Seafire, serial MB 328, was the first machine in the batch of forty-eight Mark IBs which had been converted from Mark V Spitfires in mid-1942, by Air Services Training.

Above: Dick Law, pictured after the war when he held the rank of Commander.

gunfire spotting it was usual for our Seafires to fly in pairs, with one correcting the fire and the other standing off a couple of thousand feet above keeping watch for any enemy fighters which might attempt to interfere.

The first target we were to engage was the battery at Villerville near Trouville, where there were six 155mm guns in a heavily concreted position. When I was ready, the carefully-rehearsed patter began. I called up *Warspite* on the VHF and told her "Target located, ready to open fire". She gave me a call five seconds before opening fire, then as she fired she called "Shot" followed by a figure, say "52"; the figure gave the predicted time of flight of the shells — just over fifty seconds for the firing range of fifteen miles. The battleship was a magnificent sight as she lay at anchor, loosing off four-gun salvoes with her main 15-inch guns. On the call "Shot" I started my stop-watch and headed inland, so as to have the target in clear view when the shells impacted. As they burst I would radio back a correction to bring the fire directly on to the target, say "Left 100, up 400", the distances being measured in yards. While the ship's gunners were reloading I would head back over the sea; there was no point in hanging around over enemy territory and risking being shot down and jeopardizing the whole operation, for no useful purpose.

When *Warspite* indicated that she was ready to fire again, I would move into position to observe the target and the process would be repeated.

During one of the early salvoes I was a little over-enthusiastic in positioning myself to observe the fall of the shells, with the result that some thirty-five seconds after *Warspite* had fired my Seafire suddenly shivered and I actually saw one of the giant shells, weighing almost a ton, go sizzling close past me on its way to the target. During subsequent salvoes, I made good and sure that I was well to the side of the line of fire!

From time to time the German batteries attempted to return *Warspite's* fire; when that happened we were

troop of 25 pounders on an army gunnery range and finally with a cruiser firing off the coast of Scotland. Near the end of May we moved to our operational base for the invasion, at Lee on Solent; the great event, for which we had all trained so hard, was close at hand.

On the actual day of the invasion, June 6th, I was up very early and with my wingman I arrived over Normandy soon after 0600 hours to take control of the guns of the battleship *HMS Warspite*. I should mention that for treated to the spectacle of a giant-sized tennis match. During one of these exchanges a salvo straddled *Warspite,* but she received only slight damage.

After about forty minutes of spotting my fuel was beginning to run low, and after being relieved by two more Seafires we returned to Lee. We spotted for *Warspite* during two further sorties that day.

On the second day of the invasion, June 7th, we were detailed to spot for American warships on the western flank of the bridgehead; accordingly, I found myself controlling the gunfire of the battleship *USS Nevada.* The shoot went according to plan and when the relieving Seafires arrived both my wingman and I had some fuel to spare; so we decided to seek out a 'target of opportunity' (anything on the ground that looked vaguely German) and shoot it up before going home.

The decision, casually made, nearly proved fatal for me. Looking back on that part of the sortie, I can see now that we were both grossly overconfident about the success of the invasion. We had been keyed-up for a ding-dong battle with the *Luftwaffe;* but the enemy air force had simply failed to show up and from our lofty viewpoint it appeared that the whole thing was becoming a walk-over. Now we felt that we could hardly go home without having played some more direct part in the impending collapse of the Third Reich. Below us we saw an enemy gun position and we decided that we would wipe it off the face of the earth. It was not, however, a very professional attack; confident in our superiority we took our time turning in and lining up and the men on the ground could have had no doubts regarding our intentions. Unfortunately for us the guns were 37mm *Flak,* manned by crews who certainly did not share our feelings regarding the hopelessness of their cause. As we ran in they were ready and their first few rounds of tracer were extremely accurate: I heard a rapid 'plunk plunk' as a couple of the shells exploded against my aircraft. It was immediately apparent that they had hit my radiator,

for almost at once my engine temperature guage needle began to climb steadily until finally it was hard against the upper stop. Simultaneously I caught the unmistakable stench of vapourized glycol and the engine coughed to a stop.

I pointed the Seafire's nose towards the coast as I pulled up, but it soon became clear that I had insufficient height to reach the sea; I selected some flat land a little way inland and prepared to put her down there. The actual belly landing was a bit of an anti-climax: the Seafire slid gently to a halt on the soft marshland and there was no fire or drama of any sort.

As I clambered out of the aircraft I rapidly became aware of the appalling din of battle: there seemed to be guns of all calibres firing and shells exploding — the latter, fortunately, all some distance away. In the cockpit of my noisy aircraft far above, I had been quite oblivious to the intensity of the battle below.

Then the rushes in front of me parted, and there was a very tall American negro Corporal who beckoned me over. Apparently, I had come down in an uncontested part of no-man's-land. When I reached him his first gesture was to offer me a swig from his water bottle; I was not all that thirsty at the time but I thought it good manners to accept — and I was glad I did, for the bottle contained a very reasonable vin rose. I later learned that he had been ashore only a few hours, so he must have been a pretty good organiser!

Gradually I worked my way back through the system to the beach, where I was taken out to a motor torpedo boat which took me back to England. I was soon able to rejoin my squadron and, after my salutary experience, contented myself with betting bigger guns than my Seafire's to do the work of destruction.

The success of the Normandy landings and their effect on the course of the war, are now common knowledge. Without doubt the accuracy of the heavy naval gunfire played a major part in making this possible, and I am very happy that I was able to assist in this.

14
Achtung! Jabo!

German motor transport burning in Normandy, after a fighter-bomber attack.

With the Luftwaffe able to mount only spasmodic operations over Normandy after the invasion, the Allied fighters were able to concentrate their efforts against the enemy ground forces. Achtung! Jabo! (Look out! Fighter-bomber!) became a shout to strike fear in the hearts of the German soldiers. Although tests had been carried out, the Spitfires did not carry rockets during this battle, but they were no less effective against the German armour for that. In fact it was the lack of fuel, due to the aerial interdiction of supplies, which crippled the Panzer Divisions in Normandy and not, as many sources have stated, the attacks by rocket-firing fighters. After the Falaise battle operational research teams from the British 21st Army Group combed the area and found a total of three hundred abandoned German tanks and self-propelled guns (almost sufficient to equip two Panzer Divisions). Of these only eleven (less than **4** per cent) had been knocked out by rockets. Fifty-four had been abandoned for miscellaneous reasons (mechanical breakdown, etc) and two had been knocked out by bombs. The remaining 233 (77 per cent) were undamaged or else had been destroyed by German demolition charges; lacking fuel, they could not move when the German army began its headlong retreat. The persistent strafing attacks on the

German columns of soft-skinned supply vehicles, by Spitfires and other Allied fighters using cannon and machine-guns, played a major part in creating the conditions for the victory on the ground. These German photographs, taken during the battle, provide an interesting insight into conditions on the other side of the battle line:

Top: a Spitfire seen pulling

up after a strafing run;

Above: Jabofalle (fighter-bomber-trap), a heavily camouflaged quadruple-barrelled 20mm Flak gun, awaiting an enemy to be lured into range by a tempting target nearby;

Topcentre: a German soldier standing guard over a Spitfire of No 602 Squadron which had been shot down over Normandy.

Above: A high-altitude variant like the Mark VI, the Mark VII was powered by the more powerful Merlin 61 engine. Although many of the Mark VIIs were fitted with the pointed wing tips it can be seen that this example, which belonged to No 131 Squadron, had normal eliptical tips. No 131 Squadron received its Mark VIIs in March 1944 and, at the time this photograph was taken, provided bomber escorts after the Normandy invasion, and also operated in the ground-attack role.

Left: Engine-change de-lux: fitters of No 442 Squadron RCAF doing an engine change in the field, with the luxury of a mobile crane to the hard work. If no such crane was available ground crews had to use a set of wooden shear legs with a block and tackle to hoist the engine out, then push the Spitfire clear before lowering the engine on to a trolley; refitting was the same process, in reverse. During the campaigns in North Africa, Italy, France and the Far East, the great majority of Spitfire servicing had to be done in the open where, as one fitter commented: "If it rained that was just tough luck— both you and the Spitfire got wet!"

Left: A close-up of the so-called 'Depth Charge Modification XXX', to enable the Spitfire to transport a pair of containers with a beverage in great demand in Normandy. The Spitfire was not cleared for the full range of combat manoeuvers while operating in this configuration.

115

Spitfire v Doodle Bug

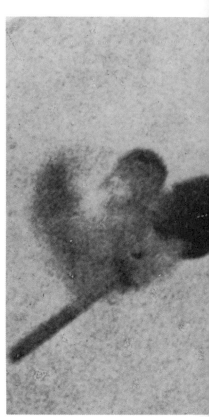

Left: One way to bring down a V 1, without risking detonating the warhead, was to topple its gyro-stabilisation mechanism by tipping up a wing; the V 1 had no ailerons and was therefore particularly vulnerable to interference in the rolling plain. Some pilots achieved the tipping by the 'brute force' method of using their own wing to knock up that of the flying-bomb; but since the V 1s were skinned in rolled steel and the wing tips of the fighters were constructed from far weaker light alloy, this method was not without hazards of its own. A rather neater method was to make use of simple aerodynamics, to achieve the same end without actually coming into physical contact with the bomb . . .

Far right: (1) the Spitfire pilot positioned his wing close over that of the V 1, thus destroying the lift on that side . . . (2) and the flying-bomb's wing dropped. The fighter remained in position causing the missile to increase its angle of bank until the crude stabilisation system could no longer cope and . . . (3 and 4) it fell out of control and the Spitfire pulled clear.

Right: An ever-present danger if attacks on V 1s were pressed to short range was that the warhead, containing nearly 1,900 pounds of high explosive, would detonate. Flight Lieutenant G. Armstrong of No 165 Squadron brought back this 'toasted' Spitfire IX after a rather-too-exciting tussle with a V 1 on July 1st.

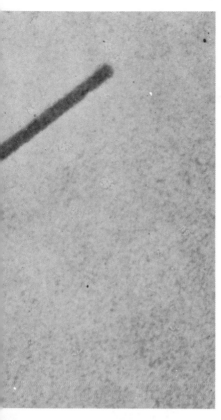

Left: In June 1944 the Germans opened their long-expected bombardment of London using V 1 flying-bombs. Although it flew straight and level, the V 1 was not an easy target to shoot down. The speeds at which these missiles flew varied greatly, with the slowest coming in at about 300mph and the fastest recorded at 440mph; thus while the slower missiles were comparatively easy for fighters to catch, the fastest outran all except the Spitfire XIVs and Tempest Vs. Moreover, since the flying-bombs were constructed mainly from sheet steel, they were less vulnerable to cannon and machine-gun fire than were normal manned aircraft. This photograph shows a V 1 receiving a strike from a 20mm explosive shell, fired from the starboard quarter.

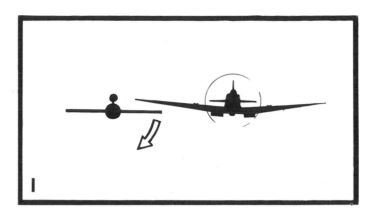

1

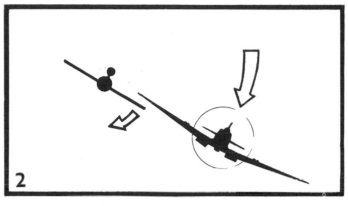

2

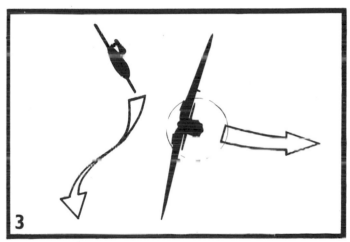

3

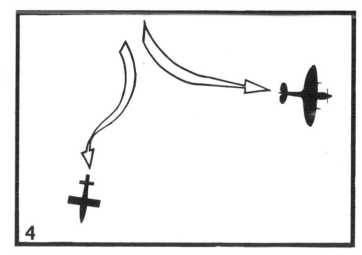

4

117

15
Foe Without Mercy
Wing Commander 'Hank' Costain, MBE

In spite of the advances made in aviation, man is allowed to use the sky on sufferance, never as a right; and, as 'Hank' Costain now tells us, the elements can regain control of their domain in most brutal fashion.

During the summer of 1944 I was a Flying Officer with No 615 Squadron, operating Spitfire VIIIs. During the battle to repel the attempted Japanese invasion of India we had been flying from Palel on the Imphal Plain; but the time came for us to pull back out of the front line for a brief rest. Accordingly on August 10th our sixteen aircraft took off from Palel with the CO in the lead, for a nice easy trip back to Baigachi near Calcutta; for a quarter of the pilots, however, the flight would be their last.

For much of the route we had underneath us puffs of thin fair-weather cumulus, and as we neared our destination we let down through them. Soon afterwards the cloud cover above us became complete, but as we had good contact with the ground everything seemed all right. Indeed it was, until straddling our path we found a thick brown storm cloud extending right down to the ground. Clearly we could

Above: Wing Commander 'Hank Costain.

Right: Hank Costain with one of the Mark VIII Spitfires of No 615 Squadron, at readiness at Palel in June 1944.

not go forwards through it and, because we had passed our point of no return, we could not go back to Palel either. So the CO decided to take us back a little way, then we could climb up through the layer of cumulus and once above it we could search for a way through the storm. But it never happened that way.

Soon after re-entering cloud there was a sudden bang, and everything seemed to happen at once: the sky turned black as pitch, my Spitfire reared up and the stick seemed to go wild in its attempts to wrench itself out of my grasp. Somehow we had slid into that dreadfully turbulent monsoon storm cloud. Within seconds I was completely out of control and with the artificial horizon toppled I had not the faintest idea which way was 'up'. Outside it was so dark that I could not even see my wing tips and the pounding of the walnut-sized hailstones on the fuselage drowned even the noise of the engine. In my earphones I heard the frenzied chatter of the other pilots as they tried to fight their way free from the storm's clutches.

Of my flight instruments only the altimeter seemed to be reading correctly, and from its spinning needles I learned that I was in a violent up-current. After going up rapidly through nearly ten thousand feet, during which my stick seemed to have no effect at all, the Spitfire bucked and entered an equally-vicious down-draft and we were plunging earthwards just as fast. I was terrified. Again, nothing I did with my controls seemed to make the slightest difference. As the altimeter reading neared 1,000 feet it became clear that this was no place for Mrs Costain's young lad. I had to bail out.

First I had to get rid of the hood, so I yanked hard on the jettison ball above my head; but the tropical heat had perished the rubber and it came away in my hand. Charming! Since the hood would not jettison I slid it fully back on its runners, then trimmed the nose fully down and undid my seat harness. Finally I let go of the stick and, as the Spitfire bunted forwards, up I went like a cork out of a bottle. At least I would have done, but not my parachute pack caught on the overhanging lip of the hood. The next thing I knew I was tumbling head-over-heels along the fuselage before ramming hard into the tailplane and shattering my leg. As the tail disappeared into the gloom I grabbed at the parachute 'D' ring and pulled it, then I glanced down to see the ground rushing up to meet me.

The canopy developed just in time, but even so the landing on my fractured leg was excruciatingly painful. As I lay in a sodden heap in that flooded Indian paddy field and began to collect my wits, my first thoughts were for the perfectly good Spitfire I had just abandoned. "Good God", I remember thinking, "What on earth am I going to tell the CO?" Luckily I was picked up by some of the locals soon afterwards and they took me to a doctor.

In less than five minutes No 615 Squadron had lost its commander and three other pilots killed and three more including myself injured; we had written-off half of our aircraft, eight of the most modern fighters in the theatre. And it had all happened without there being a Jap within a hundred miles. When it is angry, the sky is a foe without mercy.

Above: The captured
Japanese Mitsubishi A6M5
Zero-Sen fighter, Allied
code-name Zeke 52, which
flew in the comparative
performance trial against
the Seafire L IIC at the US
Navy test centre, Patuxent
River, in October, 1944.

In October 1944 Lieutenant Dick Law was sent to the US Naval Air Station at Patuxent River, Maryland, for a most interesting assignment: to take part in a comparative performance trial between the Seafire LIIC and a captured Zeke 52 — an improved version of the famous Zero fighter. Reproduced below are the conclusions drawn from the trial.

Results of Trials

The peak speeds of the two aircraft are:-

Seafire LIIC — 338mph at 5,500ft
Zeke 52 — 335mph at 18,000ft

The comparative speeds in miles per hour are:

Height	Seafire LIIC	Zeke 52
Sea Level	316	292
5,000ft	337	313
10,000ft	337	319
15,000ft	335	327
20,000ft	328	333
25,000ft	317	327
30,000ft	—	317

Climb the Zeke 52 climbs at a very steep angle and gives the impression of a very high rate of climb. The Seafire LIIC, however, has a much better initial climb and remains slightly superior up to 25,000ft.

The climb of the Seafire is at a higher speed, but at a more shallow angle.

The best indicated climbing speeds of the Zeke and the Seafire are 120mph and 160mph respectively.

Manoeuverability Turning plane — the Zeke 52 can turn inside the Seafire LIIC at all heights. The Zeke 52 turns tighter to the left than to the right.

Rolling plane — the rate of roll of the two aircraft is similar at speeds below 180mph IAS, but above that the aileron stick forces of the Zeke increase tremendously, and the Seafire becomes progressively superior.

Dive The Seafire is superior in the dive although initial acceleration is similar. The Zeke is a most unpleasant aircraft in a dive, due to heavy stick forces and excessive vibration.

Tactics: Never dogfight with the Zeke 52 — it is too manoeuerable.

At low altitudes where the Seafire is at its best, it should make use of its superior rate of climb and speed to obtain a height advantage before attacking.

If jumped, the Seafire should evade by using superior rate of roll. The Zeke cannot follow high speed rolls and aileron turns.

Conclusions The Seafire LIIC is 24 mph faster at sea level, this difference decreasing to parity between 15,000 and 20,000ft. The Zeke 52 is 10mph faster at 25,000ft.

The Seafire can out-climb the Zeke up to 25,000ft.

The Zeke is very manoeuverable and can turn inside the Seafire at all altitudes.

The Zeke fights best between 115 and 180mph IAS.

The rate of roll of the Seafire is better than that of the Zeke above 180mph IAS.

The Quest for Range

Right, Top right: Towards the end of 1943 the Flight Refuelling Company worked out a method of towing a Spitfire from a multi-engined bomber, as a means of extending the ferry range of the former; during the subsequent trials, a Wellington acted as tug. The towing line consisted of a 'Y' shaped bridle, with forked ends for attachment to the Spitfire's wings outside the propeller disc. For take-off the apex of the bridle was held by a quick-release catch to the underside of the rear fuselage of the Spitfire; this held the bridle clear of the propeller and undercarriage, preventing entangling when the Spitfire took off under her own power alongside the towing aircraft. The two aircraft climbed to their cruising altitude, where the Spitfire pilot released the bridle apex and the rest of the 700 foot long towline was paid out from the tug. The Spitfire then slowed down gradually until the line was taught, when the former's engine could be shut down. Flight trials soon proved that the towing scheme was not, however, as simple as it appeared. In a report dated February 1944 Captain Leslie Greensted, who piloted the Spitfire, highlighted the problems. Initially, the most serious was that if the Spitfire's Merlin engine was shut down or run at low speeds, it was liable to oil up; if, on the other hand, the throttle was opened sufficiently to prevent this, the Spitfire overtook the tug! To overcome this a fully-feathering airscrew was fitted—the only occasion a Spitfire was fitted with one—and the engine could be kept warm without producing excessive thrust. Other problems stemmed from the poor forward view from the Spitfire. During the spring of 1944, the towed Spitfire trials were abandoned.

Right: The first serious attempt to increase the range and endurance of the Spitfire came in the summer of 1940, when Mark I serial number P 9565 was modified to carry a fixed extra 30 gallon tank under the port wing. The handling characteristics of this aircraft were poor, however, and the report on the project stated that at an indicated airspeed of 350mph the ailerons became very heavy and 'considerable force' was needed to hold up the port wing. The following year a Mark II with metal ailerons was fitted with a similar fixed tank of 40 gallons capacity; in this form the modified Spitfire was judged suitable for service use, and was employed on operations during the latter half of 1941 by Nos 66, 118 and 152 Squadrons.

Right: The fixed extra wing tank did not find general favour, and was soon overtaken by the under-fuselage slipper tank which came in 30, 45, 90 and 170 gallon sizes. The last named, seen here, trebled the fuel capacity of the Spitfire V and made it possible for these aircraft to be flown to Malta direct from Gibraltar—a distance of nearly 1,200 miles. In this configuration the Spitfire V had a maximum still-air range of 1,450 miles, broken down as follows: climb and cruise for 940 miles using the fuel from the drop tank, at 170mph with a consumption of just over 5 miles per gallon; release the empty tank and cruise on the internal tank for 510 miles at 150 mph, with a consumption of just over 8 miles per gallon (from the point of view of range the lower speed was desirable in either configuration, but with the tank on at such a speed handling was difficult).

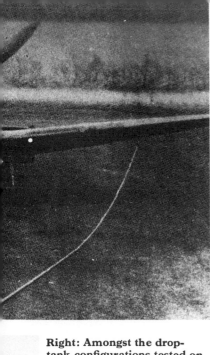

Right: Amongst the drop-tank configurations tested on the Spitfire was this one involving two 62 gallon tanks, one under each wing. Getting stores to fall away cleanly from an aircraft sometimes be a ticklish business, as can be seen from these series of photographs taken during the release trials for the 62 gallon tanks.

At 200mph (left line) the tank swung away from the Spitfire, but note that it held its position under the aircraft until after it had spun through a complete semi-circle; at one stage it was broadside-on to the airflow. At 250mph (centre line) the tank fell away cleanly. At 300mph the tail of the tank came up sharply and struck the underside of the wing, causing a severe dent (right line). The 62 gallon tank was not adopted for use on the Spitfire.

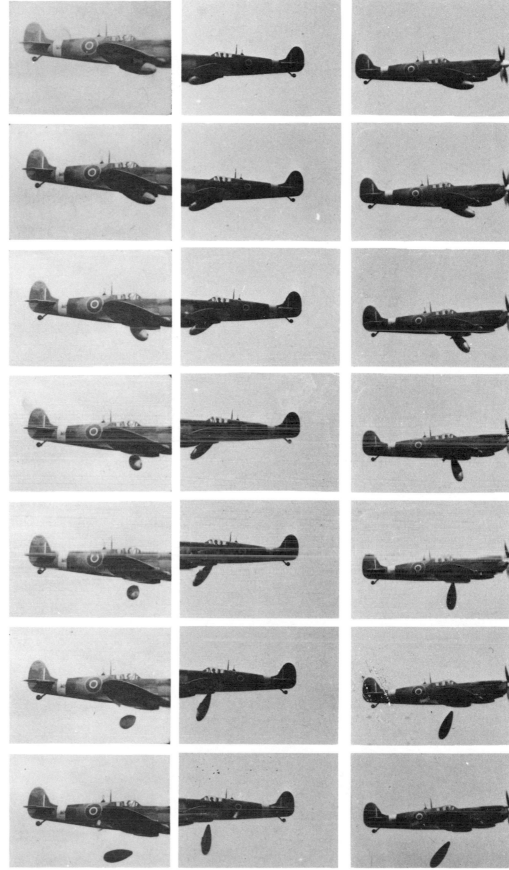

16
Spitfire Dive-Bomber
Raymond Baxter

Known to millions of television viewers for his popular science programme 'Tomorrow's World', Raymond Baxter spent most of the Second World War flying Spitfires. This section deals with his operational career during the final phase of the conflict.

In the autumn of 1944 I was a Flight Lieutenant commanding 'A' Flight of No 602 Squadron, with Squadron Leader Max Sutherland as my 'boss'. Prior to that I had flown Spitfires on operations almost continuously since the middle of 1941: in Britain with No 65 Squadron, then in the Mediterranean area with 93, and after that with No 602 Squadron during the Battle of Normandy. So by October 1944, when the squadron re-equipped with the Spitfire XVI and began re-training for the dive-bomber role, I was a fairly experienced operator.

In September 1944 the Germans began firing V2 rockets at London and the South East from launching sites in Holland. Together with the similarly equipped Nos 229, 453 and 603 Squadrons, we on 602 were given the task of maintaining vigorous patrol activity over the areas from which the

Above: Flight Lieutenant Raymond Baxter, second from the left, pictured briefing pilots of No 602 Squadron for an attack on a V 2 target in Holland.

Below: American M10 three-tube cluster launchers, for 4.5-inch rockets, in a trial installation on a Spitfire IX.

rockets were coming, mainly round The Hague. If we saw any V2 activity on the ground we were, of course, to go in and sort it out. But the Germans were good at camouflage and it was unlike them to leave anything out in the open. So, to keep up the pressure, we were given a pretty wide-ranging brief. Since we knew that the Germans were very short of petrol at that stage, it was a safe assumption that any motor vehicle seen moving on the Dutch roads was doing something to assist the German war effort — it might even be associated with the V2 bombardment. Accordingly, we were given a free hand to 'shoot at anything that moved' — though naturally we went to great pains to avoid causing casualties to the Dutch civilian population.

In addition to our offensive patrols and interdiction sorties, we often carried out pre-planned dive-bombing attacks on suspected rocket storage areas and launching sites (the Dutch resistance organisation was particularly helpful in providing intelligence on these). Sometimes such a target would appear, from the air, as no more than a ring of wheel tracks on some scrubby heath land; even a careful study of aerial reconnaissance photographs often failed to reveal more.

The usual force to attack these small targets was four or six Spitfires, each loaded with either one 500 and two 250 pound bombs, or two 250 pounders and a long range tank. From our base at Coltishall, or its satellites at Ludham or Matlaske, we would head out across the North Sea climbing to about 8,000 feet. Once we made our landfall at the Dutch coast navigation was rarely a problem, because we quickly came to know our 'parish' like the backs of our hands. As we crossed into enemy territory we were liable to be engaged with predicted fire from heavy 88mm guns. But in a Spitfire this was no great danger, provided one continually changed one's direction and altitude in a series of long climbing or diving turns; if one did it right there was the immense satisfaction of seeing the black puffs of the shells going off where one would have been.

Generally the V2 targets were defended with light *Flak*, so when we reached the target area our approach tactics would vary. Sometimes we would go straight in and attack; other times we would dodge from cloud to cloud until we were in a favourable position, then go in; other times still we would overfly the target, then nip back from out of the sun to take the defenders by surprise. We were pretty wily birds!

Once we were committed to the dive-bombing attack, the procedure was usually standard. Running in at between 6,000 and 8,000 feet we would throttle back to just below 200mph, and aim to place the target so that it passed under the wing just inboard of the roundel. As it emerged from under the trailing edge we would roll over and pull the aircraft into a 70 degree dive — which felt vertical. At this stage one concentrated entirely on bringing the graticule of the gyro gunsight on to the target, ignoring the cockpit instruments and trying to ignore the *Flak*. Accurate bombing was dependant upon accurate flying during the dive and once the target was in the sight it was important to avoid side-slipping, skidding or turning for these would have induced errors. The Spitfires would go down in loose line astern, with 30 to 40 yards between aircraft and each pilot aiming and bombing individually. In a dive the speed would build up quite rapidly, to a maximum of about 360mph before the release. When he judged the altitude to be about 3,000 feet each pilot let go of his bombs in a salvo, then did a 5G pull-up to bring the nose up to the horizontal; by the time we had levelled out we were pretty low and the drill was to make a high speed getaway using the ground for cover. The great temptation was to pull up after attacking, to see how well one had done; but that could be fatal if the Germans were alert — and they usually were. We believed in going in tight, hitting hard, and getting the Hell out of it; there was no place for false heroics. The bombs we dropped were often fitted with delayed action fuses, some of them set to explode after as long as six hours; the object of the exercise was to make life difficult for the enemy for as long as possible.

During one of our attacks on a launching site we must have caught the V2 firing crew well into their count-down. After we had released our bombs and were going back for a low level 'strafe' with our cannon, one of the great flame-belching monsters began to climb slowly out from a clump of trees. Flight Sergeant 'Cupid' Love, one of my pilots,

actually fired a long burst at it with his cannon — which must have been the first ever attempt to bring down a ballistic missile in flight!

Sometimes we would mount set-piece attacks with other squadrons, if some particularly important target had been found. On March 18th 1944, for example, No 453 Squadron provided a diversion while we put in a six-aircraft strike at zero feet on the Baatasher-Mex office building in the middle of The Hague; we had had information that the missile firing experts were housed there. It was a very 'twitchy op', because we had to attack in close line abreast. All went well, however, and we wrecked the place. Max Sutherland received a bar to his DFC for that one — and had half of his starboard elevator shot away by *Flak*.

Often we flew two or even three sorties during a single day, with a landing at an airfield in Belgium between each to refuel and re-arm. On March 18th I flew three sorties: the first was a skip-bombing attack on a road bridge north of Gouda, the second was the raid on the Baatasher-Mex building, and the third was a low level interdiction sortie against the railway between Delft and Rotterdam.

All things considered, our losses during these attacks were light. And not all of them were due to enemy action; on at least one occasion a Spitfire shed its wings after the bombs had hung up at the end of the dive, and the pilot pulled up too hard. By this stage of the war, there was virtually nothing to be seen of the *Luftwaffe*.

Just how much our efforts contributed to the gradual run-down in the rate of firing V2s at England, I never did discover. But certainly it was all damned good fun for and unmarried 22 year old.

What did I think of the Spitfire? Every single one was different, with her own characteristics and foibles; if your own was unservicable and you took somebody else's, you could feel the difference at once. During the war I never wanted to operate in any other type of aircraft; the Spitfire was a darling little aeroplane.

Hounded by Jets

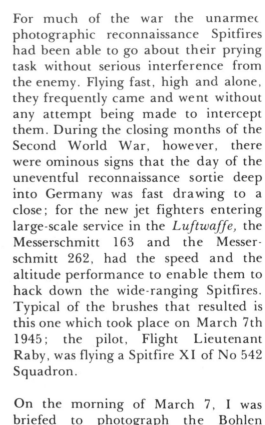

For much of the war the unarmed photographic reconnaissance Spitfires had been able to go about their prying task without serious interference from the enemy. Flying fast, high and alone, they frequently came and went without any attempt being made to intercept them. During the closing months of the Second World War, however, there were ominous signs that the day of the uneventful reconnaissance sortie deep into Germany was fast drawing to a close; for the new jet fighters entering large-scale service in the *Luftwaffe,* the Messerschmitt 163 and the Messerschmitt 262, had the speed and the altitude performance to enable them to hack down the wide-ranging Spitfires. Typical of the brushes that resulted is this one which took place on March 7th 1945; the pilot, Flight Lieutenant Raby, was flying a Spitfire XI of No 542 Squadron.

On the morning of March 7, I was briefed to photograph the Bohlen Synthetic Oil Plant, the Molbis Thermat Power Station and the Oil Storage Depot at Rositz, all being to the south of Leipzig. A damage assessment was also required of Chemnitz which the RAF had attacked two days before.

At 0930 hours I took off carrying split 36-inch cameras with full magazines and all tanks full including a 90-gallon drop tank. I was soon well above cloud and heading out over the North Sea, eventually setting course at 35,000 feet. 10/10ths cloud lay well below and continued to within ten minutes of the target area. The trip was completely uneventful except for the disconcerting factor of the thick 100 yard non-persistent contrail I was trailing behind.

At 1125 hours I arrived in the area, Leipzig was clearly visible to the north and all my targets, including Chemnitz, in full view to the south east. Chemnitz lay under a thick pall of smoke which was drifting slowly to the south, otherwise little or no cloud was visible in the sky. I felt very visible to those on the

Far left: A ground crewman fitting an oblique-mounted F24 camera into the rear fuselage of a fighter reconnaissance Spitfire, probably an FR MarkXIV of the 2nd Tactical Air Force.

Left: It has been suggested that the fitting of cameras into modified drop-tanks, to make reconnaissance pods, is a new idea. But obviously it is not, as can be seen from this 30 gallon slipper tank modified to carry an F24 camera and about to be fitted to a Spitfire FRXIV of the 2nd Tactical Air Force late in the war.

Left: A Spitfire MarkXI of No 681 Squadron, pictured at a forward airstrip in India constructed from bamboo strips and hard packed earth.

Right: A Spitfire XIs also served in the USAAF, as for example this one belonging to the 7th Photographic Group which was part of the Eighth Air Force; accompanying her in this picture is an F-5 Lightning of the same unit.

Below: Tiger in wolf's clothing: a captured Spitfire XI, bearing Luftwaffe markings. This aircraft was operated by the Sonderstaffel Wanderzirkus, a unit formed to demonstrate captured Allied aircraft to German fighter schools and operational units.

Top left: A beautiful Charles Brown study of a photographic reconnaissance SpitfireXI, taken during her flight trials with Jeffrey Quill at the controls. This aircraft later served on No 16 Squadron.

Bottom left: The diminutive Messerschmitt 163 rocket-propelled fighter, which menaced Allied reconnaissance aircraft during the final year of the war.

ground; however, I had no interference over Bohlen and Molbis, the first two targets.

It was during the first run over Rositz that, in looking behind towards Leipzig, I saw two large trails at approximately 20 and 10,000 feet respectively coming from Leipzig/Mochau airfield. Their speed was phenomenal, rate of climb about 10,000 feet per minute at an angle of about 60°. It was not long before two tiny Me 163 rocket-propelled aircraft came visible.

The first enemy aircraft drew up to my altitude and about a mile distant, passing on up to about 40,000 feet before turning off his rocket and becoming very difficult to see. This happened in what seemed to be a second, meanwhile the other Me 163 was already drawing very close and it was obvious that I would stand no chance of seeing both aircraft when they were gliding above endeavouring to position themselves. On the other hand, with the contrail flowing behind me, I was a very conspicuous target.

My first impulse was to get out of the contrail zone; I rolled over on my back, opened up to full boost and revs and

dived to about 18,000 feet where my airspeed was in the region of 500mph, then I levelled out and swinging on a violent 90° turn to port I looked back up my descending trail. One Me 163 was already diving parallel to my trail and when I saw him he was only 5 or 6,000 feet above and rapidly closing. I swung round in a sharp 180° turn as he made his pass, thereby causing us to be heading in opposite directions and drawing apart so rapidly that he was soon only a tiny speck. I again altered course and descended rapidly. The enemy came back to the area but was well above me. Realizing I was not seen I descended to 6,000 feet in a southerly direction; I tried to see the second Me 163, but was unable to do so.

The engagement lasted only five minutes and as I had obviously lost the enemy I decided to fly east. I climbed to just below trail height in order to photograph Chemnitz which was now about 50 miles to the north west. No further sign of the enemy was seen and I had no difficulty in completing my photography. At 1345 hours I landed at Bradwell Bay with 10 minutes fuel left.

The inability of the enemy to position himself owing to his high speed and lack of manoeuverability was, I thought, the most outstanding feature of this short engagement.

Left: The final mark of the Spitfire built for the photographic reconnaissance role was the Mark XIX, which was essentially an adaptation of the Griffon-engined Mark XIV fighter. This Spitfire XIX carried the identification letters of the Photographic Reconnaissance Development Unit.

Below: Now that is low flying . . . A dramatic low-level reconnaissance photograph of a German Jadgschloss radar station in Denmark, taken from a Spitfire. Radar stations were amongst the most demanding of the photographic reconnaissance targets, because close-ups were essential if the technical details of the equipment were to be gleaned.

Above, right: Spitfire IXs of No 225 (Army Co-operation) Squadron, operating over Italy. Flying over the Appenines, early in 1945. Releasing a supply container.

Below: Bomber Command Spitfire: RAF Bomber Command operated a few of these aircraft, for fighter affiliation, target towing and miscellaneous duties; this example, a clip-winged Mark V of No 1688 Flight, was photographed at Feltwell in March 1945.

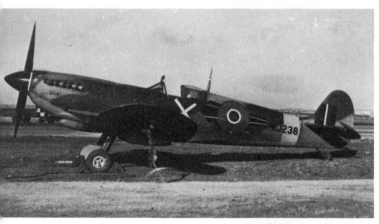

Above: This Spitfire IX, photographed at Luqa, Malta, in early 1945, carries the blue and yellow fuselage marking of No 73 Squadron.

Right: Having obviously seen better days, this Mark V was photographed shortly after hand-over to the French Air Force. The rear fuselage bore the scars of extensive re-skinning.

136

Right: During the course of her development life there was a five-fold increase in the fire-power of the Spitfire, as her armament progressed from the initial eight rifle-calibre machine guns to the ultimate four rapid-firing cannon. The diagrams below show the approximate weight of bullets and/or shells which could be loosed-off during a three-second burst (in action it was rare for a pilot to be able to hold his aim for longer); the figures are approximate because the rate of fire of weapons of the same type could vary by as much as ten per cent. Each 'shell' in the diagram represents four pounds fired.

(1) Mark I (1937): eight .303″ machine guns; three-second burst, 8 pounds.
(2) Mark VB (1941): two 20mm cannon and four .303″ machine guns; three-second burst, 20 pounds.
(3) Mark XVIII (1945): two 20mm cannon and two .5″ machine guns; three-second burst, 26 pounds.
(4) Mark 24 (1946): four 20mm cannon; three-second burst, 40 pounds.

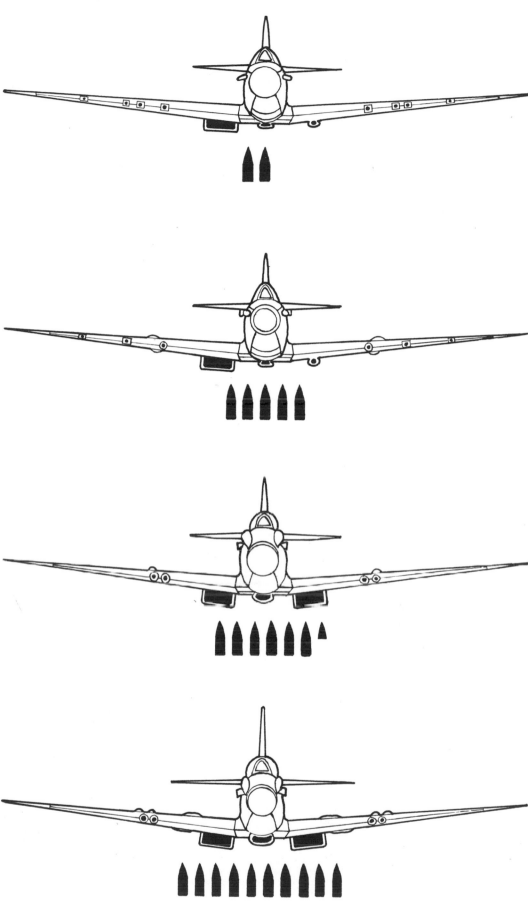

137

Spittires over Japan: included in the Air Component of the British Commonwealth Occupation Force sent to Japan after the war were two Spitfire squadrons, Nos 11 and 17. Both flew the FR MarkXIV and operated from the ex-Japanese Army airfield at Miho.

Right: aircraft of the Miho Wing in a fly-past over their base.
206
Centre right: a line-up of Spitfires at Miho.

Far Bottom right: ground crewmen refuelling one of the Spitfires prior to a reconnaissance sortie, during the cold Japanese winter of 1947.

Far top right: this MarkXIV undershot the runway at Miho and ended up straddling a storm drain; men of No 3 Repair and Salvage Unit are seen preparing to lift aircraft clear.

Below: Flight Lieutenant Ian Barrag-Smith, a Flight Commander on No 17 Squadron, seen boarding his Spitfire.

Below right: Japanese labourers at Miho pushing one of the Spitfires into a hangar.

17
When Spit Fought Spit
Wing Commander Gregory Middlebrook, MBE

A burning Spitfire of No 32
Squadron, following the
surprise Egyptian attack on
Ramat David.

Above: Wing Commander Gregory Middlebrook.

Far right: While ammunition exploded, ground crewmen struggled to push clear the other Spitfires in the No 32 Squadron park at Ramat David.

It was all a ghastly mistake resulting from navigational errors, and afterwards there were apologies. But the small battle fought over Ramat David deserves a place in this history because it was probably the first occasion when, quite deliberately, Spitfire fought Spitfire.

In the spring of 1948 I was a Flying Officer with No 32 Squadron, which operated Spitfire XVIIIs from Ramat David in what was then Palestine. On May 15th the state of Israel came into being and as part of the general withdrawal of British forces from that aread we were to depart for Cyprus the following week.

For a long time the situation in Palestine had been deteriorating, with a lot of killing on both sides. The Arabs and the Israelis were making obvious preparations for an all-out war, to begin as soon as the British troops were out of the way. For their part the Israelis were particularly keen to get hold of modern aircraft, especially Spitfires; they let it be known that they were prepared to pay £25,000 or its equivalent in other currencies, into a bank anywhere in the world, to the account of any pilot who would simulate an engine failure and belly-land on the beach at Tel Aviv or elsewhere in their territory. But in spite of this tempting offer, I never did hear of any RAF aircraft disappearing in suspicious circumstances.

During the final week we completed our preparations for the move, sending out our heavier kit and cleaning out the bar stocks; we sold off the drinks at 1 Akker (about 1p) a shot, which gave rise to some pretty wild parties! On May 21st, the day before we were due to leave, three Dakotas arrived to take away the remainder of our kit and the ground crews the following morning. During the final evening we amused ourselves burning down the Mess and several of the other buildings; Ramat David was in the area to be taken over by the Israelis and because they had been giving us a hard time we resolved to leave them as little as possible.

At this time our main worry was sabotage. For some reason the Israelis thought we were about to turn the airfield over to the Arabs, while in their turn the local Arabs were convinced that we planned to present the Israelis with our aircraft together with the airfield; as a result, we seemed to have both sides against us. To meet the threat we had British troops in a defensive perimeter round us; each night our Spitfires, and those of No 208 Squadron which shared the airfield with us, were drawn up close together on the hard standing so that they could be more easily guarded.

On the morning of what should have been our final day, May 22nd, I was up early. I was just pulling on my shorts when there were a couple of loud bangs, followed by the roar of low-flying aircraft. I dashed outside, but the aircraft — whatever they were — had already disappeared. Apparently there had been two of them, and each had dropped two bombs which had exploded near to the line of aircraft belonging to No 32 Squadron. I grabbed a parachute and dashed across to one of the Spitfires and tried to start her up. But unknown to me, to prevent any possibility of one of our aircraft being stolen, the ground crew had removed the cartridges from the Koffman starter. After five attempts to get a non-existent cartridge to fire, I gave up.

142

As a result of the attack two of No 32 Squadron's Spitfires and one of the Dakotas were set on fire. Our Spitfires had all been combat loaded with full magazines of 20mm and .5 inch ammunition and when the rounds in the burning aircraft began to cook off there were some unpleasant explosions with flying debris and the odd bullet; as a result, all but one of the Spitfires in that dispersal area suffered at least minor damage before being pushed clear.

Still we did not know the identity of the attackers. But there seemed every likelihood that they would return, so the station commander had the squadrons mount a continuous standing patrol of four aircraft over the airfield. For the rest of the day there was considerable activity as relieving Spitfires took off and those airborne came in to refuel. Because many of the aircraft now needed minor repairs, our departure for Cyprus was delayed by twenty-four hours.

Then, later that morning, I remember glancing up and counting five Spitfires swinging round as though they were about to enter the circuit. I blinked, counted again and still there were five. And that meant more trouble because I knew that at that time we had only four airborne. I ran towards some airmen nearby who were busy working by a damaged aircraft and were oblivious to the threat and shouted at them to get down. Then I glanced up to see a Spitfire diving almost straight towards me — and a couple of 250 pounders just beginning to fall clear. I hurled myself down on the hard standing and the blast of the explosions went right over me; but the rough concrete took a lot of skin off my legs and I still have the scars to remind me.

The airmen I had tried to warn were less fortunate, and we lost five killed and others injured in this new attack.

Almost immediately afterwards the other Spitfires made their bombing runs. It was all straight out of the textbook, just as though they were on a bombing range: they crossed the airfield at about 4,500 feet, each did a 120 degree wing-over into a nice 45 degree dive, released the bombs and began to climb away. They managed to wreck a second Dakota, but by that time the Spitfires on the ground were all well dispersed and camouflaged, and thus escaped further damage.

It had all happened very quickly and, since we had no radar or other means of obtaining early warning, the attackers had been able to bomb before our Spitfires could interfere. One of the airmen did some accurate shooting with a Bren gun, however, and one of the raiders was seen flying away trailing glycol and losing height. But then the 208 Squadron people, who were mounting the airborne patrol at that time, got in amongst the others and the slaughter really began. We learned afterwards that the attackers were flying Mark IX Spitfires — no match in a fight for our Mark XVIIIs — and in short order three were shot down. You could not really call it a dogfight: it was as though the raiders thought that they were the only aircraft in the sky, and made no attempt to fight back or even evade. The 208 Squadron pilots simply caught them up from behind and opened up from point blank range at sitting targets.

Soon there was only one aircraft remaining out of the second wave — and still we did not know the identity of our tormentors. So the station commander ordered the pilot in hot pursuit of the remaining raider that before he did anything else he was to establish its nationality. Accordingly the pilot pulled up alongside, saw that the markings were Egyptian, then fell back and shot it down.

On May 23rd we finally did depart for Cyprus, leaving the two sides to fight their war without our interference. The Ramat David incident was probably the first occasion when both sides in an action fought in Spitfires. After we withdrew the Israelis obtained some Spitfires of their own, and there would be other occasions when these aircraft battled with each other.

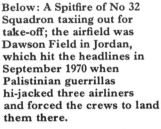

Below: A Spitfire of No 32 Squadron taxiing out for take-off; the airfield was Dawson Field in Jordan, which hit the headlines in September 1970 when Palistinian guerrillas hi-jacked three airliners and forced the crews to land them there.

Swung high
Above the terraced loveliness
Of clouds:
Poised
In the high arched
Vault of blue emptiness
They ride,
Swift minions
Of the Gods of War
from 'Fighters at Dawn'
by R. P. L. Mogg

18
Spitfires and Guerillas
Air Vice Marshal John Nicholls, CBE DFC AFC

During the Malayan Emergency two squadrons of Spitfires took part in the initial air operations against the terrorists. However the effectiveness in this role, of an aircraft designed fourteen years earlier as an interceptor, was questionable.

In June 1948, when the State of Emergency was declared in Malaya, I was a twenty-one year old Flying Officer serving with No 28 Fighter Reconnaissance Squadron which operated Spitfire XVIIIs from Sembawang on Singapore Island. With those of the similarly equipped No 60 Squadron, there was a total of sixteen Spitfires in Malaya; these, and a few Beaufighters and Sunderlands, made up the Royal Air Force's entire offensive strength in the area.

Almost from the start we and the other squadrons began sending out strikes against the jungle hide-outs used by the terrorists. In the beginning it was a rather hit and miss affair, with one far more likely to miss than to hit. The maps we carried were almost devoid of detail except along the coast; they would show dominant features such as rivers, but after a short distance inland these would peter out into a dotted line with the helpful caption "It is assumed that the river follows this line"! The reconnaissance Spitfires of No 81 Squadron would take target photogrphs for us, but since their maps were the same as our own they had similar problems of navigation. In the jungle one tree-covered hill can look depressingly like a thousand others.

I vividly remember the first time I dropped a bomb in anger. On July 2nd 1948 I went off with my squadron commander, Squadron Leader Bob Yule, to a target just across the causeway from Singapore, in South Johore. We took off at first light so that we could get in our dive attacks before the usual mid-morning layer of cumulus cloud

Above: Air Vice Marshal John Nicholls, currently the Senior Air Staff Officer at Headquarters RAF Strike Command.

Centre: Spitfire XVIIIs of No 60 Squadron, pictured at Kuala Lumpur during the Malayan emergency

Right: Leading Aircraftman Robert Collins reloading the magazine for the starboard 20mm cannon of a Spitfire XVIII of No 60 Squadron, at Kuala Lumpur.

developed. When we reached the target area we cruised round for more than half an hour looking for something resembling our briefed objective, before eventually we did attack. Diving from 12,000 feet we dropped our 500 pounders, two from each aircraft, then we carried out a series of strafing runs with cannon and machine guns. There was nobody firing back; it was really like being on the range — except that the target was far less distinct.

During the months that followed we flew several similar strikes. Most of the targets were in deep jungle, and sometimes half a dozen of us would circle for up to an hour looking for the hut or whatever it was we were supposed to hit. Then the first pilot who reckoned he had found it would bomb, and the rest of us would follow and aim at his bursts; after that he would strafe the area until we had used up our ammunition. At that time our intelligence on the whereabouts of the enemy was poor. Moreover, only rarely could our troops go in to find out what the air strikes had achieved; sometimes a week or so after the attack we might hear a report that the target basha hut had been hit by cannon shells, but by the time the ground forces reached it there was rarely any sign of the actual terrorists.

It was all rather loose inconclusive and the reasons were not difficult to understand. Guerilla fighters make the maximum use of all available cover, they travel light, they move fast and they seldom concentrate; operating in dense jungle, they are extremely difficult to find. Broadly speaking, air attacks against them can be mounted in two distinct ways: precision attacks, or area attacks. Precision attacks, by definition, require the target to be visible or to be marked in some way. Area attacks demand a great weight of attack to saturate the area. And both depend for their success upon up-to-date intelligence on the target.

The ineffectiveness of the Spitfire in these operations illustrates the sort of problem we had, using an interceptor designed thirteen years earlier to bomb

such difficult targets. Later, Lincoln heavy bombers equipped with radar took over the task of attacking the jungle hideouts, but even with their much greater bomb loads I am not convinced that they achieved much. Indeed, as Vietnam has shown, one needs a bomber the size of the B-52, laying down paterns of up to eighty-four 500 pounders, before one can make any real impression on the jungle; and even then, as I have said, one needs first-class intelligence if one is really to hit the enemy. The best way to go after men hiding in the jungle is to send trained troops after them; air strikes can drive the enemy out of areas one wishes to occupy and pacify, and into areas where they either find it hard to exist or where they are faced by superior forces. The guerilla can achieve his object only if he can subvert the people he seeks to control; deny him that chance, and he will not succeed. It was when we got round to doing that, that we began to get the upper hand over the terrorists in Malaya.

I left No 28 Squadron in mid-1949,

before the Malayan operations were placed on a proper footing. I had had a lot of fun but had not, I think, done all that much to help defeat the terrorists.

Operating against the guerillas in Malaya, we were really asking too much from the Spitfire. But I have no doubts regarding its value as an air fighter. It had that rare quality which comes from a perfect matching of control responsiveness and 'feel', which made the aircraft part of you once you were airborne. You strapped on, rather than got into, a Spitfire; your hand on the stick produced instant control reaction, and it would obey as accurately and almost as quickly as one's right arm obeys the commands from the brain. I have known a few other aircraft with this particular and highly personal characteristic: the Vampire and the Hunter followed by the F-104A Starfighter which, despite its outstanding performance in terms of speed, retained that same unique quality as a perfect fighter pilot's aeroplane. But for me the Spitfire was the first and so the one best loved.

Accidents at the operational training units were commonplace, as some of the raw pilots learned the hard way that there was more to being a fighter pilot than being able to take-off and land a Spitfire. This picture, taken at 57 OTU at Hawarden, shows what happened when a Spitfire tried to 'run over' a Master.

19
Stronger, Safer, Swifter
Eric Newton, MBE CEng FRAeS

Aviation in itself is not inherently dangerous but, to an even greater extent than the sea, it is terribly unforgiving of any carelessness, incapacity or neglect.

FLIGHT SAFETY AXIOM

In an aircraft a sparkling performance will count for little in the long run, it it is accompanied by vicious handling characteristics. Even the Spitfire had pitfalls to trap the unwary or the unlucky, though mercifully they were few; moreover, thanks to the painstaking work of the accident investigators, those pitfalls that did exist were revealed and in most cases remedied.

After a five year apprenticeship in mechanical engineering, and a brief spell in the Royal Air Force, I joined the Aeronautical Inspection Directorate of the Air Ministry in 1938. Gradually I became more and more involved with the investigation of aircraft accidents and in 1942 I was appointed an Inspector of Accidents; and I have been involved with this aspect of aviation ever since.

During the early war years the business of accident investigation was largely unexplored ground and we in the Accidents Investigation Branch (which at that time came under the Air Ministry) learned many of its essentials from the Spitfire and her generation of aircraft. Of course, if there was an accident and the cause was fairly clear, obvious pilot error or a simple component defect or something like that, then we were not called in; but if an aircraft suffered a structural failure in the air or inexplicably caught fire on the ground, then the RAF would soon get on to us to try to find out why.

Out of a total of 121 serious or major accidents to Spitfires reported to us between the beginning of 1941 and the end of the war, sixty-eight involved structural failure in the air. Initially the most common reason for such failures, with twenty-three instances in 1941 and 1942, was aileron instability. The symptoms were not at all clear-cut: the aircraft were usually diving at high speed when they simply fell to pieces. Only after one of the pilots had survived

Below: A recent photograph of Eric Newton, who still serves with the Accidents Investigation Branch.

this traumatic experience and parachuted successfully were we able to find out the cause. During his dive he saw *both* of his ailerons suddenly flip up, producing an extremely violent pitch-up which caused the wing to fail and the aircraft to break up. In collaboration with the Royal Aircraft Establishment at Farnborough we did a lot of tests and found that this aileron up-float was made possible by stretch in the control cables; in those days control tensioning was a hit-or-miss business, with no compensation for temperature. On our recommendation the RAF introduced the tensometer, which ensured accurate tensioning of the controls; this, and the almost simultaneous introduction of the new metal ailerons, cured almost all the cases of aileron instability in the Spitfire.

The next most serious cause of structural failure in the Spitfire was pilots overstressing the airframe. She was extremely responsive on the controls and one must remember that in those days there was no accelerometer to tell the pilot how close he was to the limit. So it was not difficult to exceed the aircraft's 10G ultimate stress factor during combat or when pulling out of a high speed dive; during the war we were able to put down forty-six major accidents to this cause, though undoubtedly there were many other occasions when it happened and we did not see the wreckage. Incidentally, if there was a structural failure in the Spitfire it was almost inevitably the wing that went; the fuselage was far less likely to fail first. I once asked a very senior RAF officer why the accelerometer — technically a simple instrument — was not introduced during the war. He replied that he was sure it would have had an adverse effect on the fighting spirit of the pilots. Whether that would have been so, I cannot say. But I do know that when they finally did introduce the accelerometer into service, in the Hunter in 1954, and began educating the pilots on structural limitations and the dangers of overstressing, accidents to this cause virtually ceased.

By the way, I cannot remember a single case of metal fatigue failure in a Spitfire; but that was probably because in wartime they hardly ever survived long enough to fly the necessary number of hours for this to develop.

After structural failure, the next largest category of accidents proved, on investigation, to have followed loss of control by the pilot (thirty-six cases). Of these, twenty occured in cloud and could be put down to pilot error; one must remember that early in the war, in the rush to turn out more pilots, instrument flying training was not up to the peacetime standards. A further thirteen accidents were shown to have been caused by oxygen starvation; on the early Spitfires it was easy to mishandle the oxygen system and if this happened and the aircraft was flying at high altitude the pilot passed out. As a result of our investigations and recommendations, the oxygen system on the Spitfire was modified to make it easier to operate. The remaining three accidents in the loss-of-control category were initiated by the pilot pulling excessing 'g' and blacking himself out.

Engine failures and fires contributed a further seventeen accidents, and the remainder could be put down under the 'miscellaneous' heading. An example of the latter was the case at Hethel just after the war when, as the pilot was starting up an unarmed Spitfire XVI, it exploded and burst into flames. The singed and shaken pilot managed to clamber out, and stood helplessly by as the machine burnt itself out. Everyone was baffled by the incident, so we were called in to investigate. The first thing we noted was that the leading edge of the wing on the starboard side — there was no fuel tank in that position on the Mark XVI — was peeled right back. This was obviously the seat of the explosion and we were able to trace the smoke pattern, like a line of soot, from there to the engine exhaust stubs. Then the cause became clear: the fuel filler cap was just in front of the cockpit, and as a result of careless refuelling petrol had sloshed down the fuselage and on to the wing, and some of it had become trapped in the leading edge; when the pilot climbed into the cockpit the explosive fuel-air mixture was waiting and when the engine fired — bang! Looking round, we found several other Spitfires with petrol lodged in the wing leading edge and this same accident just waiting to happen.

There were one or two accidents, and

Below: The burnt-out remains of Spitfire XVI serial TE 457 at RAF Hethel in September 1946, following the explosion of fuel vapour trapped in the leading edge of the starboard wing; note the peeling-back of the skin, indicating that this was the seat of the explosion.

some very near misses, caused by the light-weight plastic seats fitted to some batches of Spitfires. The trouble was that they were not strong enough, and if there was a heavy pilot who pulled a bit of 'G' they tended to collapse — on to the elevator control runs which ran underneath. We soon had that type of seat replaced.

As I have mentioned, we investigated a total of 121 Spitfire accidents during the war; and a further nine after it. The causes did not always fit simply into the neat categories mentioned above. For example, a pilot might lose control in a cloud and his aircraft then broke up in the ensuing dive due to aileron instability; in that case the accident would have been listed under two categories.

In the nature of my work I tend to concentrate on an aircraft's failings and ignore it if it is safe; but how safe was the Spitfire? I think the figures speak for themselves: a total of more than twenty-two thousand of these aircraft were built, and we were called in on only 130 occasions — and in not all of these was the Spitfire found to be at fault. If one considers that she was not a simple trainer built for ease of handling, but a thoroughbred fighting machine the equal of any in the world during most of her service career, there can be no doubting that the Spitfire was a remarkably safe little aircraft.

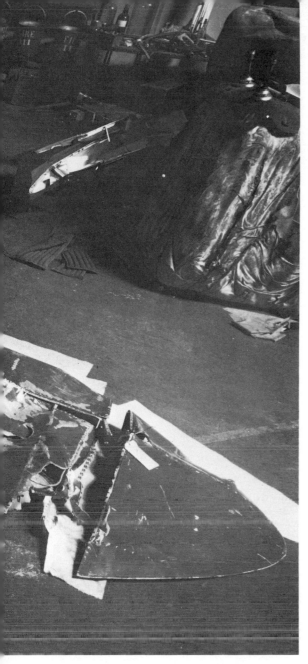

In spite of the success of Eric Newton and others like him, in making the Spitfire a safe aircraft to fly, it remains a sad fact that the great majority of Spitfire crashes were not due to enemy action but to simple accidents which did not warrant deep investigation. All too often a hastily-trained pilot's poor airmanship would place him in a position from which he lacked the skill — or the luck — to extricate himself.

Typical of such accidents, and amusing rather than tragic since the only personal injuries were to the pilots' pride, is this one from the files of the Royal Canadian navy. It illustrates clearly the dangers of pressing on in the face of deteriorating weather con-

ditions; and it shows how imprecise communications can so easily lead to embarrassment. This story is told to you the way it happened; only the names have been omitted, to protect the guilty.

A pair of Seafires was flying along the eastern coast of Canada when the weather began to deteriorate and soon the cloud base was down to 300 feet in places. The estimated time of arrival for their planned refuelling stop at Presque Ile came and went, but they were unable to establish radio contact with the tower there. Nevertheless the intrepid pair continued on, well beyond their ETA (and well beyond the extent of their maps!). At last they came to a town which they were able to identify, from the sign-board at the railway station, as Campbellton, New Brunswick — 110 miles beyond Presque Ile. With fuel running short they flew south along the coast of New Brunswick looking for a landing field and eventually found a group of hangars near Bathurst. A low level reconnaissance revealed a runway covered with packed ice and snow and the only landing aid, a wind sock, wrapped firmly around its mast.

After they had inspected the runway, the Number 2 called "Will you have first go, or will I?". The leader replied that he would "Have first crack at it". The Number 2, however, understood this as "Have a crack at it," The upshot was that both did, at the same time — and from opposite directions! The Number 2 later described what followed: "I flew a normal approach from 400 feet at 80 knots over the end of the runway. I touched down on the very edge and when I felt I had the aircraft under control, I called the leader and said "I think I've made it" — but as I said it, we collided . . . The left wings of both our aircraft were sheared off and we were spun around through 180 ."

The leader's account was similar: " . . . I touched down in the middle of the runway and was rolling to a stop when I heard the Number 2 say 'I think I've got it made'. Then we collided . . ."

Left: From wreckage such as this, the men of the Accidents Investigation Branch had to try to piece together the reasons for the accident—in this case the mid-air break-up of Spitfire Mark II serial X 4421 in March 1941. To the trained eye the upward bending of the top spar boom near the wing root, coupled with the tensile failure of the lower spar boom, was significant: it meant that the the structure had failed due to excessive positive 'G' loading, probably due to a gross application of elevator at high speed. The remaining damage to the wing occurred after this failure, during the course of the break-up or in the subsequent impact with the ground.

Curtain Calls

Left: Three Seafire Mark 47s of No 800 Squadron, the last front-line unit in the Fleet Air Arm to operate the type, showing the landing hooks in the lowered position and the contra-rotating propellers. During the summer of 1950, embarked on HMS Triumph, the Squadron took part in the initial stages of the Korean conflict; the Seafires mounted several rocket strikes, and also flew defensive patrols covering Allied shipping. In the following November Triumph returned to England where the Squadron disbanded and the Seafire passed out of front-line service in the Royal Navy.

Above right: The last front-line RAF fighter unit to operate the Spitfire was No 80 Squadron at Hong Kong, which flew the type until January 1952. In this photograph one of the unit's Mark 24s is seen at Kai Tak, wearing the black and white stripes painted on at the beginning of the Korean War.

Spitfire Mark 22s of Nos 610, 611 and 613 Squadrons of the Royal Auxiliary Air Force, led by Squadron Leader J. B. Wales, pictured in formation during a rehearsal for the Royal Air Force Display held at Farnborough in July 1950. A this time the Spitfire was fast passing out of service in Fighter Command and within a few months the remaining Squadrons would all re-equip with jet fighters.

Below: From the beginning of the Malayan emergency until the spring of 1954, the Spitfire XIXs of No 81 Squadron provided photographic reconnaissance for the anti-guerilla operations in Malaya. The final operational sortie by a Royal Air Force Spitfire was flown by this unit on April 1st 1954, almost twenty years to the day since Reginald Mitchell had begun detailed work on the design of his new fighter. In this photograph a No 81 Squadron Spitfire is seen taxying out for one of the final sorties, past a replacing Meteor PR 10.

Left: Throughout the 1950s the Spitfire continued in use for second-line tasks in several air forces, often as personal aircraft for senior officers. The black-painted Mark IX, sometimes referred to as 'The Black Widow', was used by the Chief of Staff of the Israeli Air Force, Brigadier Ezer Weitzmann; the accompanying aircraft was a Super Mystere.

The Final Act
Air Vice Marshall John Nicholls, CBE DFC AFC

In 1963 one of the few surviving airworthy Spitfires was flown in a battle trial against a Mach 2 Lightning fighter. In this section we learn how this came about, and why.

In 1963 I was the Wing Commander in charge of the Air Fighting Development Squadron (the successor to the earlier Air Fighting Development Unit), which was part of the Central Fighter Establishment at Binbrook. Earlier the CFE had taken on charge a Spitfire XIX originally intended for mounting on the station front gate; instead, she had been maintained in a flyable condition.

This was at the time of the Indonesian confrontation and, since the Indonesian Air Force operated a large number of P-51 Mustang fighters, we were very interested in discovering how best a Lightning might engage such an aircraft. In the RAF we did not have any Mustangs; but at Binbrook we did have our Spitfire with a performance which was, in many respects, similar. Thus it came about that our Spitfire came to be involved in a short battle trial pitted against a fighter which was her successor by three generations.

Of course, from the start we knew that the Lightning could overtake the Spitfire by nearly a thousand miles per hour — there was no need to run a trial to prove that. But we did find that the piston-engined fighter presented a very poor target to infra-red homing missiles, especially from the rear aspect. And, since the Lightning would therefore very likely have to follow up its missile pass with a gun attack, a high overtaking speed would have made accurate firing very difficult. On the other hand, if the Lightning pilot slowed down too much he could end up playing the slower and more manoeuverable fighter's dogfighting game and lose. None of this was new; we had learned the same lessons during trials flown between the Lightning and the Hunter. Another problem was that if the Spitfire pilot had sufficient warning of the attack he could spin round to meet it head-on — and thus present the most difficult target of all.

In the end we evolved a type of attack which was the antitheses of all I had learned from my own operational experience of fighter-versus-fighter combat in Korea: instead of trying to get above the enemy and diving on him to attack, we found it best to use the Lightning's very high power-to-weight ratio to make a climbing attack from behind and below. From that angle the field of view from the Spitfire was poor, there was a good chance of achieving surprise and the infra-red source gave the best chance for missile acquisition. If the Lightning pilot did not acquire the target or bring his guns to bear on his first pass he could continue his steep climb — which the Spitfire could not possibly follow — and when out of range he could dive and repeat the process. Using such tactics, we felt that in the end a competent Lightning pilot could almost always get the better of an equally competent Spitfire (or Mustang) pilot.

Almost certainly that trial at Binbrook was the final operational act carried out in earnest in the Spitfire's long career.

Below: A fine shot of two Spitfires of the Battle of Britain Flight of the Royal Air Force, starting up at their base at Coltishall. The date was June 6th 1969, and the aircraft were about to take-off for a flight over Normandy to commemorate the twenty-fifth anniversary of the Allied landings.

20
Spitfire Swansong
M. Maffre

Now there are but a few of them left. Only a few of those myriad Spitfires which once speckled the British sky from the Orkneys to the Isle of Wight, that droned singly or in sections, squadrons or wings across the Channel, that swept at tree-top level or thirty thousand feet from the Pas de Calais to the southern reaches of the Elbe, that swallowed sand and harried the Afrika Korps from El Alamein to Tunisia, that duelled out of lonely Malta and chased the enemy from Sicily to the Gothic Line, that patrolled the aching sunlight in the Bay of Bengal, that teetered like tipsy seamen on flimsy undercarriages aboard aircraft carriers . . .

A babble of tongues chattered in them. Canucks and Yanks and Britons nattered over their radios; expatriate Frenchmen, Norwegians and Poles whooped into their microphones at the sign of black-crossed fighters. Aussies and South Africans drawled at each other at vast altitudes . . .

Grievous things were done to the Spitfire in the name of progress. Her wings were clipped and her super-charger blades cropped for better low-level work, and the outraged bird was dubbed the 'clipped and cropped Spitty'. They added blades to her propeller so that in the end she actually had two sets, one rotating against the other. Lumbering cannons poked out of wings designed to carry machine guns. They put a hook on her tail and called her a sea bird. Once, be it known, she slung beer kegs on her bomb racks and ferried cheer to the Normandy beach head . . .

Today a vintage group of fighter pilots recall her peculiar whistling call as she arched across the sky. Nostalgia brings back the sound of her Merlin engine muttering in the misty half light of a hundred airfields, as crewmen warmed them up at dawn readiness. Some men who probably feel they live on borrowed time, still wonder how her stout iron heart achieved the mechanically impossible and brought them home alive. Those who did not know her may wonder how mortal man can cherish an undying affection for her gasolene-reeking camouflaged memory. And no one can tell them.

Introduction to Part Two

In assembling material for *Spitfire at War 2* I have tried to repeat the formula which proved successful with *Spitfire at War:* namely, to describe a series of incidents, and to present little-known historical documents which will interest those reading about the aircraft for the first time, while adding to the knowledge of enthusiasts possessing other books on the subject. And to back this with a large number of unpublished or rarely seen photographs which will please even the most expert reader.

The first chapter, 'K5054: A Mystery Resolved', presents recently uncovered evidence on the date of the first flight of the Spitfire, for which the author is grateful to Hugh Scrope, Secretary of the Vickers company. When designing the Spitfire, Reginald Mitchell and his team went to considerable lengths to produce an airframe that was clean aerodynamically and as light as possible. 'A Very Efficient Fighter' gives drag and weight analyses for the main components of the Spitfire to show how successful the designers were. For any pilot the first combat missions on which he encounters the enemy are fraught with danger, as he learns the art of survival in the hardest school of all. In 'Baptism of Fire' Colin Gray tells of one of his early combat missions covering the evacuation of British troops from Dunkirk in May 1940, which he was lucky to survive. In war some units will achieve successes with few losses, other will lose aircraft and pilots so rapidly that they have to be pulled out of the fight after a few days. In 'Thirteen Days in August' Dennis Armitage tells the story of No 266 Squadron during the Battle of Britain, and how the unit suffered so heavily that it had to be withdrawn from action after only 13 days in the south of England. After the Battle of Britain, daylight air combats became a rarity over the home counties. 'Skirmish Over Kent' describes the meeting between Trevor Gray in a Spitfire and Helmut Fischer in a Messerschmitt 110 reconnaissance aircraft in December 1940, and how the two pilots were brought together by this author nearly 40 years later. By 1942 Fighter Command was sending Spitfires deep into occupied Europe. Pilots had to learn the art of handling their engines so they could cruise at high speed and react quickly if they were 'bounced' by enemy fighters; but they had to do so without burning fuel at too high a rate. 'Correct Engine Handling – Key to Survival' tells how it was done. Also in 1942 the Spitfire fighters were sent to defend Malta. In 'Besieged on Malta' George Hows tells of his experiences as a ground crewman with No 1453 Squadron. The Seafire, the deck-landing version of the Spitfire, first went into service with the Royal Navy in 1942 but from the start there were

Spitfires flying past a clip-winged Mk V of No 401 Squadron, RCAF, at Biggin Hill in September 1943.
Public Archives of Canada

difficulties operating it from aircraft carriers. Jeffrey Quill, the Chief Test Pilot of Supermarine, wrote a lucid report on the difficulties and how they could be overcome, which is given in full in 'Problems with the Seafire'. During the war Spitfires served with numerous foreign air arms including the US Army Air Forces. In 'With the Eighth Air Force to Berlin' Walt Weitner of the US 14th Photo Squadron tells of the reconnaissance mission he flew to the German capital in a Spitfire, following the first large scale daylight bombing attack on the city in March 1944. Despite the efforts of the Air Sea Rescue service, during World War 2 pilots unfortunate enough to be forced down in the sea even close to land had no certainty they would be rescued. John Saffery tells of the difficulties he experienced after he baled out into the sea from his Spitfire in 'Anyway, it is only a Short Sea Crossing'. During the closing months of the war no part of German occupied Europe was beyond the reach of Spitfires. In 'Spitfires Over the Balkans' David Green tells of the operations by his squadron over Yugoslavia. Spitfires were flown by pilots of more than a score of nationalities, and introduced 'flying English' into their respective languages. 'Franglais for Spitfire Pilots' shows the impact this had on No 349 (Belgian) Squadron. In the late war period Supermarine developed and tested the Spiteful, intended as a replacement for the Spitfire in Royal Air Force fighter squadrons. Although orders were placed the aircraft never went into full production, however, and in 'Test Flying the Spiteful' Pat Shea-Simonds explains why.

As well as those named above, the author would particularly like to express his thanks to the following for making available material and photographs used in this book: Jay Spenser at the Smithsonian Institution in Washington, Peter Arnold, Carl Geust, Paul Lambermont, The Royal Air Force Museum, the Imperial War Museum, The Public Archives of Canada, Air Marshal Sir Geoffrey Tuttle, Grp Capt Alan Wright, Gordon Green, John Saffery, Harry van der Meer, Christopher Elliott and Jim Oughton.

Until the end of 1942 all Royal Air Force aircraft mark numbers were given in roman numerals. From 1943 to 1948 new aircraft entering service carried arabic mark numbers while the older types carried roman mark numbers. As a convention in this book Spitfire and Seafire marks up to XVI are given in roman numerals and those of later versions are given in arabic numerals.

Previous books on the Spitfire have contained lengthy accounts of the development of the aircraft, and rather than repeat these this book concentrates on less known parts of the aircraft's history. readers requiring detail on the evolution of the Spitfire through its various marks should refer to the author's book *The Spitfire Story* (Janes, 1982), accepted at the most comprehensive work on this aspect of the aircraft.

Those who flew, serviced or built Spitfires, or are interested in their story, might like to know to know of the existence of The Spitfire Society, formed to perpetuate the memory of this most famous of all fighting aircraft. Those wishing to know more should contact Grp Capt David Green RAF (Rtd), The Chairman, The Spitfire Society, R. J. Mitchell Hall, Kingsbridge Lane, Southampton SO1 0GB.

Alfred Price
Uppingham
Rutland

Spitfire IXs of No 411 Squadron RCAF at Heesch, Holland in March 1945.
Public Archives of Canada

21

K5054: A Mystery Resolved

Although the Spitfire is, arguably, the most successful fighting aircraft ever produced, some aspects of the history of its design and development have been difficult to establish with accuracy. The Supermarine company saw itself as a builder of aircraft rather than a keeper of records, and many of the prewar records it did keep were destroyed when the works was bombed in September 1940. As a result historians and writers attempting to assemble accounts on the evolution of the Spitfire have been forced to rely on secondary sources of information, personal memories and published accounts, which in many cases have been proved unreliable and which tend to perpetuate errors already made.

Even the date of the first flight of the prototype Spitfire, K5054, has been a matter for discussion. Some published accounts stated it was on 5 March 1936, others said the historic event took place on the following day. In a previous book (*The Spitfire Story*, Janes, 1982) this author reviewed the available evidence on the date of the first flight. In spite of an intensive search he had been able to secure no direct evidence written at the time or soon afterwards to support either date; the evidence available was either implicit, or else it had been recorded so long after the event that it could not be considered reliable. On balance, the meagre evidence available seemed to point to the prototype having made its maiden flight on 6 March 1936.

Having searched long and fruitlessly to resolve the mystery, this author is extremely grateful to Mr Hugh Scrope of the Vickers company for the hardest piece of evidence he has yet seen on the date of the first flight of the Spitfire. The evidence takes the form of an accounts sheet prepared for the board of Vickers, the parent company, of expenditure by its Supermarine subsidiary on 'Modified Single-Seater Fighter K5054'. The document noted that up to 29 February 1936 a total of £14,637 had been spent on the aircraft which had yet to fly.

On 2 April 1936 the board of Vickers met at Weybridge and the accounts sheet was presented. But beforehand Henry Duvall, the Company Secretary, had added a handwritten note to the sheet giving the latest cost of the new fighter as '£15,000 app', below which he noted that it 'Flew on 5 Mar 36'. From the minutes of the meeting we know that Reginald Mitchell was one of those who attended; he was a stickler for detail and it is unlikely in

K5054, the prototype Spitfire, pictured at Eastleigh in May 1936, shortly after it had been painted in its light-blue colour scheme. *Smith*

Statement of accounts submitted to the meeting of the Board of Directors of Vickers Ltd on 2 April 1936, which mentioned that K5054 had flown on 5 March. In spite of an intensive search, this is the only direct evidence the author has seen concerning the date of the historic first flight of this aircraft.

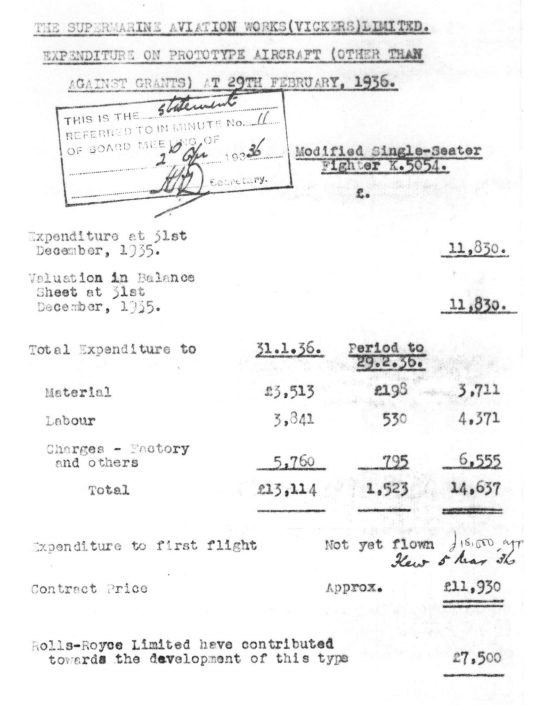

THE SUPERMARINE AVIATION WORKS (VICKERS) LIMITED.

EXPENDITURE ON PROTOTYPE AIRCRAFT (OTHER THAN

AGAINST GRANTS) AT 29TH FEBRUARY, 1936.

THIS IS THE _Statement_
REFERRED TO IN MINUTE No. _11_
OF BOARD MEETING OF
.... 2 Apr 193_6_
.... Secretary.

Modified Single-Seater
Fighter K.5054.

£.

	31.1.36.	Period to 29.2.36.	
Expenditure at 31st December, 1935.			11,830.
Valuation in Balance Sheet at 31st December, 1935.			11,830.
Total Expenditure to			
Material	£3,513	£198	3,711
Labour	3,841	530	4,371
Charges – Factory and others	5,760	795	6,555
Total	£13,114	1,523	14,637

Expenditure to first flight   Not yet flown £15,000 apr
                                                      flew 5 Mar '36

Contract Price   Approx.   £11,930

Rolls-Royce Limited have contributed
    towards the development of this type   £7,500

MB.

the extreme that he would have let pass an incorrect date of the maiden flight of his new fighter.

Although it makes only a passing reference to the first flight of K5054, in historical terms the new piece of evidence is extremely strong. Duvall would certainly have known when the first flight took place, his note was penned within a month of that date and had he got it wrong the error would certainly have been pointed out at the time and corrected. There is now little room for doubt that the date of the maiden flight of K5054, the prototype Spitfire, was 5 March 1936.

Above left:
K5054, the prototype Spitfire, pictured at Eastleigh in May 1936, shortly after it had been painted in its light-blue colour scheme. *Smith*

Left:
The prototype seen in February 1937 at Martlesham Heath, about to begin air firing trials of its eight .303in Browning guns.
RAF Museum

Below:
The prototype at Eastleigh, fitted with ejector exhausts and camouflaged; this photograph was taken some time after September 1937. *Smith*

22

A Very Efficient Fighter

K9787, the first production Spitfire, with Jeffrey Quill at the controls, pictured during its maker's trials near Southampton in May 1938. The drag and weight figures given below refer to the aircraft in the configuration shown.
RAF Museum/Charles Brown

The most notable external feature of the Spitfire, apart from its beautiful lines, is the aerodynamic cleanliness of its airframe. The table which follows gives the drag analysis of the airframe of the Spitfire I, measured in pounds at a notional speed of 100ft/sec. In each case the figures are very low for an aircraft of this period.

Profile Drag	*pounds*
Wings	20.3
Fuselage	7.3
Tailplane, Fin and Rudder	4.6
Effect of Camouflage Paint	1.5
Total Profile Drag	33.7
Induced Drag	
Lift	2.4
Washout	0.6
Total Induced Drag	3.0
Cooling Drag	
Glycol Radiator	6.0
Oil Radiator	1.0
Air Intakc	1.0
Total Cooling Drag	8.0
Miscellaneous	
Controls	1.2
Windscreen	1.2
Tail Wheel	2.0
Wing/Body Interference	1.5
Acrial Post	0.2
Gun Holes	0.5
Rivets and Joints	0.5
Total Miscellaneous	7.1
Not Accounted For	8.4
TOTAL DRAG OF AEROPLANE	**60.2**

Above:
K9787 pictured soon after delivery to Martlesham Heath for service testing, August 1938.

Left and Overleaf:
These early Mk Is are pictured at the refuelling point at Eastleigh, January 1939. K9846 was the 60th production aircraft. K9849 is being readied for engine runs with several components still to be fitted; note the serial number chalked on the fuselage. *Flight*

169

As well as being clean aerodynamically, the airframe of the Spitfire was a highly efficient structure in engineering terms. By meticulous attention to the design of each item, Reginald Mitchell and his team were able to produce an aircraft that was strong enough to perform all reasonable combat manoeuvres – and a lot of unreasonable ones. And, as can be seen from the weight break-down of the Spitfire I which follows, this strength was not achieved for an inordinate weight penalty:

Structure	pounds
Wings	820
Engine Cowling	86
Engine Mounting	58
Fuselage and Fin	426
Tailplane and Elevator	58
Rudder	18
Tail Wheel	28
Wheels and Brakes	90
Chassis and Retracting Gear	192
Controls	91
Accommodation	23
Total Structure	1,890

Power Plant	
Engine	1,412
Airscrew Hub	36
Wooden Airscrew and Spinner	96
Ejector Exhausts	30
Engine Accessories and Piping	61
Radiator	98
Cooling System	56
Cooling Fluid	142
Petrol Tanks	57
Oil Tanks	47
Total Power Plant	2,035

Load Carried	
Pilot and Parachute	200
Military Load (guns, ammunition, gunsight, etc)	685
Petrol (84 gallons)	646
Oil (six gallons)	54
Total Load Carried	1,585

Sundries Unaccounted for	335
Stressing Allowance	30
TOTAL WEIGHT	**5,875**

Right:
K9798, the 11th production Spitfire, pictured after a landing accident at Duxford in April 1939 while serving with No 19 Squadron. *Cozens*

Far right:
A pair of Mk Is of No 66 Squadron being refuelled at Duxford during the early war period. Although concentrating aircraft in this way made servicing easier, the first attacks on airfields would teach the RAF the value of dispersal.

Below:
Mk Is of No 611 Squadron pictured during a scramble take-off from Digby in Lincolnshire, January 1940. Note the small wing and fuselage roundels and the lack of fin flash, standard at this time. *Flight*

23
Baptism of Fire

During the so-called 'Phoney War', the period prior to the opening of the German offensive in the West on 10 May 1940, Spitfires had occasionally been in action against German bombers operating off the coasts of England and Scotland. But they did not encounter enemy fighters until, a few days after the offensive began, Allied troops were forced to withdraw within range of the Spitfire squadrons based in southern England. During the final week of May and the beginning of June, Royal Air Force Fighter Command endeavoured to cover the evacuation of Allied troops from Dunkirk. In the course of these operations Spitfires found themselves in action against enemy fighters of equivalent performance for the first time; now the Royal Air Force's premier fighter type had to show that it could take punishment, as well as dish it out.

Plt Off Colin Gray, a New Zealander flying Spitfires with No 54 Squadron based at Hornchurch, first went into action on 24 May against an enemy formation near Calais and was credited with one Messerschmitt 109 damaged. On the following day his unit escorted a squadron of Fleet Air Arm Swordfish attacking German ground troops advancing east of Dunkirk. The lumbering biplanes and their escorts reached the target without interference from enemy fighters, completed their attack and turned back for England. As their charges headed out to sea with no enemy aircraft in sight the Spitfires, freed of the requirement to escort them further, headed south looking for trouble. They soon found it, and in the action that followed Colin Gray's inexperience almost cost him his life.

'Suddenly we found ourselves in amongst a gaggle of 109's. I opened fire at one of them, but stopped when I noticed smoke coming back over my wings. That shook me – I thought somebody was firing at me. I pulled round hard but there was nobody there – what I had seen was cordite smoke blowing back from my own guns. I looked back at the Messerschmitt and saw Sgt John Norwell on its tail and the German pilot baling out.'

Afterwards Norwell and Gray were each credited with a half share in the destruction

Plt Off Colin Gray, whose account of the narrow escape over Dunkirk is given below. *via Bowyer*

of the Messerschmitt, but as the German fighter plunged earthwards Gray allowed his gaze to follow his falling enemy too long. The error nearly cost him his life.

'Suddenly there was one Hell of a row, like somebody running a bar along a piece of corrugated iron. The stick was knocked out of my hand and ended up in the left hand corner of the cockpit, and my aircraft flicked into a spiral dive. I grabbed the stick and hauled back on it, the Spitfire responded immediately and started to climb. I looked behind but didn't see anyone, the German pilot had not repeated my mistake of following me down. I selected 12 pounds [emergency boost] and continued my climb; the airspeed indicator read 240mph and I thought "This is bloody marvellous!" [the normal speed for a Spitfire in a steep climb was about 190mph indicated]. But then, as I continued the climb, the Spitfire began to shudder and it seemed as if it was going to stall. I couldn't understand it – the airspeed indicated still read 240mph. I eased the stick forwards, but still it read 240mph... Then I realised what had happened: my pitot head had been shot away, the needle had dropped to the 240mph position on the dial under gravity...

'I levelled out and took stock of the situation. One cannon shell had gone through the port aileron, that was what had knocked the stick out of my hand and sent the aircraft into the violent spiral dive which shook off the Messerschmitt. The airspeed indicator was out and there was no air pressure or hydraulic pressure, which meant that I had no flaps or brakes and I couldn't lower the undercarriage using the main hydraulic system. As I approached Hornchurch I blew down the undercarriage using the emergency carbon dioxide system, and saw the "undercarriage down" sticks push up through the wings and two green lights come on to indicate that the wheels were down and locked.

'The landing was very difficult. With the flaps up one came in at a different attitude than usual and, of course, I had no idea of my airspeed (the indicator still read 240mph!). The first time, I came in too fast. The station commander at Hornchurch, Wing Commander "Daddy" Bouchier, was watching my performance and was overheard to say "The silly young bugger, he's going too fast. He'll never get in!" He was right. I got my wheels almost on the ground, realised I was not going to make it and took off again. The second time I stood well back from the airfield, and dragged the aircraft in at just above stalling speed. That time I landed, and as I touched down the elevator cable finally parted and the control column collapsed back into my stomach.

'On examination of the Spitfire afterwards it was found that a cannon shell had gone through the inspection hatch in the rear fuselage and exploded inside. Splinters from the shell had slashed their way out of the skinning, leaving it looking like a cheese grater. The air bottles had been knocked out, so were the batteries. There were bullet holes up and down the fuselage and, of course, the cannon shell through the aileron. From the entry and exit holes of the bullets it was clear the Messerschmitt had dived on me from the right and above; it had been a very neat piece of deflection shooting.

'The Spitfire was put up on trestles and people from Vickers were invited to come and look at it, to see how much it had suffered. It was the first Hornchurch aircraft that had been fairly well clobbered, and still got back. Soon there would be many others.'

Colin Gray went on to become one of the most successful RAF fighter pilots of World War 2 and ended the conflict as a Wing Commander credited with 27½ aerial victories. Yet of the many actions in which he fought, for him the most memorable was that on 25 May 1940 when lack of experience so nearly put a premature end to his career as a combat pilot.

No 92 Squadron Spitfires, photographed in May 1940 during the operations over Dunkirk when the unit still used the original GR code letters.

Top:
Aircraft GR-G, serial P9372. *Wright*

Above:
Plt Off Robert Stanford Tuck boarding his aircraft; note that the underside of the port wing had been painted black, standard at this time to provide a means of identification. *Wright*

Left:
Plt Off A. Wright with his aircraft GR-S; note the dimensions of the fuselage roundel. *Wright*

24
Thirteen Days in August

Somewhat the worse for wear, a Spitfire I of No 266 Squadron (unit code UO) is photographed taxying in to its dispersal at Wittering in September 1940 after the unit returned from operations in the south of England. Note the paint peeling off the fuselage roundel. The square patch on the top of the port wing was light-green gas-detecting paint. *via Forder*

The Battle of Britain in the summer of 1940 is the action which most readily springs to mind whenever the name 'Spitfire' is mentioned. In this account Dennis Armitage, at the time a Flight Lieutenant and junior Flight Commander with No 266 Squadron, gives his memories of the great air battle.

During the initial stages of the battle the Squadron was based at Wittering in the Midlands as part of No 12 Group, and saw little action. For the unit the period of quiet came to an abrupt end during the early morning darkness of 9 August, when it received orders that at first light it was to move to Northolt for a short detachment. Led by Sqn Ldr Rodney Wilkinson, 12 Spitfires took off from Wittering at 06.00hrs and headed south. On the way the weather deteriorated, however, with banks of low cloud concealing the ground. Unable to find Northolt, the Squadron headed back north until there was a break in the overcast and put down at the first airfield it came to, at Hatfield.

'This was most sporting because someone had thought of the brilliant idea of stringing quantities of barbed wire up and down the aerodrome. At that time Hatfield was used for ground training only, except for occasional test-flights by de Havillands, and the idea of the barbed wire was that it would upset any airborne divisions which might arrive from Germany. But in practice it was amazingly ineffective. Even with Spitfires, a machine which was notoriously nose-heavy on the ground, only one of the first section to land up-ended; and even that, I think, was due to a feeling that there was something peculiar about those yards of barbed wire trailing behind which caused the pilot to make a too sudden application of the brakes [Sgt A. Eade in L1059; the aircraft suffered Category 2 damage]. After that and a few belated red Verey lights, hundreds of small boys appeared – cadets who were doing their ground training and had been hurriedly kicked out of bed – and stood in two great lines to mark out a "secret" landing run which had been left clear for de Havillands, and the rest of us plonked down one at a time without further incident.

'It was still only 6.30am but someone rustled up some breakfast for us and over this we had a good healthy argument, which our C.O. won in the end, about whether anyone had thought of sending out warning signals about the barbed wire. By 8 o'clock the clouds had cleared and we flew on to Northolt, refuelled and settled down to wait. We were told we should return home at 3pm; at 3 we were told to wait till 5; at 5 to wait till 6; and at 6 o'clock we were told to take off for Tangmere.

'The eleven of us – the twelfth man, of course, had been left behind at Hatfield –

Right:
Dunlop Urie, his injured feet bandaged, waiting to be taken to hospital. *Urie*

Below:
Spitfire X4110 had an operational flying life of just 25 minutes! This brand new aircraft was delivered to No 602 Squadron at Westhampnett on the morning of 18 August 1940. That afternoon, with Flt Lt Dunlop Urie at the controls, it took part in the large scale action fought over Bognor. The Spitfire took hits from cannon shells and suffered major damage. Although Urie managed to limp back to base, the aircraft's back was broken and it never flew again.

arrived there without further incident. We parked our aircraft, arranged to borrow ground-crews from a Hurricane squadron stationed there, fed, had a drink or two and so to bed – pyjamaless.'

No 266 Squadron's Spitfires remained at Tangmere for the next two days, during which its ground personnel arrived from Wittering. No sooner had the unit collected itself together than orders came in to prepare for yet another move, to Eastchurch on the 12th.

'The C.O., the Senior Flight Commander and myself were summoned to a most secret meeting. We were informed that we had been given special duties escorting Battles [bombers] across the Channel to bomb concentrations of "E-boats" which were now assembling along the French and Dutch coasts. It sounded horrid for the lads in the slow and aged Battles although not so bad for us. We were to operate from Eastchurch, on the Isle of Sheppey in the Thames Estuary, which would be ready for us the next day.

'In the meantime, in view of the greatly increased activity around Portsmouth, we might be called on to patrol the aerodrome if necessary but under no circumstances were we to engage the enemy if we could possibly avoid it – they wanted to be sure there would be a full squadron to go to Eastchurch next day.'

Plt Off Bob Doe of No 234 Squadron, one of the top-scoring RAF pilots during the Battle of Britain, credited with 15 victories. *Doe*

The orders to keep out of action were smartly superseded a couple of hours later, when a large force of Junkers 88's of Kampfgeschwader 51 attacked Portsmouth at mid-day. No 266 Squadron scrambled 12 Spitfires and in the action that followed it claimed four enemy aircraft destroyed, two probably destroyed and nine damaged. Two of its Spitfires were lost and one pilot, Plt Off Dennis Ashton, killed. After refuelling at Tangmere, the unit's remaining aircraft took off for Eastchurch as planned.

'We arrived at Eastchurch to find two squadrons of Battles and another half squadron of Spitfires [No 19] had arrived earlier that day, and after dinner Flight Commanders and above were summoned to a conference of war in the Group Captain's office.

'We were told the general scheme and apparently only two things were lacking. One was a special information service which was going to tell us where to find the fruitiest targets, and the other snag was that [the Battles] had not got any bombs. However, the G/C had reason to hope that both these things would be added unto us by after lunch the next day and in the meantime he suggested we might all have a really good night's rest – breakfast at 9.30am and another conference about 10 o'clock. It was actually 7.05 hours when the first bomb arrived. Not ours!'

The attack on Eastchurch was carried out by Dornier 17s of Kampfgeschwader 2 and caused severe damage to the airfield buildings. No 266 Squadron lost one airman killed, and one officer and five airmen injured. One of its Spitfires suffered damage.

'We held a brief council of war and decided to station six Spitfire pilots permanently in their machines. Until the raid we had every reason to expect we should get warning of the approach of the Luftwaffe – why we did not we never discovered – but there was no radio station at Eastchurch and our own R/T sets were, of course, no use until we were airborne, so with the telephone wires down communications were sticky.

'Fortunately the [other] aircraft were practically undamaged, but unfortunately all of our spare ammunition boxes had gone up with our hangar where they were stored – fully loaded, incidentally, which had all helped to make the fire interesting'.

On the following day, 14 August, the Squadron moved to Hornchurch.

15 August was one of the hardest-fought days of the Battle of Britain and No 266 Squadron was heavily engaged. The unit claimed three enemy aircraft destroyed and one damaged but lost two pilots killed, Plt Off F. Cale and Sgt F. Hawley. Armitage himself had a very narrow escape and suffered leg injuries:

'There had been the usual shemozzle which had eventually sorted itself out into one or two Spits, and three or four 109's buzzing round in tight circles, and I had just had the pleasure of seeing the three that I had been closeted with diving down towards the sea with one of them smoking nicely. Another

"possible", perhaps even a "probable", but not a "confirmed" because I was not silly enough to follow him down in case there was another waiting for me up in the sun – and there was. I have no idea how he slipped under my tail, but suddenly I heard a loud bang, something hit me in the leg, and there was a fearful noise of rushing air. Under these circumstances one's reactions are automatic, even though one has no idea what the Dickens has happened. I whipped into a vertical turn, looking fearfully up towards the blazing sun and then, as confidence returned, I spotted what was probably the cause of the trouble diving away, already some 5,000ft below. I realised that the noise was simply due to my perspex hood having been blown out and, that apart, my machine seemed quite manageable. My left leg was quite numb from the calf down; I put my hand down gingerly to feel if my foot was still there and, reassured on this point, I headed for home.

'On landing I found a cannon shell had exploded inside the fuselage, the spent head of the shell having found its way under the armour plating behind the seat and struck me on the leg. One of the elevator control wires was hanging on by a single thread and another cannon shell had just caught my port wing tip.'

The next day, 16 August, was even worse for No 266 Squadron. During a frenzied combat with Messerschmitt 109s near Canterbury Sqn Ldr Wilkinson, Sub Lt Greenshields (a Fleet Air Arm officer seconded to the RAF) and

Plt Off Bower were all killed; Flt Lt S. Bazley, the senior Flight Commander, baled out with burns; Plt Off Sodden was injured and his Spitfire wrecked during a crash landing; and one aircraft was damaged. One enemy aircraft was claimed destroyed and three probably destroyed.

In the course of just two days' fighting the unit had lost its three senior officers and five other pilots killed or injured; seven Spitfires had been destroyed and two damaged. Dennis Armitage, as senior surviving officer on the Squadron, had to take charge. With his engineering warrant officer he surveyed the damaged Spitfires in the hangar, amongst them the one in which he had been injured.

'One of the E.O.'s pet rules was the one about non-cannibalisation of aircraft. Many a time we had waited and waited with three or four unserviceable machines in the hangar, when all but one could have been put into the air by pinching the necessary parts from the remaining machine. But now things were different; we went to any lengths to get a machine flying again, patching and making-do in a thousand ways. And our straight-backed E.O. did not hesitate to cast aside his life-long principles, though I think it still hurt him to do so. And incidentally, for a whole month, he himself worked from dusk till dawn without a break, and most of the daylight hours as well.

'The jagged hole in the fuselage was nearly a foot in diameter. The E.O. shook his head and with one accord our eyes strayed towards another machine in the hangar with a badly

Left:
Sgt P. Mitchell of No 65 Squadron with his Spitfire *Pampero II* (YT-D). The ground crewman is fitting the blinker in front of the cockpit, to shield the pilot's eyes from the exhaust glare during night flying. *Glaser*

Below:
A section of Spitfires of No 66 Squadron taking off from Gravesend, September 1940. *Times*

Right:
Rare shot of a Spitfire II of No 421 Flight, pictured late in 1940. The unit code letters were L.Z not LZ. This unit was formed towards the end of the Battle of Britain to fly 'Jim Crow' armed reconnaissance operations to report on the position, altitude and composition of German formations on their way to attack Britain. *Elliot*

damaged starboard wing. I nodded and he nodded – no words passed but I knew that the starboard wing, the only undamaged part of my airframe, would be transferred by dawn.'

On the evening of 17 August No 266 Squadron took delivery of seven new Spitfires to make up the aircraft lost during the previous two days' fighting. There were no replacement pilots, however, and by now the unit was desperately short. Despite his injured leg Dennis Armitage had to lead the Squadron in the air as well as on the ground.

'My leg was very stiff and I had to hobble about with the aid of a stick and be helped into my Spit, but once there I was all right. Fortunately there is no place other than bed where full use of the legs is so unimportant as in an aeroplane.'

The restoration of No 266 Squadron to its full complement of aircraft brought only temporary relief, for on the next day the unit was again hit hard.

On the afternoon of 18 August the Squadron was involved in a skirmish with Me 109s near the coast and claimed one enemy aircraft destroyed, one probably destroyed and one damaged. Afterwards Dennis Armitage led his 11 Spitfires in to land at Manston to refuel and re-arm. No sooner had the last of the aircraft landed, however, than the airfield was strafed by 16 Me 109s of Jagdgweschwader 52. The commander watched as Sgt Don Kingaby had a narrow escape:

'He was the last but one to land and seeing the German fighters diving on him began to run for cover, but tripped and fell. Then for a few breathless seconds he rolled along the

ground with the bullets kicking up the earth not a foot away as the German tried to swing his aircraft to get his sights on.'

A bullet nicked one of Kingaby's fingers and another of the pilots suffered shock, but those were the only injuries suffered by the Squadron. Its Spitfires were less fortunate. Two were set on fire and burned out ('it's amazing how fiercely an aluminium aircraft will burn if it once gets going') and six others suffered damage. Of the 11 aircraft that had taken off from Hornchurch that morning only three returned in the afternoon.

On 19 August the weather broke and for the next five days there were no large scale air operations over southern England. On the 21st, having seen no further action, the Squadron received orders to withdrew north to Wittering to re-form. During its time in the south of England the unit had seen intensive action on four separate days and claimed nine enemy aircraft destroyed, six probably destroyed and 11 damaged. But in the achieving this it had lost six pilots killed (including the commander) and five wounded (including both flight commanders), out of the 19 pilots on strength at the beginning of the period. Twelve of its Spitfires were destroyed and eight damaged. For No 266 Squadron, it had been a very unlucky 13 days in August.

25
Skirmish Over Kent

By the third week in December 1940 the hard-fought daylight actions of the Battle of Britain were at an end. To counter the threat of attack by enemy fighters-bombers on London, pairs of squadrons of Spitfires now flew standing patrols over Kent during the daylight hours. But as autumn drew to an end the Luftwaffe appeared to have abandoned even this form of attack. Now enemy air incursions by day over southern England were restricted mainly to reconnaissance aircraft trying to sneak through the defences to photograph targets. Flying fast, high and alone, these aircraft presented difficult and fleeting targets. To catch them the Spitfire squadrons had to expend a disproportionate effort, as can be seen from the attempt on the morning of 21 December 1940 . . .

At 10.35hrs that morning there were blue skies over much of the south of England as No 64 Squadron based at Hornchurch received orders to put up a dozen Spitfires to mount a standing patrol in the Maidstone area. One of the squadron's pilots, Plt Off Trevor Gray, later told the author:
'After taking off from Hornchurch we flew to the so-called Maidstone patrol line which ran from Maidstone to the south coast. Once in position we patrolled at 15,000ft, the maximum we could sustain without using up our limited oxygen. Then it was a case of waiting for the enemy to come to us, but there was very little activity at this time.'

Five minutes after Gray and his comrades were airborne, the No 11 Group controller ordered a further dozen Spitfires, from No 611 Squadron based at Southend, to join them at the patrol line. One Spitfire was forced to return early with engine trouble but the remaining 23 aircraft flew up and down the patrol line in separate formations, engines throttled back to conserve fuel.

This was the position at 11.09hrs, when Leutnant Helmut Fischer and his radio operator Unteroffizier Kurt Schaefer of the 7th (Long Range Reconnaissance) Staffel of Lehrgeschwader 2 took off from Grimbergen near Brussels in their Messerschmitt 110 and headed for Southend. The clear skies over the south of England had been reported earlier in the day by German weather observation aircraft, and indicated near-perfect conditions for high altitude reconnaissance. Fischer's orders were to reconnoitre the Thames estuary for shipping and photograph Detling airfield.

Stripped of armour and all forward-firing armament except for two machine guns, the Messerschmitt rose swiftly to its penetration altitude of 33,000ft. Once there Fischer levelled out and allowed his speed to build up to the maximum for continuous cruising, 350mph. The German aircraft quickly covered the 60-odd miles from the Belgian coast to Margate, where the crew spotted a 20-ship convoy in the estuary. Kurt Schaefer tapped out a coded message to base reporting the find. The reconnaissance aircraft continued up the Thames estuary with Fischer and Schaefer systematically scanning the sky around them for any sign of enemy fighters trying to intercept the lone intruder. If the threat could be seen in time there was a good chance the Messerschmitt could outrun the opposition.

The Messerschmitt continued along the Thames Estuary as far as Southend without interference, then swung south to photograph Detling. And, as luck would have it, Detling lay directly under the line the Spitfires were patrolling. For some reason the fighter pilots had received no radio warning from the ground on the presence of the German aircraft in the area; the first they knew of it was when they saw the long white condensation trail high above. Trevor Gray takes up the story:

'We had been on patrol for some time when we noticed a condensation trail above us, heading south. Sqn Ldr Don Macdonell, the squadron commander, took us up after it. When he saw we were not gaining on it fast enough he ordered us to break formation – then we could go after it at the speed of the fastest Spitfire and not the slowest.'

In each of the 23 Spitfires the pilot pushed his throttle 'through the gate' for emergency combat power and headed after the intruder at maximum climbing speed. The relatively tight cruising formations disolved quickly, as the faster aircraft in each squadron began to pull away from the slower ones.

Left:
A remarkable photograph of Spitfires, taken from the vertical camera in Helmut Fischer's Messerschmitt 110 during the high speed chase across Kent on the morning of 21 December 1940, showing a gaggle of Spitfires of No 64 or No 611 Squadron climbing to intercept the German reconnaissance aircraft. The aircraft are flying south-southeast, having just passed over Snodland near Chatham. *Fischer*

Below:
Close-up of an Me 110 of 7. (Long Range Reconnaissance) Staffel of Lehrgeschwader 2, pictured at Brussels–Grimberghen. *Fischer*

began to trail oil and the port undercarriage leg flopped out of its housing. Fischer hauled his aircraft round in an attempt to drive off the tormentor, but had to break away when another Spitfire swung into a threatening position behind him. With yet other enemy fighters nearing his altitude, it was obvious there was no future for Fischer where he was. He rolled the Messerschmitt on to its back and pulled it into a steep dive, to build up his speed rapidly. Then he rolled the wings level and continued for the coast in a high speed descent. Hard on his heels Trevor Gray followed, firing short bursts whenever he had the enemy in his gunsight. This continued until the Spitfire's ammunition was exhausted, and it peeled away.

Now there were more than a dozen Spitfires in an extended stream edging towards the diving Messerschmitt, the fastest at the front of

By this time Kurt Schaefer had spotted the gaggles of Spitfires climbing to intercept, and started a running commentary on their relative positions. Fischer pushed his throttles wide open and headed south trying to keep himself between the sun and the enemy fighters. In this way he hoped to present as difficult a target as possible, while setting up a lengthy high speed chase which would run the single-engined fighters short of fuel before they could get into firing positions. Afterwards the German pilot reported:

'By increasing revolutions on both engines to 2,500rpm and retracting the glycol radiators, I increased speed and at the same time gained more height. Meanwhile I saw two of the fighters breaking away from the formation and gain altitude rapidly. The radio operator gave me a running commentary of the altitude and range of the pursuing fighters. In a very short time (4–5 minutes) a couple of Spitfires reached a position about 150 metres above me and started the attack.'

At the controls of the leading Spitfire was Trevor Gray, who managed to get 500yd behind the tail of the enemy aircraft. Finding it impossible to close the range further, he loosed off a series of bursts at long range. But the fire was accurate and almost immediately the Messerschmitt's radio operator was mortally wounded. Other rounds smashed away part of the hydraulic system, the aircraft

the queue and slowest at the rear. Replacing Gray at the head of the stream was Flt Lt Barry Heath of No 611 Squadron:
'I came within range of the enemy at 32,000ft and was about to attack when he dived steeply. I dived after him, waiting until about 20,000ft while a Spitfire did an astern attack. I then fired a 5–6 second burst, closing from 300yd to 100yd. At 5,000ft I had to pull out as I could no longer hold my plane in the dive.'

After Heath completed his attack it was the turn of Flt Sgt Maurice Choron of No 64 Squadron:
'The aircraft we were chasing went into a very steep dive in an attempt to get away. There were three Spitfires in front of me, and we all followed him in a steep dive. Two Spitfires were near enough to open fire. I was following

Left:
Plt Off Trevor Gray. *Gray*

Below:
SH-E, the Spitfire Trevor Gray flew during the action on 21 December 1940. *Gray*

the enemy aircraft, and got the impression that he was seriously hit from the manner in which he spiralled as he went down. However, he slowly pulled out of his dive and at 8,000ft I was within firing range – 400yd closing to 300yd. I had set my sight for a span of 60ft and fired four bursts with the enemy aircraft right in my line of fire, using 30° forward deflection and dipping the nose of my aircraft during each burst in order to be sure of hitting the enemy aircraft. I could not see my fire hitting him, though I am positive it did so. At about 2,000–1,500ft my safety glass froze up and I could no longer fire with any certainty of hitting, so I broke off my pursuit.'

During the rapid descent from the cold air at high altitude, into air with a higher moisture content lower down, frost now began to form on the inside of the canopies and windscreens of several of the Spitfires. Plt Off J. Lawson-Brown of No 64 Squadron managed to carry through his attack in spite of this problem:
'I only had a view of about 3in diameter when I had cleaned the safety glass with Glycol solution – the rest of the safety glass and some of the perspex was frozen up. I made a quarter attack at 700ft firing one short burst at 250yd range when I was about 5 miles out to sea off Eastbourne. I then came in below astern, and fired two short bursts at 250yd range and closing in, two more bursts at 50ft range. During this attack the enemy aircraft lost height steadily from 300ft to 50ft. With the fourth and final burst of this attack I raked the enemy aircraft from stem to stern by pulling the stick back, and I then had to break off to port and make a steep climbing turn to avoid being forced into the sea by the enemy aircraft. I circled once, but as I could not see anything I set course for Hornchurch.'

After crossing the coast between Eastbourne and Bexhill Fischer headed out to sea at full throttle, dodging in and out of the banks of haze which lay close to the surface. The high speed chase continued for a few miles longer, before one by one the Spitfires were forced to break away as their fuel began to run short. Since the Messerschmitt had not been seen to crash, it could be claimed only as 'damaged'.

Some of the Spitfires had used so much fuel during the pursuit that they were now unable to return to base. Fighters put down to refuel at the forward airfields at Lymne, Hawkinge and Manston. Maurice Choron ran out of fuel near Tunbridge Wells and his aircraft was wrecked in the crash landing which followed. Barrie Heath also ran out of fuel and, attempting a wheels-down landing on a field near Rye, his aircraft suffered considerable damage when it turned on its back. None of the British pilots suffered injury however.

Once he had shaken off the pursuers Fischer remained at low altitude, throttled back to cruising speed and made his way towards the forward airfield at Mardyk near Dunkirk. There he used the emegency air system to extend his undercarriage and made a normal wheels-down landing in the damaged Messerschmitt. The machine had collected 32 hits during the various attacks and the German pilot had indeed been lucky to survive the encounter.

The action had an interesting sequel in 1979, when Helmut Fischer and Trevor Gray met for a second time. On this occasion, however, the German pilot was accorded a cordial reception when he called with his wife at the Surrey home of his one-time opponent. The two men, who had done their utmost to kill each other 39 years earlier, were able to speak as friends on the events of the past.

Trevor Gray (left) and Helmut Fischer pictured in 1979 after they had been brought together by the author. *Gray*

An Air of Battle

Photographs of operational Spitfire IIBs, the cannon-armed version of this mark, are rare. The 'give-away' for the Mk II is the small blister on the starboard side of the engine cowling immediately behind the spinner, covering the redesigned reduction gear fitted to the Merlin XII engine.

Above left:
Plt Off Gene Potter of No 71 (Eagle) Squadron sitting on the cowling of his Mk IIB at North Weald in 1941. The blanket over the rear fuselage conceals the squadron's XR code letters.   *Salkeld*

Left:
P8332, a Mk IIB of No 222 Squadron.   *RAF Museum*

Below left:
Ground crewman cleaning the port 20mm cannon of a Mk VB of No 72 Squadron at Biggin Hill, September 1941.

Below:
WAAF mechanics helping the pilot to strap into a Spitfire IIA of No 411 (Canadian) Squadron at Digby in October 1941.
Canadian National Archives

Right:
Yellow-nosed Spitfire: AR219, a Westland-built Mk I, was flown as a 'bounce aircraft' by instructors at No 57 Operational Training Unit at Hawarden.
RAF Museum

26
Correct Engine Handling – Key to Survival

In August 1942 the Air Tactics department at the Air Ministry issued the document which follows, as a guide to Spitfire pilots on the optimum engine settings to use when flying over enemy-held territory. Long range sorties had to be planned carefully to meet the diverging requirements of fuel economy, and the need to maintain the highest possible cruising speed in areas where formations were liable to encounter enemy fighters. If Spitfires were 'bounced' while flying at low speed it could take up to two minutes for them to accelerate to maximum speed, during which time they were extremely vulnerable. To reduce the risks while over enemy territory formation leaders were advised to cruise at speeds considerably higher than those for optimum fuel consumption. For a given cruising speed and altitude, different settings of boost pressure and engine revolutions could give substantially different rates of fuel consumption. For example, a Spitfire V cruising at 10,000ft at 281mph (True), with +2lb boost and 2,650rpm, burned fuel at a rate of 35gal/hr; but by flying at the same speed and altitude with +3¾lb boost and 2,000rpm, consumption was only 29gal/hr. Flying at the same altitude at maximum continuous cruising speed, 331mph (True) with +6lb boost and 2,650rpm, consumption was 70gal/hr. During combat, the maximum emergency power setting of +16lb boost and 3,000rpm guzzled fuel at 150gal/hr. A thorough knowledge of which power and rpm settings were best, for particular stages of the mission, could spell the difference between life and death for a Spitfire pilot.

HOW TO MAKE FULL USE OF THE PERFORMANCE OF THE SPITFIRE V, VI AND IX

1. This memorandum . . . is intended to bring to the notice of all concerned the necessity of making full use of the power available in our Spitfire aircraft. It applies equally, in principle, to all our fighter aircraft operating against an enemy whose performance is equal or superior to our own.

2. At the present stage of the war, the enemy in France is equipped with the FW 190, a fighter with an excellent rate of climb and good acceleration. To defeat this aircraft and to avoid casualties on our side, our aircraft must fly as fast as possible whenever they are in the combat zone.

3. In the past, pilots have been told to fly at low rpm and high boost to economise in petrol. All pilots must know the correct rpm and boost at which to fly to obtain the longest duration of flight or range; a Table at Appendix 'A' gives the various durations at different

Right:
Spitfire in trouble: combat photos taken from the Messerschmitt 109 of Major Gerhard Schoepfel, commander of III Gruppe of Jagdgeschwader 26, during the action on 27 June 1941 when he claimed a victory. *Schoepfel*

Far right:
Spitfire V of No 234 Squadron being dismantled by a German salvage team after it made a belly landing in northern France in April 1942. *via Ethell*

adjustments of rpm and throttle for the Spitfire VB and VC (Merlin 45 and 46).

4. Wings must still fly at the most economical rpm when they are flying under the enemy RDF [radar] screens but it is essential, as soon as they are liable to be detected, that they open up to maximum power for formation flying.

5. The acceleration of the Spitfire is relatively poor. It is therefore dangerous to cruise at, say, +2 boost and 1,900rpm when the Hun is about, because the time taken in accelerating to maximum speed will allow him quickly to draw into firing range.

6. It is fully realised that the speed of formations depends on the ability of the worst pilots to keep up. This is only a question of training and practice. At present, +5 boost and 2,650rpm are the maximum boost and rpm settings known to be used successfully by a wing. On this occasion, the pilots said that they could have gone faster, and this is definitely a step in the right direction.

7. It is recommended that when planning operations it should be decided at what speed the aircraft should fly and at what point in

Ground running a Mk V of the 309th Squadron, 31st Fighter Group of the US 8th Air Force. This unit flew operations from Westhampnett during the summer and autumn of 1942. *VMI Collection*

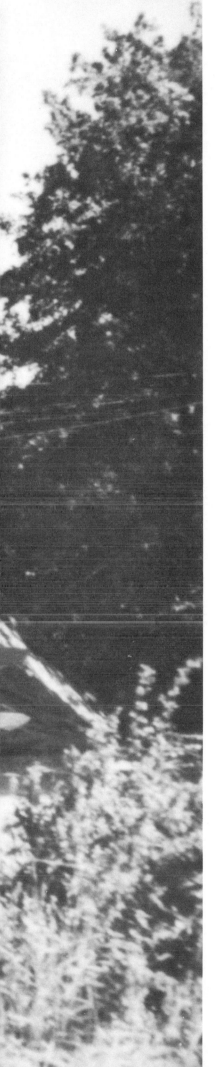

the operation wings should open up to maximum speed. After opening up to maximum speed, they should not throttle back to economical cruising speed until they are well clear of the area in which they may be attacked.

8. Spitfires are now modified to give +16 emergency boost. It must be impressed on pilots that this gives a great increase of speed under 21,500 feet and 18,250 feet for Merlin 46 and 45 engines respectively, and that if used for combat only there is no risk of engine failure.

SAFETY FAST – OR PRUNE'S GUIDE FOR LIVING

(i) Don't loiter. When you can't keep up don't blame your leader: pull your finger out and cut corners.

(ii) Low revs and high boost will bring you safely back to roost.

(iii) Don't wait until you see the Hun before you decide to get a move on. It will take a couple of minutes for your Spitfire to respond after you open up, and by that time whatever you do will be irrelevant. When you are liable to meet the enemy always fly at maximum cruising speed.

(iv) If you want to live on the other side, you must move fast; but equally, if you want to come back again you must save petrol. You will find your engine happier at, say, +4lbs and 1,700rpm than at +1lb and 2,650 rpm.

Both these adjustments give the same A.S.I. [indicated airspeed] but if you fly at +4lbs and 1,700rpm you will save seven gallons of petrol an hour. It is possible to get full throttle and +4lbs above 10,000 feet by reducing the revs until the boost falls to +4lbs. Use full throttle and minimum revs above full throttle height for any desired A.S.I. This gives the best combination of fast cruising and minimum consumption.

(v) When you are travelling at full throttle, and full power is suddenly wanted, it is only necessary to push the constant speed lever fully forward to get full revs and boost. To return to high speed cruising at best economical conditions, reduce your *revs* and not your boost.

(vi) When being briefed, always ask at what revs and boost you should fly. This will naturally depend upon the length of the sweep, but don't forget that:

(a) *when hard pressed* you can fly at +16 boost and 3,000rpm without any danger of [the engine] blowing up,

but

(b) your consumption will be 150 gallons per hour. Study the Table in Appendix A and know how much petrol you are using.

(vii) Finally, when unlikely to be engaged always fly minimum revs and under +4lbs boost; but when in the vicinity of Huns, fly maximum everything and in *good time*.

APPENDIX A
SPITFIRE VB AND C (MERLIN 45 AND 46): APPROXIMATE PETROL CONSUMPTION FIGURES AT VARIOUS BOOST AND REV SETTINGS

A.S.I.	T.A.S	Height	Boost	Revs	Consumption per hour [galls]
250	255	2000	$+4\frac{1}{2}$	2000	42
230	234	2000	$+2\frac{3}{4}$	1800	35*
		2000	$+\frac{1}{2}$	2650	40
200	203	2000	$-\frac{1}{2}$	1800	31*
		2000	$-2\frac{1}{2}$	2650	35
295	331	10000	$+9$	3000	88
		10000	$+6$	2650	70
250	281	10000	$+3\frac{3}{4}$	2000	42*
		10000	$+2$	2650	47
200	225	10000	$-1\frac{1}{2}$	1800	29*
		10000	-3	2650	35
283	368	20000	$+9$	3000	88
268	350	20000	$+6$	2650	70
258	300	20000	$+3\frac{3}{4}$	2650	65
240	310	20000	$+3\frac{3}{4}$	2400	50
230	300	20000	$+1\frac{1}{2}$	2400	46*
		20000	$+1$	2650	48
200	263	20000	$-1\frac{3}{4}$	2200	36*
		20000	$-2\frac{1}{2}$	2650	40
216	335	30000	0	3000	47
180	283	30000	$-3\frac{1}{4}$	2850	41*
		30000	$-3\frac{1}{4}$	3000	43

Consumption at +16lbs boost and 3,000rpm = 150 gallons per hour.
* = Fly at these settings.

PRU Spitfires

Above:
Spitfire PRIC P9426 of the Photographic Reconnaissance unit, pictured after a belly landing at Heston in mid-1940. Note the standard-type roundels and fin flash, unusual on reconnaissance aircraft. Apart from the lack of radio mast and the bulged canopy, the 'give away' that this is a PRIC is the small bulge above the port wing which covered the pump for the 30gal blister tank fitted underneath. The two vertical cameras were housed in a similar blister under the starboard wing. *Tuttle*

Right:
Spitfire PRIG with its pilot, Flg Off Gordon Hughes. Clearly visible are the port-facing oblique camera pointing 13° below the horizontal, the bulged sides of the cockpit canopy and the absence of the radio aerial. This version was used for low altitude photography beneath cloud, when the very pale pink colouring merged with the light background and made detection from the ground difficult. *Tuttle*

Left:
Flg Off Bill Panton pictured with his PRIG. *Green*

Below:
PRIG R7117 photographed at Benson in 1941. This version usually carried a port-facing oblique camera behind the cockpit; either it was not fitted to this aircraft, or it was one of the few with the camera facing to starboard. Other non-standard features on R7117 are the lack of bulges on the canopy, the presence of the radio mast and unusually prominent markings on the wing upper surfaces and fin. *Tuttle*

Above and Right:
Sq Ldr Alistair Taylor preparing to board, and running up the engine of his PRIF at Benson. The aircraft was painted in standard PRU blue. The pilot's heavy clothing but lack of Mae West suggests he was about to make a high altitude flight not involving a sea crossing. *Tuttle*

197

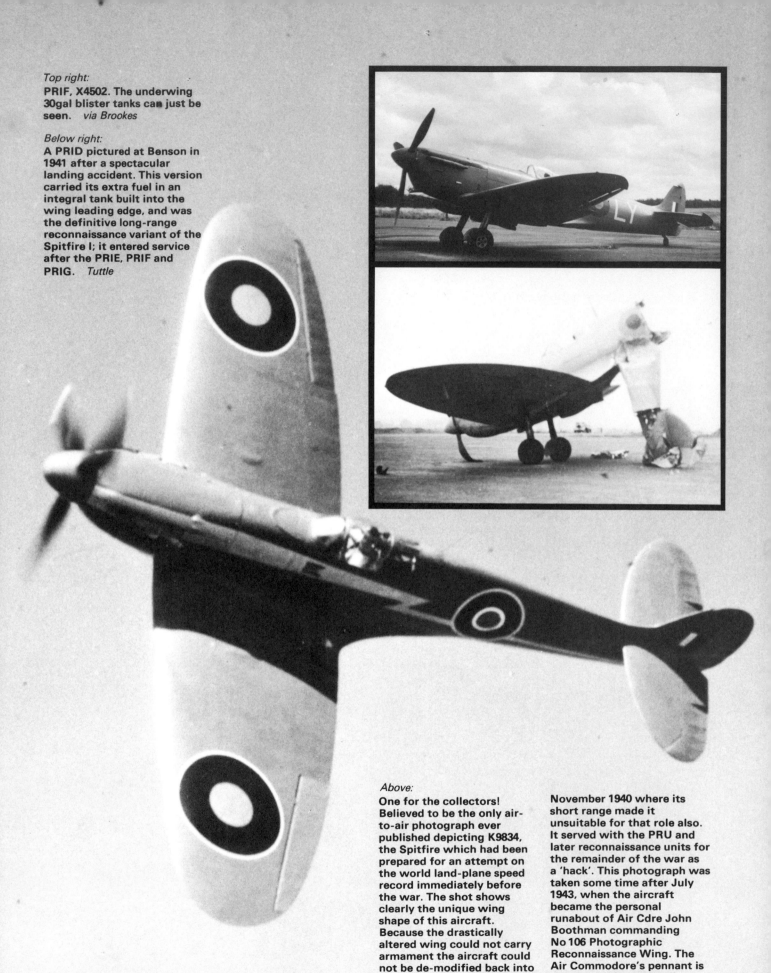

Top right:
PRIF, X4502. The underwing 30gal blister tanks can just be seen. *via Brookes*

Below right:
A PRID pictured at Benson in 1941 after a spectacular landing accident. This version carried its extra fuel in an integral tank built into the wing leading edge, and was the definitive long-range reconnaissance variant of the Spitfire I; it entered service after the PRIE, PRIF and PRIG. *Tuttle*

Above:
One for the collectors! Believed to be the only air-to-air photograph ever published depicting K9834, the Spitfire which had been prepared for an attempt on the world land-plane speed record immediately before the war. The shot shows clearly the unique wing shape of this aircraft. Because the drastically altered wing could not carry armament the aircraft could not be de-modified back into a fighter. It was delivered to the Photographic Reconnaissance Unit in November 1940 where its short range made it unsuitable for that role also. It served with the PRU and later reconnaissance units for the remainder of the war as a 'hack'. This photograph was taken some time after July 1943, when the aircraft became the personal runabout of Air Cdre John Boothman commanding No 106 Photographic Reconnaissance Wing. The Air Commodore's pennant is clearly visible on the silver flash running down the fuselage. *Saffery*

27

Besieged on Malta

Before the war George Hows had trained as an agricultural engineer, and in 1940 he volunteered for the Royal Air Force and trained as an engine fitter. After a brief period with a Hampden bomber squadron, in April 1942 he was posted to Egypt. A few months later, holding the rank of Aircraftman 1st Class Fitter IIE, he arrived on the besieged island of Malta where he was one of the ground crewmen who sweated to keep airworthy the small force of Spitfires on which the island's survival depended. It was a job that would test his improvisational skills to the utmost . . .

'Early in August I was posted to Malta which was then nearing the most critical period of its siege. We flew in by night in a Dakota and, after holding off for about an hour because an air raid was in progress, we were unceremoniously dumped at Luqa and the aircraft made a hasty getaway. No sooner had we set foot on the island than the sirens sounded again. With the other new arrivals I was hustled away from the runway and into a cave which was being used as a shelter.

'The following day I was assigned to No 1435 Flight which operated Spitfire Vs. Just to the east of Luqa airfield was a patch of waste land known as Safi strip, where our Spitfires and the aircraft of other units were dispersed in improvised blast pens made out of 4-gallon petrol cans filled with sand and erected to a height of 12–14ft. Working under a corporal, my task was to carry out 25-hour and other inspections on the Spitfires as they became due. Also we did those engine repairs which were beyond the fitters assigned to the aircraft, as well as engine changes, fault diagnosis and engine tuning. All of our work had to be done in the open, in the blast pens. As well as this routine work, we patched up the Spitfires which had been damaged in battle to keep as many as possible flying. Sometimes the pressure was such that we had to cut corners; bullet holes in the aircraft were often patched over with bits of cloth, even pieces of paper, doped in place. Later we were able to do a smarter job – if the Spitfire survived that long.

'That summer we were desperately short of spare parts and ground equipment. Any air-

craft which crash landed and was damaged beyond repair was a Godsend, providing us with virtually our only source of spares. Everything, apart from the simplest of tools, was in short supply. I remember there was only one Rolls Royce Merlin tool kit for the whole of the Safi dispersal area. The only crane we had was a home-made affair, made of pieces of scrap angle-iron bolted on the chassis of an old lorry and incorporating a hand operated cable winch. Necessity was indeed the mother of invention.'

Compounding the problems of those trying to keep Malta's dwindling force of Spitfires serviceable were the frequent attacks on the airfields by German and Italian aircraft.

'At the beginning I was terribly scared by the almost continual air attacks on our dispersal area. But fortunately we had plenty of slit trenches and caves, all of our offices and workshops were in caves.

'The Junkers 87 Stuka dive bombers would concentrate on the ships in the Grand Harbour and the heavy bombers came over most nights. The worst of our tormentors were the low flying Messerschmitt 109s, which came in unannounced during the day to bomb and strafe us. But like everyone else, after about ten days I became used to them. We learned to ignore the sirens and took cover in the slit trenches only when the red flag was hoisted to indicate an imminent danger of attack to Safi itself. As things got hotter the flag stayed up for so long that we could get hardly any work done; so we ignored that too.

'The deep cave shelters which had been blasted out of the solid rock gave considerable protection, and surprisingly few people were injured during these attacks. I have been in caves when they suffered direct hits from bombs, and all we felt was a slight shudder. The main problem in the caves was from the damp, which created health problems when people slept in them for months on end.

'Frequently the runway at Luqa was cratered. Standing by ready to fill in the holes would be a gang of soldiers from the Lancashire Fusiliers with a lorry kept filled with rubble – of which there was never any shortage. An old Valentine tank was used to drag

LAC George Hows, whose account of the siege of Malta appears below.

Spitfire VCs on the aircraft carrier USS *Wasp* during the ship's two sorties in April and May 1942 to deliver fighters to reinforce the defences of Malta. The Spitfires George Hows serviced on Malta during the siege had all flown in from aircraft carriers.
all USN

Above:
Moving up from the hangar, to be ranged on deck ready to take off at first light the following morning.

Left:
His aircraft restrained by the deck crew, the pilot carries out the pre-take-off checks.

Top right:
The deck control officer drops his flag and the pilot pushes forward his throttle before releasing the brakes; already the lift is on its way down to the hangar to pick up the next aircraft.

Bottom right:
Take-off.

200

clear any aircraft which was wrecked on the runway; it also made a pretty good roller, to compact the rubble in the crater and level it off. Our runway repair teams had the whole thing down to a fine art. It was a rough and ready process, but the runway had to be made serviceable quickly if our aircraft were to be able to land. After a period of such treatment the runway got very rough and pitted, however, and this caused a lot of wear to the Spitfires' tyres. But, such was the loss rate in the summer of 1942, few Spitfires outlived their tyres. On problem after each raid was that there would be numerous splinters from bombs and shells lying all over the runway. So early each morning a detail of about 40 men known as the "Shrapnel Party" would walk shoulder to shoulder down the length of the runway to pick up metal pieces of aircraft, bombs or AA shells.'

At about the time George Hows arrived No 1435 Flight was expanded and re-designated No 1435 Squadron, under the command of Sqn Ldr Tony Lovell. One of the most successful pilots on the unit was Flt Lt Henry McLeod, a Canadian who that summer was credited with 6½ enemy aircraft destroyed or probably destroyed, and one damaged.
'In the Squadron there was a tremendous esprit de corps. If one of our Spitfires brought

Right:
After their arrival on Malta in desert camouflage, many of the Spitfires had dark blue-grey paint daubed over the light brown parts of the camouflage to make them less visible from above when flying over the sea. Note that this aircraft has also had its two inner cannon removed and wooden bungs fitted in their place. *Jefford*

Below:
Spitfire Vs of No 1435 Squadron in their blast pens at Safi. Instead of the more usual two-letter identification code, this unit used only the letter 'V'. *Hows*

down an enemy every man felt he had a share in it be he cook or copper, "wallah" or technical ground staff. Everyone was part of a team with a common cause, to beat the enemy and get back home. Discipline was self-imposed, nobody wanted to let the side down. We never knew what it was to have somebody put on a charge, there weren't such things.

'During the Siege uniform dress simply ceased to exist, it was a question of what one could get hold of. Hardly two people were dressed the same. Often one would see an airman wearing an R.A.F. tunic and Army trousers, and that would be his "best" uniform.

'Towards the end of August the Siege really began to bite, following the near-destruction of a long-awaited supply convoy. Our rations, which had been small enough when I arrived, were cut first to one half and then to one third of normal British Army rations. Breakfast would be a slice of bread and lunch was a ladleful of watery bully-beef soup. The main meal of the day, supper, would usually be a thin slice of bread with some bully beef and a small portion of potatoes with sometimes – if we were lucky – some dried vegetables but seldom enough to allay one's hunger. At Safi village just off the airfield an old woman ran a black market eating house. We had to pay five shillings for a rather foul pancake made out of flour and water, fried in Spitfire hydraulic oil which we had to bring ourselves; and we had to queue for the privilege.

'The worst parts of the Siege were the almost continual bombing and the shortage of food. By November 1942 things were getting very bad, the heavy anti-aircraft guns were limited to a few rounds each day; it must

have been terrible for the gunners to have to sit under cover for the rest of the day after they had fired their allocation of rounds, but there was no alternative. During the Siege we always seemed to have enough fuel and ammunition for our Spitfires, but everything else was in short supply. Motor fuel was so short that bus services on the island had to be suspended. I remember seeing Lord Gort, the governor of Malta, coming to visit Luqa on his bicycle – that was a great morale booster for those who saw him. Very little mail got through to the Island and news from home was sparse and spasmodic. Things became a little easier after a convoy got through in September. With the arrival of another convoy in December we knew the worst of the Siege was over. But it was not until February 1943 that people began to receive parcels from home, many of which had originally been sent for Christmas 1941.'

From then on the air defences of the island became progressively stronger, while the enemy air attacks tailed off to the point where the sounding of a siren became something of an event. No 1435 Squadron was heavily involved in flying missions in support of the invasion of Sicily in July 1943, and the landings on the mainland of Italy two months later. Gradually the Allied forces advanced up the toe of Italy, moving further and further away from Malta.

'In October 1943 we received orders to move to Italy. We loaded our hotch-potch collection of ground equipment and vehicles on tank landing craft which took us to the port of Taranto. We called ourselves "Fred Karno's Air Force". You should have seen our convoy:

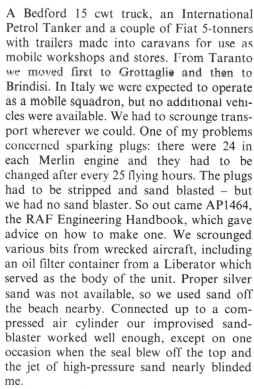

A Bedford 15 cwt truck, an International Petrol Tanker and a couple of Fiat 5-tonners with trailers made into caravans for use as mobile workshops and stores. From Taranto we moved first to Grottaglie and then to Brindisi. In Italy we were expected to operate as a mobile squadron, but no additional vehicles were available. We had to scrounge transport wherever we could. One of my problems concerned sparking plugs: there were 24 in each Merlin engine and they had to be changed after every 25 flying hours. The plugs had to be stripped and sand blasted – but we had no sand blaster. So out came AP1464, the RAF Engineering Handbook, which gave advice on how to make one. We scrounged various bits from wrecked aircraft, including an oil filter container from a Liberator which served as the body of the unit. Proper silver sand was not available, so we used sand off the beach nearby. Connected up to a compressed air cylinder our improvised sandblaster worked well enough, except on one occasion when the seal blew off the top and the jet of high-pressure sand nearly blinded me.

'There was always a shortage of hand tools, though we were sometimes able to get these from an American squadron in exchange for blankets or a bottle of Scotch.

Top left:
Line-up of Spitfire IXs of No 1435 Squadron at Safi in October 1943, shortly after the unit re-equipped with this version before moving to Italy. *Hows*

Above:
Spitfire IXs of No 1435 Squadron at readiness at Brindisi, Italy in late 1943. These fighters were often scrambled to engage German reconnaissance aircraft, and had been carefully polished with bees wax for maximum performance. *Hows*

Left:
Spitfire V JK707 lying on the beach near Salerno in September 1943. The aircraft belonged to the 307th Squadron, 31st Fighter Group, US Army Air Forces. The official US caption to the photo reads: 'The Curtiss P-40 (foreground) was shot down by mistake by our Anti-Aircraft...' *USAF*

Right:
**Makeshift servicing
arrangements for No 1435
Squadron aircraft at Brindisi.
The workshop on the left had
been a packing case for an
Auster aircraft; the mobile
workshops behind the
Spitfire were constructed
from packing cases bolted to
captured Italian
vehicles.**   *Hows*

Below:
**Spitfire Vs of No 225
Squadron being serviced 'in
the field' under primitive
conditions, at Lago, Italy in
March 1944.**
Canadian National Archives

Bottom:
**Mk IX of No 154 Squadron
pictured after landing at the
newly completed airstrip at
Alto, Corsica in April 1944.**

'While we were at Brindisi our commander, Sqn Ldr Ronald Webb at that time, launched a campaign to improve the performance of the Mark IX Spitfire. "Webby", as he was known to us all, was a fantastic New Zealander who inspired us to get on with the job with a minimum of fuss. With my corporal I carefully tuned up the engine of his personal aircraft, K for Kathleen. We stripped off the dope (which weighed about 200 pounds) and applied a thin coat of paint over the engine cowling to prevent glare from the sun. Somebody got hold of several pounds of pure beeswax and when the Spitfires were at readiness the ground crews would polish them to get maximum performance.

'Although our squadron was originally intended as an interceptor unit, later the Spitfires were fitted with bomb racks for two 250 pounders. With these they attacked road and rail targets, and shipping across the Adriatic off Yugoslavia and Albania. We felt it was a way of exacting revenge for the "stick" the Germans had given us on Malta.

'We followed the ground forces up through Italy, moving to Foggia and then to Falconara. We were at the latter on 2 May 1945 when the German forces in northern Italy surrendered. On the day before VE day we moved back to a small village just outside Naples, where the Squadron was to be disbanded. The mayor and our CO got together and decided the village should have a victory parade. So we all turned out in the afternoon and marched through the main street, headed by the village band. Then we halted in the centre of the village and the mayor delivered a long speech in Italian, none of which we understood apart from the final sentence which was to the effect that the bars in the village would be open to us for free drinks that evening! On the next day No 1435 Squadron was disbanded. With a total of 150 pilots, groundcrew and administrators, it had been an efficient and dedicated fighting unit. I am proud to have served with it from the first day of its existence until the last.'

Spitfire VIII JF880 of No 417 Squadron RCAF undergoing servicing at Fano, Italy in December 1944.

Spitfires with Red Stars

Above and Right:
A Spitfire V of the Red Air Force, one of those delivered early in 1943, pictured at a display of Soviet wartime equipment. The loop aerial above the rear fuselage belonged to the RPK 10M radio compass, a piece of equipment not previously seen on the Spitfire. Because the loop was fixed athwartships, the pilot had to turn the aircraft to take bearings. *via Guest*

Below right:
Spitfire PRIV in Soviet markings. As well as the standard red star national markings on the fuselage and tail, this aircraft also carries one on the engine cowling. Almost certainly this aircraft was one of the four Spitfire IVs detached to Vaenga in northern Russia in the autumn of 1942, to fly photographic reconnaissance missions over northern Norway. When the detachment ended the two surviving Spitfires were handed over to the Soviet Air Force. *via Guest*

28
Problems with the Seafire

The Seafire entered service with No 807 Squadron in June 1942, and first went into action in the Mediterranean the following autumn. It soon became clear that the naval derivative of the Spitfire was not really strong enough for the rough and tumble of deck operations; this, combined with problems of control near the stall and a landing speed higher than previous aircraft operated by the Royal Navy, resulted in numerous deck landing accidents. The Seafire rapidly gained a reputation as a bad naval fighter, but with no other British aircraft available with a comparable performance the Royal Navy had little choice but to use the type.

Jeffrey Quill, the Chief Test Pilot at Supermarine Aviation Ltd, was seconded to the Fleet Air Arm with the rank of Lieutenant Commander to investigate the problems encountered with Seafire deck operations. In February 1944 his analysis of the problem, 'Report on Seafire Deck Landing', was submitted to the Fifth Sea Lord, Rear Adm D. Boyd. The document breaks down the problems into their component parts in a lucid manner, and casts new light on both the Seafire and the general problem of deck-landing high performance aircraft at that time. The contents of the document are included here in their entirety.

MA970 was the first Seafire IIC, the naval version of the Spitfire VC, fitted with the strengthened wing and provision to carry four 20mm cannon or the more normal two cannon and four machine guns. Unusual for an early model Seafire, the aircraft is depicted here fitted with four cannon as it rests on the test catapult at Farnborough.

REPORT ON SEAFIRE DECK LANDING

It is thought that there are four main factors which contribute to the success and practicability of deck landing on ships under conditions as they exist today. These are:–

(1) The method of approach.
(2) The view from the aeroplane.
(3) The 'Speed contrability' of the aeroplane.
(4) The robustness of the aeroplane to withstand the degree of rough usage which may be expected on the deck under seagoing conditions.

No (1) is entirely up to the pilots and D.L.C.Os [Deck Landing Control Officers – the 'Batsmen' who guided aircraft in to land]; the remainder depend on the suitability of the design of the aeroplane.

It is proposed in this report to deal with the above four factors in so far as Seafire aircraft are concerned, with an additional section at the end dealing with some miscellaneous points which directly or indirectly affect the issue.

SECTION 1 THE APPROACH

The success of a deck landing in any aircraft depends very largely on a suitable method of approach being employed. This is particularly the case in Seafire aircraft in which, to get the best results, a fairly high degree of accuracy on the part of the pilots and D.L.C.O.s is necessary.

Broadly speaking, there are three separate methods of making an approach in a Seafire, which are as follows:–

Firstly, the straight approach for some distance dead astern.

Secondly, the 'crab' type of approach which follows a flight path dead astern of the ship, but provides an improved view by pushing the nose of the aircraft away to starboard, and

Thirdly, the approach made from a steady left-hand turn arriving from the port quarter, straightening up to the deck only for the last few yards of the approach.

The first two methods are, in the opinion of the writer, both unsatisfactory. The dead straight approach brings the aircraft straight through a Seafire blind area, which lies some distance astern of the ship. That is to say, when the Seafire is in that area and pointing straight for the ship, the pilot is completely blinded. The result of getting into this blind area is in nearly every case the same: the pilot, finding himself suddenly unable to see either the deck or the D.L.C.O., allows his aircraft to wander off towards the starboard quarter in order that he may regain his view of the deck over the port side of his aircraft, and, by the time he has done this, he is getting very close to the ship and must at the last minute make a sort of 'S' turn in order to

arrive at the deck at all. The result is always the same, and may frequently be witnessed when watching pilots carrying out their initial deck landing training. The aircraft arrives on the deck from the starboard side, following a line of direction across the deck towards the port side, frequently also with drift to port, and thereby putting a severe side load on the tyres and undercarriage, and the back structure as well. Furthermore, should he fail to pick up a wire or break his undercarriage, the chances are that he will go over the port side. Any question of teaching or encouraging Seafire pilots to make approaches from dead astern should be ruled out absolutely.

The 'crab' approach is merely a modification of the straight approach; the idea being that when the pilot finds himself in the blind area he gets round the difficulty by bringing his aircraft on in what is virtually a left-hand side slip, which enables him to see the deck and the D.L.C.O. over the port side of his cockpit. This is all very well for skilled and experienced pilots, but it must be realised that at the best of times a deck landing approach is made at a speed which, in normal conditions, would be regarded as being dangerously close to the stall. The Seafire has very good control characteristics and lateral stability right down to the stall, provided the flight path is straight, but to introduce an element of yaw at speeds close to the stall is a highly dangerous procedure unless the pilot is very sure of himself in the matter of accurate speed control. The accepted way of putting an aeroplane into a spin is to stall it and then apply yaw. Therefore, to ask comparatively inexperienced pilots to fly their Seafire at a speed within a few knots of the stalling speed and then deliberately to apply yaw, is simply asking for trouble.

It is therefore very strongly the opinion of the writer that the best way to avoid the blind area and provide the pilot with a comfortable view of the deck throughout his entire approach is to teach him to bring his aircraft in from the port quarter in a gentle left-hand turn, which is maintained down to a distance very close to the round-down, thereby successfully getting in ahead of the Seafire blind area which lies astern of the ship and which can cause so much trouble. It must not be thought that the degree of the left-hand turn necessary to achieve the desired result is very high. The final line of approach may be described as being from 'fine leg' and the turn automatically resolves itself into straight flight at the last minute, due to the relative speed of the ship to the aircraft.

Achieving the correct line of approach is, of course, entirely a matter of judgement, and can only be achieved by first explaining thoroughly to pupils and pilots exactly what is required and then giving them practice in carrying it out. It depends on the pilot making his turn-in from the down wind leg at precisely the right moment which in itself will vary with the windspeed over the deck and the distance abeam of the ship at which the pilot has made his circuit. The pitfall is trailing; that is to say, the pilot, while endeavouring to come in off a gentle turn, misjudges his approach, arrives lined up with the deck too far astern, thus getting into the blind area, whereupon he wanders off to the starboard quarter, and the result is the same as it would have been if he had made a straight approach all the way. The only way to practice pilots in this is to work them up during their A.D.D.L. [Aerodrome Dummy Deck Landing] training to a point where their ultimate distance of straight approach on to the runway is getting

down to an absolute minimum. At the end of his A.D.D.L. training, a pupil should be capable of judging his approach to the runway off a steady left-hand turn, which he should be able to correct accurately at the very last moment. If he becomes used to making the last 300 or 400 yards of his runway approach from a dead straight line, he will inevitably have difficulty when he goes to land on a ship.

Apart from the foregoing remarks, there is another powerful argument in favour of this type of approach which cuts the straight way down to a minimum, and this is that when ships are working in company, aircraft which trail astern of their own carrier are using up too much sea room and too much time. A landing circuit which trails astern is a menace to itself and to any ships which may be operating astern of it and, for that reason, even if the view from a Seafire was so good that it was a practical proposition to make a dead straight approach, such an approach would still be bad carrier technique.

The following are considered to be reasonable rough rules for Seafire deck landing:–

(1) Circuit height – 300/400 feet.
(2) Fly ahead of the ship for 10 to 15 seconds according to the windspeed before commencing circuit.
(3) Keep circuit small.
(4) Lower hook, undercarriage and flaps during circuit before getting abeam of the ship on the down wind leg.
(5) While still ahead of the beam, slow down to 80 knots and watch for moment to commence turn-in, which can only be a matter of judgement, but it will be easier to judge it when you have nothing else to concentrate on.
(6) When on the port quarter during your turn, settle down to your correct speed (70 to 75 knots with a [Seafire] IIC); keep steady rate of descent; watch the D.L.C.O. and your speed and make up your mind that you are going to arrive from the port quarter and NOT the starboard quarter.
(7) If you have difficulty in seeing the batsman, put your head out of the port side of the cockpit.
(8) Wear Mark VII or Mark VIII goggles.

SECTION 2 PILOT'S VIEW

The method of approach outlined in the previous section is designed specifically to provide the pilot with an adequate view of the deck during his approach and landing.

The conclusion to be reached is therefore the pilot's view from a Seafire is not adequate to permit a straight approach to the deck.

If, however, a correct turning approach is made, the view is not too bad.

During the latter part of the approach, however, it is considered advisable that the pilot should put his head out of the side of the cockpit to look round the left-hand side of the windscreen.

To do this Mark VII or Mark VIII goggles are essential and should be compulsory.

Furthermore, pilots doing A.D.D.L.s ashore should be trained to do their A.D.D.L.s with their heads out of the cockpit in order to accustom them to landing in this manner.

A detail which has considerable bearing on the question of view is the type of exhaust manifold fitted.

The triple ejector type with fish tail flame dampers is very bad indeed, and frequently obscures the pilot's view of the batsman. The triple ejector type without flame dampers is better, but the multi ejector type is the only really satisfactory type. It is appreciated that this fact is realised by the authorities, but at the same time there are still a very large number of the unsatisfactory manifolds in use in the squadrons.

However, in general it can be said that the deck landing view of a Seafire is not so bad as it has sometimes been made out to be, but it can be bad if a wrong approach is made.

It is not thought to be a major factor contributing towards deck landing difficulty, other defects in the aircraft, which are dealt with hereafter being, in the writer's opinion, far more important.

SECTION 3 SPEED CONTROLABILITY

This is the quality in an aeroplane which is dependent on the features of its design which renders it either easy or difficult to fly at a steady and accurate speed under conditions of a deck landing approach. Factors in the design which go towards providing either good or bad speed controlability are, firstly, a good degree of fore and aft stability at low speeds and, secondly, the provision of plenty of drag when in the flaps and undercarriage down condition, or, more simply, a low lift/drag ratio.

Now it is in the above respects that I feel bound to report that the Seafire is decidedly lacking. The fore and aft stability during the approach at low speed is very poor, with the result that the aeroplane tends to vary its speed considerably if the pilot allows his attention to wander for a moment. Also, when in the flaps and undercarriage down condition, the machine is still far too clean aerodynamically, and generally lively; if you are going a little too fast you cannot stop, and if you are going a little too slowly and put on a slight burst of engine, the response is so immediate that before you know where you are you are liable to be going too fast again.

Therefore, to maintain that steady speed, steady altitude, and steady rate of descent which are so essential in deck landing, the pilot has to exercise a considerable nicety of touch on both the stick and the throttle. In fact, a degree of skill is required which, while being perfectly well within the capacity of most pilots, is regrettably not to be relied on altogether.

It is the opinion of the writer that the poor speed controlability of the Seafire is the chief cause of trouble with such pilots who do have trouble with Seafires. As an example, the American Hellcats and Corsairs although they are very much heavier aircraft and approach the deck very much faster are, in fact, generally considered easier to land on and it is my opinion that their good speed controlability contributes towards this easiness of deck landing more than anything else.

In view of the suggestions made above, i.e. that the Seafire is inclined to be difficult to control on a steady speed and yet, owing to its lack of drag, must be controlled very accurately, it is thought that slow flying practice, apart from A.D.D.L.s, should form a fairly large part of the Seafire pilot's deck landing training ashore.

Needless to say, the remarks on the subject of stability and drag have been communicated to the designers, who are fully aware of the situation. Seafire Modification No 109, an alteration to the design of the elevator, has already been introduced with a view to improving fore and aft stability, but it is not yet in full use in squadrons and it is thought that retrospective action in introducing this modification should be pushed ahead.

SECTION 4 ROBUSTNESS OF THE AEROPLANE

By comparison with the types of ship-borne aircraft produced in America, the Seafire would appear to be a somewhat delicate structure which is very easily prone to minor damage on landings which would not have damaged an American fighter. This is to a very large degree true, but it must be borne in mind that everything to do with an aircraft is a compromise and there is no question of something for nothing. One of the main principles which has governed development of the Spitfire aircraft is the reduction of weight right down to the lowest practicable limit, and it is only by adhering to this principle that the rate of climb of the aeroplane has been kept superior to the enemies' (and the Americans') contemporary development. What the correct compromise is, between strength to withstand excessively rough treatment on ships and maintenance of good performance in the air, is very difficult to decide. It would appear that in so far as the Fleet Air Arm is concerned

slightly too much strength has been sacrificed in the Seafire in order to maintain a first rate performance, and that in the case of the American fighters too much performance had been sacrificed in order to provide the tremendous robustness which they seem to achieve for deck work. For example, if you cut down the load of petrol on a Hellcat or a Corsair to give it the same fighting range as the Seafire IIC, the performance in climb of those two aircraft is still vastly inferior to that of the Seafire LIIC, indicating that their structure weights and power loadings are far too high to be able to cope satisfactorily with opposition from shore based enemy fighters.

Above:
Landing accident on HMS *Indefatigable* in April 1945, when Seafire S-117 failed to engage a wire, jumped the barrier and rammed into a Firefly and an Avenger in the forward deck park before coming to rest hanging over the side. One man was killed. *Scales*

Left:
HMS *Slinger* at Brisbane, Australia in August 1945 about to leave with replacement Seafire IIIs for the British carriers operating off Japan. Note the bars added to the roundle in this theatre, and the fold just inboard of the wing tips.
Scales

It may be quite rightly argued that the American fighters are required for long range escort work, which will probably not involve them with shore based opposition, and that, therefore, the poor climb performance can be accepted in the interests of the other advantages but, in the case of Seafires which are short or medium range interceptor fighters and assault force fighters, it is felt that it is not reasonable to expect the same degree of robustness and general resistance to rough handling, as the performance requirements are necessarily so much more severe in order to be able to deal with the best that the enemy can put up in the way of fighter opposition from land, and that, therefore, if the Navy have a requirement for an aeroplane which is to equal the best of contemporary R.A.F. development, they must inevitably have a higher rate of damage and unserviceability when operating from ships. This, however, is not in any way intended to infer that the Seafire cannot be greatly improved on in its resistance to bad deck landings, etc., by making use of the knowledge and experience which has been gained up to date. It is evident, for example, both from statistics and from trials that have been carried out, that the present type of splined undercarriage leg does not absorb sufficient energy to prevent damage to the other parts of the structure and that although the new type torsion link leg is an improvement, there is still room for further improvement, which no doubt can be achieved without paying too much in weight. It is held that there is at the moment far too much damage resulting to Seafire undercarriages as a result of what may be termed 'reasonable landings', and that the whole question of developing suitable undercarriage legs, from whatever source, should be tackled energetically.

A lot of minor damage to arrester hooks and to the frames round the snap-up gear, and to the snap-up gear itself, is experienced in service. It can be established from Cine films that the hook snaps up after hooking a wire in less than 1/24th of a second; furthermore, accidents occur at present due to the hook bouncing on contact with the deck and not picking up wires while it has the chance. This was pointed out to Messrs Supermarines, who designed a hydraulic damper to attach between the hook arm and the fuselage. This was fitted to aircraft and flown by me on H.M.S. Pretoria Castle. It had the effect of reducing the force with which the hook snapped up and should, if adopted in service, alleviate the damage to snap-up gears and surrounding frames. As regards the anti-bounce question, this device was tried out by building a ramp across the deck about 18″ abaft No 1 wire, which was intended to cause the hook to bounce over the wire. In every case where the hook struck the ramp when the damper

215

was fitted, it rode over the ramp without bouncing and still picked up No 1 wire. This is merely mentioned as an indication of what can be achieved in the way of reducing minor damage without necessarily resorting to large increases in weight. It is felt that with regard to all further Fleet Air Arm development the provision of a sting type hook, as fitted to most American aircraft, should be obligatory. These hooks are better in every way; in most cases they avoid too much lift of the tail when the wire is picked up but, primarily, they hang down from what is the lowest part of the aircraft and, therefore, their tendency is to pick up an earlier wire than the normal type hook, even if the aircraft is held too high.

MISCELLANEOUS POINTS

(1) D.L.C.O.s

The importance of making a correct type of approach has been mentioned before, and it applies perhaps more to Seafires than to some other aircraft, but yet is still of the utmost importance to all types.

This brings up the question of the D.L.C.O.'s contribution towards achieving these two things. The importance of correct and consistent batting cannot be overestimated. A good deck landing is made by the combined efforts of the pilot and the D.L.C.O.; if either makes a mistake a bad landing is likely to result, but here there is one thing that is important to remember and that it is comparatively easy for the D.L.C.O. to correct a pilot's error, but it may be impossible for the pilot to correct a D.L.C.O.'s error.

There must be very few pilots indeed who would care to try and land a modern type of aircraft on the deck of a carrier without the aid of a D.L.C.O. The landing, therefore, must be regarded as a joint effort, and it is it is essential that the D.L.C.O.s should be as competent and as carefully trained as the pilots themselves. Pilots who are carefully trained to obey the bats reach a stage where they obey them so quickly and instinctively that if the bats make a serious mistake the pilot is very liable indeed to crash. The writer himself in carrying out landings for the purpose of giving practice to a pupil D.L.C.O. experienced the fact that the reaction to obey the bats was quicker than the reaction to query the signal, with the result that he allowed himself to be batted into the rundown, thereby damaging the hook. It might almost be said, therefore, that the bats can hypnotize the pilot into committing suicide and are consequently a most potent weapon in the hands of an untrained or unskilled officer. The following points are therefore submitted for consideration:

(1) Careful selection of Pilots for Training as D.L.C.O.s

Squadron cast-offs due to incompetence, nerves, etc, will not do. Batting is hard work, frequently dangerous, and requiring long periods of concentration and expenditure of energy. A batsman is quite useless unless he holds the confidence of the pilots in his ship and, therefore, his past flying record should be such as to earn their respect and not their amusement.

(2) Standardised and Thorough Training

This goes without saying and it is realised that Easthaven [the training school for Deck Landing Control Officers] have this matter in hand. At the same time it is felt

Unusual company: a Seafire III in formation with a Grumman F6F Hellcat and a captured Japanese Mitsubishi J2M2 Raiden (Allied code-name 'Jack'), during comparative trials flown from the US Navy airfield at Patuxent River, Maryland. *USN*

that not enough D.L.C.O.s are passing through Easthaven and that there are too many 'quacks'.

(3) Limited Periods of Service as D.L.C.O.s
If the best type of pilot is to be attracted towards the job of D.L.C.O., there must be an assurance that the job is of limited duration and that it forms a definite step in his progress as a squadron officer and that it will not constitute an indefinite delay in achieving what should be his ambition, namely, to command a squadron. At the moment the average young pilot regards, and with some justification, batting as a dead-end or backwater for tired and finished pilots. He would be horrified at the idea of being sent on a batting course because he would regard it as having put paid to his flying career for an indefinite period, possibly for ever. This impression must be removed if the best type of pilot is to be attracted towards a period of service ad D.L.C.O. The ability to be a batsman must come to be regarded as an extra qualification which assists in the career, rather than as a 'stooge' job.

(2) Seafire Wing Tips
Some squadrons of LIIC aircraft have had their wing tips removed and a certain amount of argument has taken place as to the wisdom or otherwise of this step. It is claimed that the removal of the wing tips has the effect of reducing the tendency in a Seafire to float, thereby reducing the chances of barrier accidents. There is no doubt something in this, because theoretically the removal of a portion of non-flapped wing area decreases the lift/drag ratio, which is desirable for deck landing. However, it is thought that the deterioration in the handling qualities of the aeroplane from other points of view which also affect the deck landing when the wing tips are removed, outweighs any slight advantage which may be gained during landing.

Removal of the wing tips produces tangible advantages in:–
   (1) Aileron control.
   (2) Hangar stowage.
   (3) A possible slight advantage in reduction of float.

The disadvantages consequent upon their removal are as follows:–
   (1) Increased landing speed.·
   (2) Aggravation of the root stall (particularly in steep turns).
   (3) Loss in take-off performance.
   (4) Loss in rate of climb.

It is the writer's opinion that the advantage claimed in reduction of float is speculative; the other two advantages claimed are agreed.

However, it would appear that provided the long wing tip aircraft can be handled in the hangars and on the lifts, there is no justification for making an alteration to the aircraft which reduces the efficiency of the wing and cuts down performance and manoeuvrability in turning circle, and inevitably increases the speed of entry into the wires during a deck landing.

We already know the trouble that has been experienced in landing Seafires in low wind speeds. It has been necessary to cut the diameter of propellers in order to stop them striking the deck when the aircraft pitches owing to high speed of entry into the wires; this reduction of propeller diameter is necessary, but it costs performance to a certain degree. Therefore there would appear to be no logical reason for introducing another modification which further reduces performance while at the same time increasing the speed of entry into the wires, thereby taking away some of the advantages which have been gained by cropping the propellers. There is no doubt that pilots flying short wing tip aircraft have to approach the deck faster than those flying long wing tip aircraft. Only in the most special cases where it is essential to have the advantage in aileron control, should the cropping of wing tips be permitted.

(3) Jettison Tanks
The position of the jettison fuel tank cock and jettison lever [low down on the starboard side of the cockpit, below the undercarriage selection box] renders them difficult to operate, bearing in mind the special conditions which prevail after taking off from the deck of ships working in company. As all aircraft inevitably take off individually, pilots have to pay a great deal of attention to the question of forming up rapidly and in the right formation and not getting mixed up with other ships' aircraft. This has been communicated to the designers.

(4) Airspeed Indicator Calibration Facilities
It is thought that insufficient attention is paid to the accurate functioning of airspeed indicators. Deck landing approaches with Seafires are made to within very fine limits of speed. One hears pilots discussing the question of speed to within matters of one or two knots, but in many cases they have no idea of what degree of accuracy exists in their instruments. All ships should be supplied with the necessary calibration equipment and orders should be issued providing for frequent and accurate use.

(Sgd) *J. K. Quill*
Lt Cdr (A)
RNVR

29

With the Eighth Air Force to Berlin

Right:
Walt Weitner with *High Lady*, the Spitfire he flew to Berlin on 6 March 1944. *Weitner*

Spitfire XIs operated by the US 7th Photo Group based at Mount Farm near Oxford.

Below:
PA944 taking off.

*Reginald Mitchell had intended the Spitfire as a short range interceptor fighter but, such was the versatility of his design, it was also to prove one of the most effective photographic reconnaissance aircraft of World War 2. Operating at extreme altitudes, reconnaissance Spitfires ranged far and wide over German-occupied territory, bringing back thousands of valuable photographs. A few Spitfire PRXIs were supplied to the US 8th Air Force and equipped the 14th Photo Squadron, 7th Photographic Reconnaissance Group based at Mount Farm near Oxford. In this account Walt Weitner, who as a Major commanded the unit, describes the mission on 6 March 1944 when, flying his personal Spitfire *High Lady*, he conducted the post-attack reconnaissance immediately following the first full-scale US daylight attack on Berlin. His was the first US-operated reconnaissance Spitfire to fly over the German capital.*

A reconnaissance mission to Berlin would take the Spitfire PRXI almost to the limit of its effective radius of action from even the nearest airfield in England. So beforehand Walt Weitner flew *High Lady* to the Royal Air Force airfield at Bradwell Bay near Clacton, where the aircraft's tanks were filled to capacity: 84gal in the two main tanks in front of the cockpit, 132gal in the integral tanks built into the leading edge of each wing, and 90gal in the 'slipper' drop tank under the fuselage. This gave a total fuel load of 306gal, more than *four* times the capacity of the tanks of the prototype Spitfire when she made her maiden flight almost exactly eight years earlier.

Once the refuelling was complete Weitner, wearing several layers of thick clothing to keep out the cold at high altitude, climbed into *High Lady* and strapped in. At 13.30hr, as briefed, he took off.

'With a full load of fuel and that narrow undercarriage, the Spit would "lean" disconcertingly during turns when one taxied. But once you got off the ground and got a little speed she really perked up, she would leap away. Once the gear was up and you pulled up the nose, boy would she climb!

'I took the direct route for Berlin, heading out on 086° over the North Sea towards Holland. Thirty-nine minutes after take-off I passed my first check-point, The Hague, at 39,000 feet. There was 5/10ths cloud cover below, through which I could make out the Zuider Zee.

'The Spitfire was easy to handle at very high altitude. This one was well trimmed and stayed pretty level. One had always to have hold of the stick, but it needed hardly any pressure. In the reconnaissance business you do not fly straight and level for long, you are continually banking to search the sky all around for enemy fighters and check the navigation.

'With all the extra clothing, the parachute, dinghy, life jacket, and oxygen mask, the narrow cockpit of a Spitfire was no place for the claustrophobic! The heavy flying clothing kept me pretty warm, though my extremities did begin to get a bit cold. The temperature outside was about −60°F, and from time to time I would stamp my feet to get the circlation going.

'Throughout the flight at high altitude my Spitfire left a long condensation trail. I could have avoided it by descending below 22,000 feet, but I did not think that was the thing to do on a deep penetration like this. I thought the best bet was to cruise near to the ceiling of a Messerschmitt 109; then, if I had to go up, I had a little margin of altitude I could use. The Germans must have known I was up there but nobody was paying any attention to me. I thought that if enemy fighters did come after me they would have to leave trails too, and I would get plenty of warning.

'As I passed over Hannover the skies were clear and I decided to make a photo run over the city. The intelligence people could always use such photos. There were trails ahead at

PA950 doing a low altitude 'beat up' of the airfield. *Weitner*

Right:
One of the photographs taken by Weitner during his mission to Berlin on 6 March 1944, showing smoke rising from fires in the Zehlendorf district of the city.

Below:
Weitner receiving congratulations after the mission from Lt Col George Lawson, the commander of 7th Photo Group.

about my level, but they were moving on an easterly heading and obviously not aware of my presence.'

The reason for the Germans' lack of interest in the lone Spitfire is not hard to fathom: almost every available Luftwaffe fighter in the area was in action against the force of more than 600 Flying Fortresses and Liberators and their escorts now battling their way westwards back to England, after the attack on Berlin. Over the VHF Weitner could hear snippets of conversations from the distant combats: 'Three Me's at 12 o'clock, 2,000 feet above us. Let's go!'. . . 'One lone bomber down there, shall I escort him home?'. . . 'Here comes one at you, Joe. Dive! I'll tag him.'. . . 'Good show! He's smoking now!'

As the Spitfire neared Berlin, however, the Luftwaffe finally reacted to the intruder high over the Fatherland. Glancing in one of the mirrors in the side-blisters of his canopy, Walt Weitner suddenly realised he was no longer

alone. 'I saw three black forms, also trailing, following an uncomfortable 1,500 yards behind, their altitude just below my own.' The discovery came at a bad time for the American pilot. He was running his engine on the drop tank and from his calculations he knew it was almost empty; but since it had no fuel gauge the only indication when it was dry would be when the engine started to splutter – which might leave him without power at a critical time. He thought of switching to one of the wing tanks and dropping the slipper tank, but the mission required all the fuel the aircraft could carry; if he released the tank it would mess up his fuel calculations and might force him to abandon the mission short of the target. Nor would it solve the problem to switch the engine over to one of the wing tanks for the time being leaving the slipper tank in place, because the latter contained insufficient fuel for him to be sure it would resume feeding if he re-selected it. As an old flying saying puts it: 'The three most useless things to an

aviator are the runway behind, the sky above and the fuel he cannot use . . .' Walt Weitner decided to try to outrun the enemy fighters using the last of the fuel in the drop tank, and see what happened.

'I pushed the throttle forward as far as it would go without selecting emergency power, eased up the nose and began to climb. The whole time I nervously held the tank selector valve, ready to switch to one of the internal wing tanks the moment the engine faltered. As I climbed through 40,000 feet I could see that the German fighters behind me had split: one went on my right and two on my left, to box me in. And at that moment the engine coughed. I immediately selected internal fuel and the engine caught right away.

'At 41,500 feet I levelled off and my indicated airspeed increased to 178mph [a true airspeed of about 360mph]. After what seemed forever, but was probably only 2 to 3 minutes, the German fighters began to fall back and slid out of sight. Had they come any closer

221

I should have gone to emergency boost, but it never got that desperate.'

Almost certainly the enemy fighters were Messerschmitt 109s fitted with nitrous oxide power boosting to enhance their high altitude performance, belonging to one of the special high altitude interception units. From German records there is evidence that the aircraft which attempted to intercept Weitner belonged to 1st Gruppe of Jagdgeschwader 3, based at Burg just to the south of the Spitfire's track.

Still keeping a wary eye for the enemy, Weitner checked his navigation and prepared for the first photographic run on the target. 'By now the target was only a few minutes away. I could see the huge Lake Mueritz, some 50 miles north-north-west of Berlin, away to the north but I could not yet see the city itself because of the smoke and industrial haze. I looked around and noted with relief that the enemy aircraft appeared to have abandoned the chase.'

Because the Spitfire lacked a pressurised cabin Weitner had no wish to remain at maximum

altitude longer than necessary, so he eased the aircraft back down to 38,000ft. Then he suddenly caught sight of the enemy capital laid out beneath him. The time was 15.30hrs, exactly two hours since he had taken off from Bradwell Bay.
'There was quite a lot of haze, but I could see the sun glinting off the red brick and tile houses. If the German fighters re-appeared I might be able to make only one photographic run so I planned to make the first from almost due north, down wind, to get a good line of photos without drifting off the target. I rolled the Spitfire on its side to line up the string of lakes I was using as check points, levelled out using the artificial horizon and switched on the cameras.'

In the rear fuselage of the Spitfire the two vertically-mounted F.52 cameras, each with a 36in telephoto lens, clicked at five-second intervals to photograph a three-mile wide strip of ground beneath the aircraft. During the photography accurate flying was essential: even a small amount of bank could cause gaps in the cover, and 10° would be sufficient to miss a target altogether. Any correction to the aircraft's flight path had to be made in the five-second intervals between photographs.
'My orders were to photograph the bombers' targets and I had been given aerial photos of the city taken previously by the RAF, with the targets marked on them. But I could see smoke rising from places other than my assigned targets so I decided to photograph the sources of the smoke also. The whole time I kept checking the sky behind my tail, as I expected further interference from the enemy fighters. But none showed up. There was some flak, I could see the smoke bursts mushrooming, but none of it was close.
'I spent about 25 minutes over Berlin, during which I made runs from different directions and took about 70 photographs. Then a solid layer of cloud began moving over the city from the east, and as fuel was beginning to run low I set a course of 297° for home.'

On the return flight Weitner had another drama with his fuel. The order of using the Spitfire XI's fuel was, first, that in the drop tank; next the pilot used the fuel in the wing leading edge tanks, alternating between the two at 15 minute intervals so that the aircraft did not get out of trim; then he was to switch to the lower main tank and finally to the upper main tank. As the last of the fuel in the wing tanks was consumed, the Merlin coughed briefly. Weitner switched to the lower main tank and the engine's even roar resumed. How long it would continue to do so was a moot point, however, for the American pilot was disconcerted to see the needle of the fuel gauge

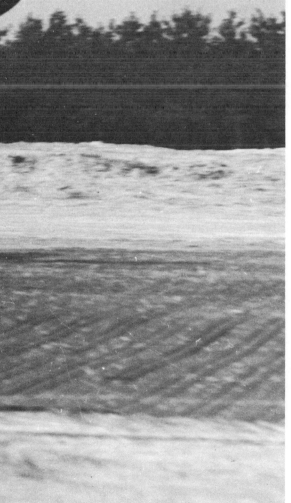

hard against the zero mark. Could there have been a fuel leak, leaving the aircraft with insufficient to regain friendly territory? Or might it be simply that the gauge had frozen up?

'I discovered why I had toiled over maths for so long without learning its true value! Some rapid calculations almost proved the main tanks *had* to be full. During these reveries nothing of a threatening nature showed itself except a few far-off trails to the east. Soon the cloud covering the English coast was within gliding distance, and all was well again. Over the North Sea I descended to 30,000 feet and called "Gangplank" [Bradwell Bay] on the VHF for a homing. Over the coast of East Anglia the gas gauge suddenly came to life showing about 20 gallons. At my altitude I knew I had enough fuel to reach Mount Farm without having to land at the coast to take on more.'

Weitner descended to Mount Farm with the engine throttled back, made a low pass over the airfield, pulled round hard into finals, lowered his flaps and undercarriage and landed. *High Lady* had been airborne for four hours and 18 minutes.

'On entering the dispersal area the gas and the maths ran out simultaneously, leaving a spluttering and dead engine on my hands just a few safe feet short of "according to plan". . .'

Above and left:
PRX 1s of No 400 Squadron RCAF operating from Schneverdingen, Germany in April 1945.
Public Archives of Canada

A Spitfire PR19 at high
altitude carrying a 170gal
drop tank. *Saffery*

Photographic Reconnaissance

I depend on you, Spitfire, here in this world
Of clear attenuated atmosphere,
The fields of France eight miles below
The sky blue-black, mysterious, above,
And trailing us, the traitorous path of mist
For every Hun to see.

I depend on you, Spitfire. We have no guns
To spit our hate at Me 109s,
Only our wits with which to dodge the Hun
As, self-dependent like a hunted fox,
We set ourselves above the mark
And watch our camera click.

Alone together in the vastness of the sky
The target of a hundred thousand eyes
In each of them the lust to kill
That tiny, potent, speck that's you and me.
I realize now the fox assuredly
Disdains the efforts of the hounds.

by Wg Cdr Nigel Tangye

30

'Anyway, it is only a Short Sea Crossing'

One of the most lonely places on earth is a one-man dinghy out at sea when there appears to be no prospect of immediate rescue. On 15 June 1944 Sqn Ldr John Saffery commanding No 541 Squadron, a photographic reconnaissance unit based at Benson, learned the truth of it after he was forced to bale out over the Straits of Dover. The quotations are from the report he wrote shortly after his rescue. The aircraft involved was RM633, a Spitfire PR19 of the initial production batch.

'On June 15 I was briefed for a target in the Ruhr. After I had got into my flying kit, I decided to wear a new pressure waistcoat which had been given to me to try out the day before. This waistcoat, which can be inflated and used as a Mae West in an emergency, is designed to assist the pilot to get sufficient oxygen into his lungs at great heights.'

The initial batch of Spitfire 19s did not have pressurised cabins; the waistcoat provided counter-pressure around the pilot's chest to assist him to exhale when breathing oxygen under pressure.

'Among other gadgets it has a small electric lamp attached to a scull cap, that winks automatically for 72 hours. When I was strapped into the Spitfire I discovered that the new waistcoat had not been fitted with the quick release attachment for the dinghy lead. As time was short I tied the dinghy lead on to the leg strap of the pressure waistcoat and remarked to the airman who helped me in, 'Anyway, it is only a short sea crossing.' These very nearly joined the list of famous last words.

'I climbed to 30,000 feet quickly as there was a tail wind of 120mph at that height, then levelled out and reduced to 2,100rpm. Towards the top of the climb I looked over the gauges and everything was normal. I crossed out at North Foreland about 25 minutes after take-off. A few minutes later I saw that I was not getting quite the speed I had expected and at about the same time I had a feeling, twice in quick succession, of a sudden lack of traction, rather like slipping a car momentarily into "neutral". I looked round the cockpit and saw that my oil pressure was

reading 5lbs [the normal reading was about 80lb/sq in]. The oil and coolant temperatures were both reasonable so I thought perhaps it was just instrument failure. Nevertheless, I turned back for England an called Manston to say I was returning with engine trouble.

'When I next looked at the instruments the oil pressure was nil and the temperature was rising, though not alarmingly. I moved the pitch lever to the fully coarse position and began to descend. At about 23,000ft the aircraft began to feel rather peculiar and on looking at the dashboard I found to my astonishment that the rev. counter was reading 4,000rpm.'

This was the maximum reading the gauge would show – the normal maximum rpm for the Griffon was 2,750. Almost certainly there had been a failure of the control mechanism for the constant-speed propeller.
'I hastily switched off and continued the descent in a glide at about 180 IAS [180mph, indicated airspeed]. I got another vector from Manston and could see the English coast but I began to doubt whether I could reach it as I was losing height very fast. At about 12,000 feet I told Manston I could see them

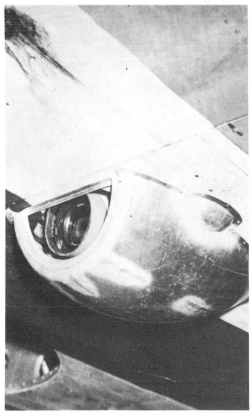

Far left:
Sqn Ldr John Saffrey, whose sea-survival account follows. Saffrey

Above:
A PR19 of No 541 Squadron pictured in mid-1944, similar to the one from which John Saffrey parachuted. This early production aircraft lacked the pressurised cabin fitted to later examples of this version. Saffery

Left:
A forward-looking oblique camera fitted under the port wing of a Spitfire PR19; a similar installation under the starboard wing permitted stereo photographs to be taken while flying towards the target. A few PR19s of No 542 Squadron carried this installation during the summer of 1944. IWM

and asked whether they could see me. There were chalk cliffs on the coast, which meant that an undershoot would be disastrous, and as there was no future in ditching a Spitfire, I called up Manston and said that I was going to bale out. My height was 5,500ft.

'I pushed back the hood, unplugged the radio and oxygen, took off my oxygen mask and undid the Sutton harness [the seat straps]. I saw that I was then doing 140 IAS, so I pushed the nose down until there was 200 on the clock, then rolled the aircraft over with the nose well above the horizon. I let the nose come down, eased the stick forward and dropped out at about 4,500ft.

'I saw the [invasion] stripes on the fuselage slide past me and then looked for the handle of the ripcord. The parachute opened immediately. I saw the aircraft dive straight into the sea and burst into flames. This was reassuring as I thought that the column of smoke would be seen.

'I went into the water drifting sideways, bobbed up again and got rid of the parachute. I then saw the dinghy pack floating beside me. It had burst open on impact and the dinghy was half out. I grabbed the bottle [containing compressed carbon-dioxide], pulled out the pin, shook the dinghy out of the pack and began to inflate it. When the dinghy was fully inflated I remembered that I had not blown up the Mae West part of the pressure waistcoat, so I inflated that too.

'I climbed into the dinghy and lay on my face, puffing and blowing. I turned over to get into a sitting position and found myself back in the sea again. I got in a second time and turned over very cautiously. I then found that the dinghy pack cover had become detached from my harness and I could not find it anywhere. With it had gone the mast, sail, paddles, rations and, worst of all, the rockets and smoke candles.

'As I was rather exhausted, I sat back for a time and could see a big convoy about 3 or 4 miles west of me sailing northwards. Beyond it, about another 5 miles away, were the cliffs of England. It was about 06.40 hours and the morning was warm and sunny with a fresh south-westerly breeze. There was a slight chop on the sea and quite a lot of water in the dinghy. I baled for a bit, threw the drogue over the side and fastened the weather apron about half-way up. I saw a buoy about a mile to the north and tried paddling towards it with my hands but soon gave it up as futile and exhausting. About half an hour after getting into the dinghy I saw a Spitfire go right overhead and guessed that he was looking for me. Soon after I saw two Thunderbolts and later an Avenger which also went overhead. This went on all day and was exasperating. I very much regretted the loss of my signal rockets because I was sure that I would have

been spotted in the first hour if I could have made any kind of signal. I tried to use my goggles as a heliograph but without success. I think the search was probably made harder by the sun glinting off the choppy sea, which must have made one little 'K' Type dinghy very inconspicuous. I noticed that the drogue was always out to the port side and was pulling the dinghy broadside to the sea, so I pulled it in and found that the dinghy automatically kept head to sea very well indeed.

'By noon I had drifted north-eastwards out of sight of the buoy, and I could only just see the coast of England when I rode on the top of a wave. The sea was getting higher so I baled 100 times with the baler, reducing the water in the dinghy to about 1½-ins in depth, and then fastened the weather apron right up. I did not put the weather cape over my head as I still had my helmet on and wanted to look about me. About every four hours I gave the dinghy ten puffs of the bellows pump. It was not really necessary but it gave me something to do.

'The Avenger kept up the search right through the middle of the day and I saw him go past me out to sea on one side and then return the other side several times. I was spotted by a number of birds, particularly by a very pretty little tern with red legs and beak who would have landed on my head if I had not upset his approach by moving. There was also a puffin who was greatly intrigued and swam around inspecting me from every angle. He eventually got to within about three feet of me where he bobbed about for quite a time first on one side and then the other. Two porpoises also rolled past but did not come closer than about 20yd – to my relief. In the afternoon the sky clouded over and the swell got longer and higher but although the wind seemed to be freshening it was still quite warm. Some of the seas were breaking and I was periodically soaked, but rather to my surprise I did not suffer from cold. I was wearing ordinary blue battle dress, a woollen pullover, a big woollen sweater, long woollen stockings, flying boots, gauntlets, helmet and Mae West and this outfit kept me very comfortable except for a rather chilly section around the thighs, which were only covered by the battle dress trousers. The search seemed to lower and intensify in the evening and I saw two Spitfires at about 500 feet pass within a mile or two again and again. Sometimes they were even closer. It seemed to me that any aircraft in which the lookout could lie in the nose and search straight ahead, would be a better search aircraft than a single-engined type. About this time I thought of opening my flying rations, but I was not really hungry and I feared that the eating might make me thirsty. I had no water and no prospect of getting water so I decided not to eat anything until the next morning. At about 19.00 hours I saw a Walrus doing a careful search low down about 5 miles south of me. Then when he was about a mile away he headed straight for me and I thought he had seen me, but just about 400 yards short he turned to port and returned the way he had come. As he was very close and only about 300ft up, I was very disappointed.

'The Air Sea Rescue people put on a terrific search and kept it up all day. If I had not lost my signals they would have found me quite early, as they were always in roughly the right area.'

By now dusk was falling, so Saffery pulled on the scull cap and switched on the small emergency lamp.
'Everything was soaking wet and I did not really expect it to work. I then put the weather cape over my shoulders, held the weather apron up to my face and tried to get some sleep. About 30 minutes later I heard a terrific racket nearby, peeked out and saw an M.T.B. about 30 yards away. I was thrown a line and taken aboard.'

The crew of the motor torpedo boat had seen the lamp winking on the pilot's helmet. Once on board the craft Saffery was taken below decks and stripped of his wet clothing, rubbed down with towels, wrapped in blankets and filled with rum, then put to bed while the boat completed its patrol.

The incident shows well the difficulties of locating a dinghy from the air if there was any sort of sea running and the survivor had no smoke markers, flares or radio beacon. The problem persists to the present day. It was indeed fortunate for John Saffery that the naval patrol boat chanced upon him, had it not done so his chances of survival would have dropped markedly with each hour that passed.

Rare reconnaissance bird. Pink-painted Spitfire FRIX of No 16 Squadron, pictured shortly after D-Day. This aircraft carries a single oblique camera looking to port just behind the cockpit; the cannon have been removed, leaving only the four .303in machine guns as a token armament. *Taylor*

Spit on Floats

Right:
W3760, the first Spitfire V floatplane, pictured in its original form shortly before it began flight trials from Southampton Water in October 1942. In addition to the floats the aircraft was fitted with a fin extension below the rear fuselage and a four-bladed propeller. The armament was not fitted. In common with other development Spitfires the aircraft carried a spin-recovery parachute in a container at the base of the fin and had a rudder horn balance guard at the top of the fin. Note that at this initial stage the floatplane retained the normal-type carburettor air intake and fin. *Smithsonian*

Below:
W3760 pictured in January 1943, after the fitting of armament, a fin of increased area and a late type tropical air filter with an extended lip.

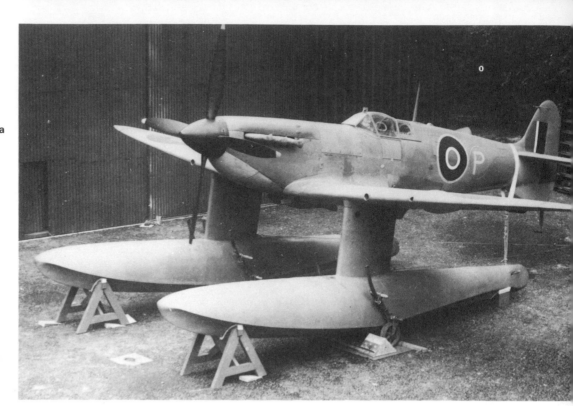

31

Spitfires Over the Balkans

Now President of the Spitfire Society, David Green was a Flg Off in March 1945 when he was posted as 'A' Flight Commander to No 73 Squadron whose main base was at Biferno in Italy. At the time the unit was flying Spitfire IXs in the fighter-bomber role, in support of partisan forces in Yugoslavia battling with the Germans. In this account he gives his impressions of operations in this theatre, and how the end of the war came suddenly for him.

Although its main base was at Biferno, by this stage of the war No 73 Squadron was one of several Balkans Air Force units which used the airstrip at Prkos near Zara (now Zadar) in Yugoslavia as a forward operating base.

'There was a unique little war going on in Yugoslavia, it was the first time partisan operations had been employed on such a large scale. Although there were no regular forces defending Prkos and there were German troops all over the area, we did not feel particularly threatened. There was a row of mountains between us and the enemy forces and we figured we would have plenty of warning if they tried to advance in our direction.'

Other units using Prkos at that time were Nos 253 and 352 Squadrons with Spitfires, Nos 6 and 351 Squadrons with rocket-firing Hurricanes and No 249 Squadron with Mustangs.

Normally the Spitfires of No 73 Squadron would take off from Biferno in the morning, land at Prkos to refuel, fly two or more sorties from the forward base, landing there to refuel and re-arm between each, then return to Biferno in the evening. David Green flew his first missions in this way on 22 March in PV852 (aircraft letter 'B'). He flew to Prkos, refuelled, then took off to attack the German headquarters at Gospic, about 30 miles north of the airstrip. Afterwards he returned to Prkos, took on more bombs and attacked Gospic again. After these raids he noted in his logbook 'bags of accurate flak'. Later in the day he flew two road reconnaissance sorties from Prykos, then returned to Biferno.

David Green explained the dive-bombing tactics employed by No 73 Squadron during these operations.

'Carrying two 250lb bombs the Spitfire made a very fine dive bomber. It could attack accurately and didn't need a fighter escort because as soon as the bombs had been released it was a fighter. The briefing beforehand had to be good enough for us to be able to fly right up to the target even if we had never been there before, identify it and bomb it – because the flak was often accurate we didn't want to spend time circling in the target area before we went down to attack.

'We normally operated in sections of four, and would fly to the target at 10,000 feet in finger-four battle formation. We would make for an Initial Point decided at the briefing, a distinctive point on the ground in the target area with, ideally, a linear feature like a road, a river or a railway line leading to the target itself. By the time it reached the IP the formation would have increased speed to 260mph Indicated [about 305mph True] and we would be flying in loose echelon to starboard, ready to begin the dive. As the target came into view I would position it so that it appeared to be running down the line of my port cannon. As the target disappeared under the wing I would hold my heading, and when the target emerged from under the trailing edge I would pull the aircraft up to kill the forward speed, roll it over on its back and let the nose drop until the target was lined up in the gunsight graticule. That way one got the Spitfire to go down in the correct angle of dive of 60 degrees. It is a pretty steep dive, it felt as if one was going down vertically. The other aircraft in the section, Nos 2, 3, and 4, would be following me down still in echelon. It was important to trim the aircraft nose-down, otherwise the pressure on the stick would become enormous as the speed built up and the Spitfire tried to pull itself out of the dive. During the dive the speed built up rapidly and it was important to keep an eye on one's height, because the altimeter lag was considerable. When the altimeter read 5,000ft above the target altitude, indicated, that meant the true altitude above the target was about 4,000ft. I would let go my bombs and call

"Bombs gone!"; the other chaps in the section would then release theirs. At the time of release the aircraft would be doing about 420mph Indicated [about 450mph True].

'If there had been little or no flak the desire to see the results of the bombing was usually so great that I would pull hard on the stick to bring the aircraft out of the dive and into a slight climb so that I could look over my shoulder to see where the bombs had gone. But if we were being fired at, we would use our high forward speed to get us down to ground level where there was cover.'

David Green flew a series of similar attacks on 22 March. On the 24th and 25th he flew to Prkos to refuel, then escorted Dakota transports flying into landing strips deep in German occupied Yugoslavia. On each occasion the Spitfire escorts would orbit while the Dakotas landed, off-loaded their cargo and took on wounded, then took off again. During his mission on the 25th, David Green was airborne for two hours 25 minutes. On the 28th he bombed a German position near Otoka, on the 30th flew two attacks on Ostrazac, and on the 31st flew three missions to attack enemy positions at Gospic, Krupa and Ostrazac.

David Green spent most of April on a detachment to the Italian Air Force and returned to his squadron early in May. By then aircraft were staying overnight at Prkos. On the 3rd he flew a bombing and strafing mission against Lipke, on the 4th similar missions against enemy positions at Liubljana and Zelchi.

'We were never worried by enemy fighters. People did see them on the odd occasion, but it was very rare. By this time one felt that most of the fighting was going on in the hinterland. Zagreb, for example, was hotly defended by flak and our chaps did see the odd fighter there. But they never made any attempt to interfere with our aircraft.'

Operations continued in this way until the evening of 6 May, when David Green and other pilots in the Officers' Mess tent at Prkos heard on the BBC News that the war in Europe was over and the German High Command had ordered all of its forces to surrender to the Allies the following morning.

'We had been slotted for the dawn mission the next day, so I called the operations tent on the field telephone and said "Its all over, isn't it, you won't want us to fly tomorrow." Back came the answer "Yes we do, we've got an armed recce for you." I said "The war's over, they have just said so on the radio." And back came the reply "It isn't necessarily

Inset:
Flg Off David Green, whose account of operations over the Balkans follows. *Green*

Right:
David Green, in the aircraft nearest the camera, leading a section of four Spitfires IXs of No 73 Squadron to the take-off point at the forward operating base at Prkos in Yugoslavia in the spring of 1945. Each Spitfire carries two 250lb bombs. *IWM*

over for us. We don't know if the German forces here know the war is over. We want you to go and find out."

'The next morning I was briefed for a reconnaissance quite different from any I had ever flown. With my section I was to search roads and railway lines in northern Yugoslavia leading out of the country, to see what if anything the enemy forces were doing. Our people wanted to know, first, if the German troops in Yugoslavia were indeed surrendering. And if they were, whom were they trying to surrender to? Were they going to stay where they were and surrender to the Yugoslavs or the Russians? Or were they trying to move north and surrender to British and American forces moving into Austria?

'To me it seemed unlikely we would see anything – up till then we had seen very little of the German troops from the air. If they moved it was usually in small numbers, they were very good at camouflage and difficult to spot. Normally we didn't see any activity on the ground until we began an attack and they started to fire at us. For the reconnaissance our aircraft were to carry the normal armament including bombs, but we were not to engage in offensive action unless we were fired at first or threatened.

'With my section I took off from Prkos at first light. I remember thinking this was a funny sort of a mission: nobody could tell me what a surrendering army would look like. We couldn't shout out the cockpit to ask! The only way I could think of to discover whether they were surrendering was to show ourselves and see if they opened fire.

'Initially we headed due east into the brightening sky, past Kazanci and the Makljen Pass as far as Sarajevo. Then we turned north-west and flew along the road past Zenica and towards Banja Luka. With my wing man I flew low up the road between 150 and 500 feet, weaving back and forth with the other pair giving us top cover. There was hardly any activity on the ground and no light flak. It was a clear day, with good visibility and the sun just climbing over the mountains. Below us was the usual lovely Yugoslavian countryside, a bit like south Wales with its moderate hills and valleys and rolling countryside.

'We had just looked at one valley, and pulled up over a line of hills to look at the next. And suddenly, there in front of us, was this enormous convoy of German vehicles extending along the road as far as the eye could see – what in modern parlance we would call a "ten-mile tailback". Some of the vehicles were horse-drawn, they were all heading north at a walking pace.

'As soon as I saw them I told the pilots to increase speed, fuze the bombs and set guns to "fire" in case we ran into trouble. Under normal conditions we would have climbed to height for a dive bombing attack. But now my job was to find out whether they were surrendering.

'We thundered up the road at 100ft at about 300mph, snaking back and forth. It must have looked fairly threatening to the German troops as we ran in. As soon as they saw us a white Verey light arced away from one of the vehicles, leaving a trail of white smoke in the still morning air. Men ran away from the slowly moving convoy, waving their empty hands above their heads while others waved white towels and sheets. The trucks and carts were piled with kit and had men sprawled on top riding wherever they could. Not a shot was fired or a weapon raised, and it was clear these people knew the war was over and had no wish to continue fighting. We flew up the convoy for about 8 miles without reaching the head, with similar signals of surrender all the way. I did not see a single hostile act anywhere. I got the impression that there was a gang of chaps who could not wait to get home. We pulled up and circled the vehicles, and the white flags continued to wave.

'For us there was a lot of curiosity value – it was the first time we seen Germans that we hadn't attacked. For the whole of my adult life, since 1938, I had grown up convinced that all Germans were dangerous; and for the previous six years we had been killing each other. And now all of that had come to an end. Suddenly I wondered "What are we going to do tomorrow?"

'The other pair of Spitfires had been giving top cover, but when it was clear there was going to be no fighting I called them down to have a look too. And they did, we just trailed in line astern past the convoy. When I had seen enough, I led the formation into the climb and radioed back to base the position of the convoy and the fact it was not hostile.

'We formed up in a box and climbed quietly and undramatically away from the enemy of yesterday. Their task was to surrender to the West and keep out of the hands of the Reds. Ours was to return to base – and then see what the future held for us all. There was one small job to be done first. Our bombs were fuzed and had to go. Leading the formation round in a wide sweep to port we coasted out south of Rijeka, past the low lying islands of Cres, Losinj and the oddly named Krk, and out over the clear, clean sea. I put the formation into a shallow 30 degree dive, then we let go our bombs in a salvo.

'I looked back over my shoulder as we climbed away, opening the canopy for the view and some fresh air. The water was already settling where the eight bombs had fallen. We had made what was perhaps the last modest bang of the war in Europe. It was time to go home.'

32
'Franglais' for Spitfire Pilots

The Spitfire brought together men of many nations and produced a comradeship of the air that surmounted national differences and introduced 'Flying English' into many languages. The reader might care to savour the following passage written immediately after the war, by a Belgian Spitfire pilot of No 349 Squadron, in the 'Franglais' spoken by personnel on the unit, many of whom had served with the Royal Air Force for more than four years. At the time of the flight described, July 1945, the Squadron was operating from Wunstorf in Germany.

'Ce matin, pendant que je prenais mon porridge au breakfast, le flight commander est venu me detailer pour un show. Je n'étais pas très keen d'aller encore faire de la line astern ou du close vic pendant une heure mais il fallait bien puisque je venais de rentrer d'un forty-eight en Spit.

'A neuf heures, le three tonner est venu nous prendre au billet pour nous conduire à l'intelligence. Le squadron leader in charge nous a tout d'abord donné une idée du general set up pour le fly past en mettant un emphasis particulier sur le fait que Three-four-nine allait se trouver à l'outside des turns to port et que, en conséquence, ils devaient pousser leur throttle past the gate pour catcher up avec les Typhies de la Six-O-nine, les leaders des sections devaient rester à une dizaine de wingspans les uns des autres, plus ou moins en line abreast car il faisait très bumpy. Le press tits était fixé à dix heures, après quoi le three tonner nous conduisait au dispersal pour un briefing au squadron.

'Nous devions rester tout le temps sur 'A' channel, excepté en cas d'emergency pour un homing urgent.

'A dix heures moins dix, nous étions tous dans nos taxis, strappés in prêts à partir. Au premier essai de mise en marche, mon prop stoppait après deux tours. Je primais encore un peu, mais devais m'arrêter après deux ou trois dopes pour ne pas l'overprimer. Je pressais les tits encore une fois. Des flammes sortaient de mon exhaust, mais je continuais de presser. Press on regardless! Le voilà parti. Il ne me restait plus de temps pour tester quoi que ce soit; le mécano me wavait le all clear, et j'allais taxier out.

'J'arrivais sur le runway quand les autres étaient déjà lined up pour le take off. Je prenais vite ma place de yellow three, juste au moment où le leader donnait le thumbs up.

'Nous voilà partis en l'air. Un virage près du deck nous rapprochait très vite de la blue section qui avait décollé avant nous, mais néanmoins il nous fallait un certain temps avant d'être lined up properly. Le group leader settait course juste au-dessus du lac; pendant ce temps la Three-fifty arrivait balls out to catch up avec la formation.

'Peu de temps après le set course, Red two callait up pour dire que son engine était rough et qu'il devait retourner à la base. Le spare prenait immédiatement sa place.

'Le show passait very smoothly et au bout d'une demi-heure, le Wing est revenu à la base.

'Le break était canif. La red section a breaké immédiatement, la Blue passait en dessous de la Yellow section, qui continuait tout droit. Les atterrissages n'étaient pas trop mauvais à part yellow two, qui draggait in son taxi, donnant l'impression de faire un low level cross country.

'A dispersal, mon slow running cut out m'a encore donné un peu de trouble, mais je l'ai signalé dans le seven hundred.'

Below:
Spitfire IXs of No 349
(Belgian) Squadron.   IWM

Right:
A pair of Spitfire LFIXs of
No 443 Squadron RCAF, one
with clipped wings and the
other with standard wings,
pictured in April 1945 over
their base at Schneverdingen
in Germany. The unit code of
this squadron was 2I.
Public Archives of Canada

Below right:
RAAF Mk VIII, A58–505 of
No 79 Squadron pictured at
Biak, New Guinea, April 1945.
Hegge

Left:
Mk VIII of No 457 Squadron RAAF bearing the unit's 'shark's mouth' insignia taxying out of Labuan, Borneo in October 1945, prior to the Squadron's return to Australia.
Australian War Memorial

Above and Below:
Mk VIIIs of No 548 Squadron RAF, operating over Darwin, Australia early in 1945.
Glaser

Griffon-Powered Development Spitfires

Above right:
DP845, the first Spitfire powered by a Griffon engine, flew for the first time in November 1941. Initially designated a Mk IV, it was redesignated as Mk 20 before it finally became the prototype Mk XII.
Smithsonian

Right:
DP851, the second Griffon Spitfire, made its maiden flight in August 1942 designated a Mk 20. This aircraft featured a strengthened wing with a revised internal structure. Initially this aircraft was powered by a Griffon II engine with single-stage supercharging. Later it was re-engined with a Griffon 61 with two-stage supercharging and redesignated as a Spitfire 21. This photograph shows the aircraft as a Mk 21 shortly after it resumed flight testing in December 1942, when it was fitted with a four-bladed airscrew; later still the aircraft was fitted with a five-bladed propeller.
Smithsonian

Right:
JF321, one of the six Spitfire VIIIs which early in 1943 were re-engined with two-stage supercharged Griffons to become pre-production Mk XIVs. As well as an enlarged fin, this particular aircraft was fitted with contra-rotating propellers.
Smithsonian

Bottom right:
PP139, the second prototype Mk 21, flew for the first time in July 1943. This aircraft differed markedly from the first prototype being fitted with revised ailerons with balance tabs, revised main wheels with doors to fair off the wheels when retracted and an enlarged fin.
Smithsonian

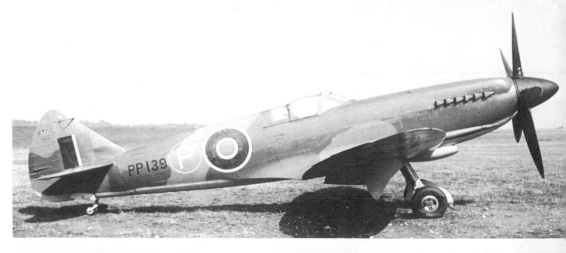

242

Late Production Spitfires

LA187, the first production
Mk 21, flew for the first time
in July 1944.   *IWM*

Mk 21s undergoing final
assembly at South Marston
at the end of the war.
Vickers

Right:
A few Mk 21s were fitted with contra-rotating airscrews and delivered to the RAF for testing. This close-up shows details of the installation.

Below:
After the war LA188, the second production Mk 21, was stripped of armament and used for high speed diving trials at Farnborough.
Crown Copyright

Left:
PK312, the prototype Spitfire 22, flew initially with Mk XIV-type tail surfaces. It is seen here with the enlarged 'Spiteful-type' tail.
Smithsonian

Above:
PK431, an early production Mk 22, seen with its original small tail surfaces shortly before completion at Castle Bromwich. *Vickers*

Right:
After the war Spitfire 22s served with most squadrons of the Royal Auxiliary Air Force. These belonged to No 613 (City of Manchester) Squadron and were pictured in 1948 or early 1949. *Smithsonian*

Below right:
PK713, one of the few Mk 24s built. Apart from the serial number, externally this particular aircraft is identical to the late production Mk 22s. But later Mk 24s were fitted with the shorter-barrel Mk V Hispano cannon.

Late Mark Seafires

Left:
NS490, the prototype Seafire XV, was the first Griffon-powered Seafire and corresponded to the Spitfire XII. *Smithsonian*

Below:
SR572, a Seafire XV, landing on HMS *Illustrious* after the war. The Mk XV was the first Griffon-powered Seafire variant, and later production aircraft featured the sting-type arrester hook seen here. In front of the tail wheel was a fixed strut to prevent the wheel fouling the arrester wires.
RAF Museum/Charles Brown

Right:
The Seafire 17 was similar to the Mk XV but featured a cut-down rear fuselage and bubble canopy, and an extended-stroke undercarriage.
RAF Museum/Charles Brown

Far right:
Following the Mk 17, the designation of Seafire mark numbers was revised, and the next version to appear was the Mk 45. TM379, the prototype Seafire 45, was a Spitfire 21 'navalised' by Cunliffe-Owen Aircraft Ltd. The main changes were the installation of naval radio equipment, the fitting of the string-type arrester hook, modification of the main wheel fairings to prevent their fouling the arrester wires and the fitting of a fixed guard in front of the tail wheel for the same purpose. The aircraft was an interim development type and did not have folding wings. *Smithsonian*

Below:
TM379 seen later in its career fitted with a Griffon 85 engine driving contra-rotating propellers. With the original fin the aircraft displayed a measure of lateral instability and in an attempt to cure it this particular Seafire was fitted with an enlarged fin and rudder, which gave the tail an outline quite different from normal. The new surfaces were still not large enough, however, and later aircraft were fitted with the fully enlarged Spiteful-type tail unit.
Smithsonian

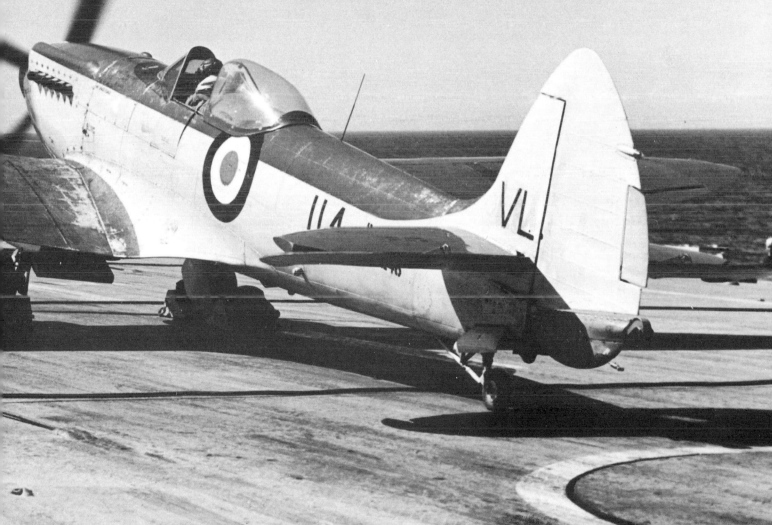

The Seafire 46 was the naval equivalent of the Spitfire 22 with a bubble canopy, though the contra-rotating propeller and enlarged tail surfaces were fitted as standard. Like the Mk 45 this version lacked folding wings and only a few were built pending the development of the definitive Mk 47 version.
RAF Museum/Charles Brown

The Mk 47 was the definitive version of the Seafire. Although outwardly similar to the Mk 46, it featured a system of wing folding quite different from that of earlier marks; on the first 14 aircraft the wings had to be folded manually, but later aircraft were fitted with hydraulic jacks for this purpose. All production aircraft were of the fighter-reconnaissance version, with provision for a vertical camera behind the cockpit and an oblique camera pointing left or right. These photographs were taken during the deck trials with an early production aircraft on HMS *Illustrious* in March 1947.
RAF Museum/Charles Brown

Right:
Photographs by Charles Brown taken on *Illustrious* in May 1947 showing Mk 47s landing (not all of the same aircraft). The aircraft picks up the hook and is plucked out of the sky; as it slams down on the deck the long-stroke oleo legs absorb the landing forces. The aircraft is drawn smoothly to a halt by the arrester wires, and even before it comes to rest the deck crew are sprinting out to free the hook.
RAF Museum/Charles Brown

Above:
VP464, a standard production Seafire FR47, wearing the late-1940s light green/medium grey naval colour scheme standard on Royal Navy aircraft, pictured during its maker's flight trials. Under the outer wings this aircraft carries a pair of 22.5gal fixed blister tanks stressed for combat.
Smithsonian

Seafire FR47 on the ground catapult at Farnborough fitted with rollers for the rapid centralisation of the aircraft on the track, in October 1947. The aircraft is rigged for a heavy-weight launch and carries two 22.5gal combat tanks under the wings, a 50gal drop tank under the fuselage and two 500lb bombs. Note the details of the new type of catapult shuttle, the underwing hooks and the bridle connecting them; also the hold-back system fitted to the tail, which incorporated a weak link which broke when the combination of engine thrust and catapult force were sufficient to get the aircraft to flying speed. The photos also show clearly the carburettor air intake extended to immediately behind the spinner, a recognition feature of production Mk 47s.
Crown Copyright

Spitfires and Seafires Abroad

Spitfire IXs of the French Air Force in Indo-China.

Above:
MJ341 of Groupe de Chasse 2/4 'La Fayette' operating from Hanoi, French Indo-China in December 1947.
Goyat

Right:
Mk IXs of GC 1/4 'Dauphine', MJ671 'E' and TD202 'P', flying a combat mission from Nha Trang late in 1947 or early in 1948.

Below right:
Aircraft of GC 1/6 'Corse' at Tourane in October 1950.

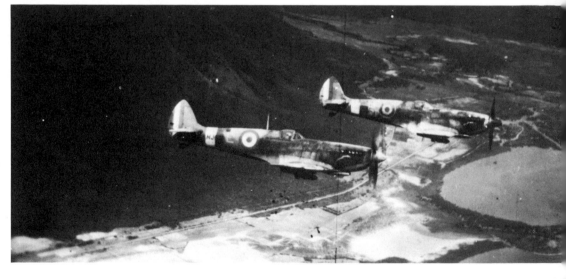

Spitfire IXEs of No 332
Squadron of the Royal
Norwegian Air Force, based
at Gardermoen near Oslo in
1948. Aircraft 'A-CI' carried
its serial number NH193 both
on the fin and on the fuselage
forward of the cockpit.
RAF Museum/Charles Brown

Spitfire IXs of No 322
Squadron of the Royal Dutch
Air Force pictured at
Semarang airfield, Java in
what was then the Dutch
East Indies. This unit
operated during the war of
independence which
preceded the foundation of
the state of Indonesia in
December 1949.

Above right and Right:
Spectacular end of MK993 in
January 1949, after it ran off
the runway at Semarang
following a brake failure and
ended up in a paddy field; the
pilot was unhurt.
van der Meer

After the war the Royal Canadian Navy received 35 Seafire XVs, some of which were operated by No 803 Squadron.

Left:
Aircraft 'H' taking off from HMCS *Warrier* during 1946.

Below:
Also on *Warrier* in 1946/47, the deck crew push back aircraft 'L' to disengage the hook from the arrester wire; although a first glance it appears this aircraft has clipped wings, in fact the outer wing panels had been painted in a lighter colour than the rest of the machine. Note the maple leaf above the fin flash.

Above:
16 April 1947 and a nasty moment for Seafire XV PR504, 'B', after taking the barrier and ending up on its nose; the slipper tank has been torn from the fuselage, spilling fuel over the deck. The crash crews are rushing in with extinguishers to smother the area in foam to prevent a fire.

Right:
Seafire XV PR479 photographed in September 1948 when it belonged to the 1st Training Air Group of the Royal Canadian Navy. It is seen here taking off from Rivers, Manitoba with a rack of 25lb practice bombs under each wing. A non-standard feature of this particular aircraft is the mast behind the cockpit, to support a wire aerial to the tail for the high frequency radio.
Public Archives of Canada.

33

Test Flying the Spiteful

Patrick Shea-Simonds – usually called Shea – learned to fly at the Reading Aero Club in 1934, and gained a commission in the Fleet Air Arm in 1940. Early in 1942 he was appointed Workshops Test Pilot at RNAS Halston where he qualified as an Engineer Officer and was also able to fly every type of aircraft operated by the Royal Navy. In June 1943 he joined No 1 Course at the Empire Test Pilots' School, Boscombe Down, which he completed in February 1944, and was then posted to 'C Flight' at Boscombe engaged in performance testing. Early in September 1944 Frank Furlong, the Deputy Chief Test Pilot at the Supermarine company, was killed while flying the prototype Spiteful and Shea accepted an offer to take his place. In this account Shea tells of his experiences flying the new fighter, and why it was not accepted into service.

The prototype Spiteful, NN660, had in fact been a hybrid aircraft with a Spitfire XIV fuselage and tail married to a completely redesigned wing of the luminar flow type. Shea arrived at High Post, the Supermarine test airfield, five days after Furlong's death and

Left:
Lt Patrick Shea-Simonds, known to all as Shea, whose account of test flying the Spiteful follows, pictured during the war.
Shea-Simonds

Below:
NN664, the second prototype Spiteful, which Shea flew for the first time on 9 April 1945. Later in its career this aircraft was fitted with the enlarged tail surfaces, though it remained unpainted throughout. *Smithsonian*

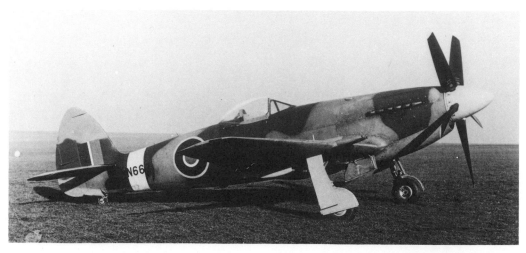

Right:
NN667, the third and last prototype Spiteful, fitted with an extended carburettor air intake. *Smithsonian*

Far right and Overleaf:
Shea demonstrating RB515, the first production Spiteful 14, for the camera of Charles Brown. The revised shape of the new laminar-flow wing of this aircraft is clearly evident in these photos. *RAF Museum/Charles Brown*

while the accident was a matter of some controversy.

'Frank had been coming back to High Post in NN660 when he met up with one of the production test pilots flying a Spitfire XIV, and the two amused themselves with a mock dogfight. Suddenly Frank's aircraft rolled on its back and went straight into the ground. Afterwards the inevitable happened: the pilot wasn't alive to answer back, so the accident was put down to "pilot error". There was a lot of bad feeling about this amongst the firm's test pilots, it was felt that Frank was not the sort of chap who would have pulled too much "g" and lost control of the aircraft. I had known Frank earlier and I felt the same, but of course I was in no position to comment on the accident because I had not seen it nor had I flown the Spiteful. So, for a time, the matter had to rest there.'

Following the crash of the prototype the Spiteful test programme had come to an abrupt halt, but there was plenty of work for the pilots testing late-mark Spitfires and Seafires. The first task for Shea was to complete the maker's trials of the Seafire XV, before the aircraft went to Boscombe Down for service trials.

In January 1945 NN664, the second prototype Spiteful, was ready for testing. This aircraft was the first 'real' Spiteful, with the redesigned fuselage as well as wings. Jeffrey Quill carried out the initial trials with the second prototype, in the course of which he encountered a problem with the aircraft's controls which seemed to explain Furlong's crash.

'The Spiteful had aileron control rods (instead of the cables on the Spitfire), and these should have given more positive control. But during a test flight in the second prototype while Jeffrey was doing a tight turn to the left and pulling "g" he suddenly found his stick locked hard over. He gave the stick a bash with the palm of his hand which freed it, and after that everything was all right. But had he been at low altitude, as Frank had been, it could

have been very nasty. Jeffrey felt that this could well have been the cause of Frank's accident, and was able to get the court of inquiry to reverse its initial finding that the cause of the accident was "pilot error"; later Frank was awarded a posthumous King's Commendation for his work as a test pilot. After that the control rods of all Spitefuls were very thoroughly checked for freedom of movement, and we never had a recurrence of the problem.'

Shea made his first flight in NN664 on 9 April 1945 and from then on became heavily committed to the Spiteful test programme. 'There were obvious similarities with the Spitfire, but there were also many differences. The cockpit layout of the Spiteful was quite different, it was no longer a "Spitfire cockpit". The most obvious change was the seating position, which was more reclined. Sitting in the seat, one's feet on the rudder pedals felt as if they were "up in the air". Several of the shorter pilots did not like the new seating position. But being 6ft 6in tall, sitting in a Spitfire even with the seat fully down I always felt rather squashed in. I found the Spiteful cockpit much roomier and the view over the nose was definitely better than in the Spitfire.

'The next noticeable thing was that the wide track undercarriage of the Spiteful made the feel of the aircraft on the ground – during taxying, take-off or after landing – very different from that of the Spitfire. A lot of people grizzled on about the Spitfire's narrow track undercarriage, and it certainly wasn't ideal for deck operations. But it did have a curious sort of "bicycle stability" and once the aircraft was rolling it tended to go straight in the direction in which it was pointing. The Spiteful was different, during taxying and landing runs it tended to wander off course and one had to rely on differential braking to keep the aircraft going straight.'

Normally the Spiteful's lack of directional stability on the ground was only a minor irri-

tation. But during a test flight in the new fighter Shea suffered a hydraulic failure while airborne, and found himself in a potentially embarrassing position.

'The undercarriage, brakes and flaps were all hydraulically operated in the Spiteful (on the Spitfire the undercarriage was hydraulically operated, but the brakes and flaps were pneumatically operated). I knew I could get the undercarriage down with the carbon-dioxide emergency system, but I would have no brakes or flaps. Since I had to make a flapless landing I decided to go to Boscombe Down, where the runway was much longer than the one at High Post. I got the aircraft on the ground all right and was trundling down the runway, but as the speed fell away the rudder became less and less effective and the aircraft started to wander to one side. With no brakes, the only thing I could do was give a quick burst of engine to put a bit of slipstream over the rudder and get the aircraft going straight again. I ran on down the runway with a series of ever-decreasing "blips" of the engine, gradually getting slower and slower. The Spiteful ran off the end of the runway going at a walking place, and came to rest without damage on the grass.

'As I got used to the Spiteful I found it not unpleasant to fly. It took off all right and its high speed performance was quite good. To be frank I never liked the "feel" of it as much as I liked the "feel" of the Spitfire, but by then I had a lot of hours on Spitfires and Seafires and they were such beautiful aircraft to fly that it would have been difficult to find anything else that felt as nice. But the main snag with the Spiteful was its low speed handling. The Spitfire had "washout" along the wing [ie the angle of incidence was greatest at the wing root, and decreased progressively toward the tip]; if you held a Spitfire straight and level and throttled back and eased back on the stick, the stall started at the wing root and worked its way out toward the tips. If you continued to hold the aircraft straight, it could be made to sink in a stalled glide with even a measure of lateral control.

'The approach to the stall in the Spiteful was quite different. With the laminar flow wing there was no "washout", and in fact the stall seemed to begin at the tips and work its way in. You didn't get a violent wing drop, but you did get a wing drop and there was pronounced "kicking" of the ailerons. As a warning of an incipient straight stall it was reasonable enough, but it felt nothing like as pleasant as the Spitfire. Approaching a stall, the Spiteful felt as if it was about to do something nasty. On the flare-out before landing, for example, it felt as if it was balanced on a pin and might tilt one way or the other

at any moment. In fact the aircraft didn't finally do anything unpleasant, but it felt as if it might and that was disconcerting until one got used to it.

'Oddly enough the spinning characteristics of the Spiteful were surprisingly good – it was practically impossible to keep the aircraft in a sustained spin. It would go into a violent flick with the nose right up in the air, rather in the same way as the Spitfire, but would often flick itself right out of the incipient spin. You didn't have to worry about taking full recovery action, if you just let go of the controls it would usually come out on its own. Even if you held the controls in a spin-inducing position, the Spiteful would be trying to recover by itself.

'Because of the low speed handling characteristics encountered with the Spiteful we spent a lot of time trying to improve matters on the second prototype and early production aircraft. In due course these aircraft were all fitted with new wings having slightly blunted leading edges, and enlarged tails. We also tried out root spoilers and modifications to the ailerons. The various modifications finally adopted did improve the aircraft's low speed handling, which became noticeably pleasanter. But these improvements were all made at the expense of all-out level speed, with the result that the performance of the Spite-

ful ended up little better than that of the Spitfire 22.'

One reason why the high speed performance of the Spiteful showed no great improvement over that of the late-model Spitfires was that the redesigned wing fitted to the Spitfire 21 and later marks proved to have greater strength and better high speed characteristics than had originally been expected. Initially it had been thought that the wing would run into aileron reversal problems at airspeeds below 500mph and that a new stronger wing of laminar flow profile would be needed if Spitefuls were to be able to exceed this speed safely.
'The idea of the laminar flow wing was very fashionable during the mid-war period as a means of achieving low drag at high speeds. But when it was tested on the Spiteful, the new wing did not give much improvement in performance over the late-type Spitfires. The theory of the laminar flow was all right, but only so long as the wing profile had been manufactured to very fine tolerances and the whole thing was kept free of dirt or minor dents. It needed only a squashed mosquito on the leading edge, and the airflow over that part of the wing went for a Burton!'

With the end of the war in Europe the Royal Air Force lost interest in the piston-engined interceptor: the new jet fighters promised to be considerably more effective and the order for 150 Spitefuls was cancelled. But nobody had yet landed a jet aircraft on an aircraft carrier, and the poor throttle response of the early jet engines threatened to make a missed approach hazardous. With the war in the Pacific likely to continue well into 1946 the Royal Navy had a clear requirement for a piston-engined fighter with the performance of the Spiteful. Less than a week after the Royal Air Force cancelled its order the Admiralty signed a contract for a similar number of its navalised version, the Seafang.
'At the time the war against Japan seemed likely to go on a lot longer, and the Seafang would probably have been a better naval fighter than the Seafire. With the improved forward view over the nose deck landings would have been a lot easier. And it had a very much more robust wide-track under-carriage – during an arrested landing the tendency of the aircraft to "wander" after touch-down would not have mattered. Even with the modifications made to the wing and the tail to improve low-speed handling, the performance at high speed would have been comparable with or slightly better than that of the latest-model Seafires.'

During a flight on 28 September 1945 Shea experienced a near-catastrophic engine failure in RB515, the first production version of the

RB515 pictured after Shea's belly landing at Farnborough on 20 September 1945 following the near disastrous engine explosion.
Shea-Simonds

Right:
Close-up of the wrecked engine of RB515; note the broken supercharger impeller embedded in the side of the cowling. *Shea-Simonds*

Far right, Top:
RB516, the fifth production Spiteful 14, pictured during weapons trials at Boscombe Down. This aircraft featured the lengthened carburettor air intake. Under the fuselage is a 180gal drop tank, and under the wings are four Triplex rockets each comprising of 7.2in howitzer shell with three 3in rocket motors. *Oughton*

Far right, Bottom:
RB518, the sole Spiteful F16 built. Fitted with a Griffon 101 engine with a two-stage three-speed supercharger, in 1947 this aircraft attained a true airspeed of 494mph at 28,500ft, the highest recorded by a British piston-engined machine. *Smithsonian*

Spiteful. He had taken off from High Post for a handling and longitudinal stability test at 30,000ft. Up to 28,000ft the climb was normal and he reduced boost and rpm to bring the aircraft to maximum cruising speed in level flight at 30,000ft. The indicated airspeed slowly increased to 240mph indicated when: 'Suddenly there was a loud explosion and I saw something [in fact a piece of the engine] fly past the cockpit on the starboard side. At the same time the engine began to vibrate very violently, oil began to stream back over the windscreen and cockpit hood. The engine rpm counter was hard against the upper stop reading 4,000rpm – obviously the propeller had "run away".'

The constant speed unit for the propeller had failed and put the blades into fully-fine pitch, thus allowing the engine to overspeed far beyond its safe limits. The Griffon was in the process of shaking itself to pieces . . .
'I took what action I could to deal with the situation: I brought the constant speed control lever back to positive coarse pitch, closed the throttle, pulled the engine cut-out, turned off the fuel and switched off the ignition. At the same time I pulled the nose of the aircraft up, reducing speed to 140mph Indicated. I then opened the cockpit hood, released my safety harness and prepared to abandon the aircraft as I fully expected the engine either to disintegrate completely or to be torn from its mounting. The vibration and high rpm persisted, while oil and glycol streamed around and into the cockpit and I saw a crack develop in the starboard side of the cockpit immediately aft of the windscreen side panel.
'It had been drummed into us at Boscombe

Down that aircraft which went wrong during tests were valuable bits of evidence, and it was the test pilot's job to get them back on the ground in one piece if possible. So although I was ready to bale out, I decided to hang on and see if the aircraft could be saved. After about 15 seconds the rpm fell rapidly, the airscrew came to a stop and the vibration ceased.
'I called Boscombe Down on the radio and informed them that my engine had blown up and I was preparing for a forced landing. By this time I was over the Swindon area, which like Boscombe and High Post was covered in cloud. To the east the skies were clear and as I did not feel like letting down through cloud with the engine out, and could see Farnborough clear and within gliding distance, I decided to land there and informed Boscombe. I had plenty of height and once the vibration ceased the Spiteful handled quite well as a glider. By the time I had descended to 5,000 feet it was obvious that the aircraft wasn't likely to catch fire – if a fire was going to start it would have done so before then. So I re-fastened my harness and started to approach the long runway at Farnborough from the south west. I knew this would bring me in for a down-wind landing, but the surface wind was light and I preferred to approach the airfield over open country rather than over the town.
'It was obvious that the hydraulic systems were no longer working fully and I had no idea what damage had been done to them. So, rather than risk finding that only one undercarriage leg would extend, I decided to land the aircraft with the wheels up. I selected flaps down and worked the hand pump until

VG471, the first Seafang F31,
was virtually a hooked
Spiteful and carried little
naval equipment. The aircraft
was delivered to the RAE
Farnborough early in 1946
and is depicted following
modifications to the
windscreen and rudder.
Smithsonian

resistance ceased, at which point I had about ¼ flap.

'I made my final approach and landed wheels-up on the grass alongside the main runway. Surprisingly, the touchdown was the least dramatic part of the whole business. The Spiteful had a large wide-span radiator under each wing and slid along the grass on these; it felt just like putting down a flying boat on water. As I touched down I saw the fire tenders and ambulance driving down the runway practically in formation with me."

On examination of the aircraft it was found that the first stage of the Griffon engine's supercharger had disintegrated completely. There had been considerable damage to the hydraulic, glycol and oil pipes at the rear of the engine, as well as to the cowling and fillets in the vicinity of the supercharger. On the starboard side part of the crankcase had shattered and at least one of the connecting rods had broken. A few days later Joe Smith, Supermarine's Chief Designer, sent Shea a copy of a letter the company had received from Sir Arthur Sidgreaves, the Managing Director of Rolls-Royce, in which he wrote:
'The failure resulted in pieces of the engine being forced through the cowlings, and due to the inertia forces I understand the engine was nearly torn from the airframe. There was also the possibility of fire, so that the pilot would have had every reason to abandon the aeroplane and descend by parachute. The fact that he held on and successfully landed the machine is of great value because it enabled the evidence to be retained and an examination made as to the cause of the trouble, whereas in so many of these instances of failure the evidence is lost.'

Subsequently Shea received a more formal recognition of his feat, in the form of a King's Commendation for Valuable Service in the Air. RB515 suffered surprisingly little damage as a result of the accident and, after repairs and the installation of a new engine, it later resumed flying.

In October 1945 Jeffrey Quill and Shea demonstrated the Spiteful during a display of the latest military aircraft at Farnborough. As the latter recalled, the newest Supermarine product was rather overshadowed:
'Jeffrey flew the Spiteful on the first day and I flew it on the second. The occasion was a bit embarrasing for us, however, because Geoffrey de Havilland stole the show with his very impressive demonstration of the Vampire. It was clear that the writing was on the wall for the piston-engined fighter.'

Because of the continuing Naval interest in the Seafang, and also because the Attacker

VB895, the sole Seafang FR32, was fitted with a contra-rotating propeller and hydraulically folding wings which were to have been standard on production aircraft. Piloted by Mike Lithgow, this aircraft underwent deck landing trials on HMS *Illustrious* in May 1947. *RAF Museum*

jet fighter under construction used essentially the same laminar-flow wing, testing of the Spiteful continued.

'From October 1945 most of my time on Spitefuls was spent mainly in NN664 doing high speed dives – by that time she had been fitted with the larger tail. Much of this work was taken up exploring the aircraft's lateral control characteristics and measuring the stick forces required to apply various amounts of aileron. For this the aircraft was fitted with a stick force recorder and I had to note down the readings and rates of roll on my knee pad.

'Supermarine wanted the figures to calculate the lateral reversal speed, because a similar wing was to be fitted to the Attacker jet fighter then being built. We established that with a generous safety margin the limiting diving speed of the Spiteful was 525mph Indicated at 5,000ft. The aircraft handled well up to that speed and there were no difficulties about pulling it out of the dive. However, this was little better than the limiting speed of the late-model Spitfires or Seafires [the Seafire 47 fitted with folding wings had a safe limiting diving speed of 500mph]. In fact, it was confirmation that the Spitfire wing was a darn sight better and more efficient aerodynamically than had been supposed. And, at the same time, the supposed advantages of the laminar flow wing proved illusory.'

Shea continued test flying the Spiteful until February 1946, when he left Supermarine after having amassed 82 hours flying on the type. Mike Lithgow took over from him as Deputy Chief Test Pilot and did much of the testing of the Seafang, before the production contract for that aircraft was also cancelled

'In my view two things killed the Spiteful as a service fighter: first of all, Boscombe Down took against it from the word go because of its low speed handling characteristics. They were looking at it from the point of view of the average squadron pilot, and had to consider how he would cope with the aircraft. When I was at Boscombe we had to guess the capability of that mythical human being and there was a tendency to assume that he was more of a clot than he actually was. It was not that the Spiteful was really dangerous to fly at low speeds, it just did not feel very nice to anyone flying the aircraft for the first time and particularly so if one was comparing it with the Spitfire.

'The other problem was that the laminar flow wing failed to produce any substantial increase in performance. Had the Spiteful been, say, 30 or 40mph faster than the Spitfire 22, I am sure there would have been far fewer complaints from Boscombe about the low-speed handling characteristics of the aircraft.'

End of an era. Spitfire 22 PK542 pictured in formation with the first pre-production Supermarine Swift fighter in 1951.
RAF Museum/Charles Brown

Appendices

Appendix I
Technical Data

Mk V B

Engine	One 1,440 h.p. Rolls Royce Merlin 45 inline
Span	36 ft 10 ins
Length	29 ft 11 ins
Height	11 ft 5 ins
Weight empty	5,065 lb
Weight loaded	6,650 lb
Crew number	One
Maximum speed	374 m.p.h. at 13,000 ft
Service ceiling	37,000 ft
Normal range	1,135 miles
Armament	Two 20 mm. cannon and four .303 machine guns, one 500 lb or two 250 lb bombs

Mk XIV

Engine	One 2,050 h.p. Rolls Royce Griffon 65 inline
Span	36 ft 10 ins
Length	32 ft 8 ins
Height	12 ft 8 ins
Weight empty	6,600 lb
Weight loaded	8,500 lb
Crew number	One
Maximum speed	448 m.p.h. at 26,000 ft
Service ceiling	44,500 ft
Normal range	850 miles
Armament	Two 20 mm. cannon and four .303 machine guns; up to 1,000 lb of bombs

Spitfire: Comparison of Marks

		I		II		III		IV		VA	
Span	Ft in.	36	10	36	10	36	10	36	10	36	10
	Ft in.									32	2
Length	Ft in.	29	11	29	11	29	11	29	11	29	11
Height	Ft in.	11	5	11	5	11	5	11	5	11	5
Weight	Lb	5,784		6,527		NV		7,178		6,417	
Speed	m.p.h.	355		357		NV		372		374	
	m.p.h.									357	
at	Ft	19,000		17,000		NV		NV		13,000	
	Ft									6,000	
Ceiling	Ft	34,000		37,200		NV		39,600		37,000	
	Ft									36,500	
Range	Miles	NV		500		NV		NV		1,135	

		V B		V C		VI		VII		F VIII	
Span	Ft in.	36	10	36	10	40	2	40	2	32	2
	Ft in.	32	2	32	2						
Length	Ft in.	29	11	29	11	29	11	31	0	30	4
Height	Ft in.	11	5	11	5	NV		NV		NV	
Weight	Lb	6,650		6,785		6,797		7,875		7,767	
Speed	m.p.h.	374		374		364		408		408	
	m.p.h.	357		357							
at	Ft	13,000		13,000		NV		25,000		25,000	
	Ft	6,000		6,000							
Ceiling	Ft	37,000		37,000		NV		43,000		43,000	
	Ft	36,500		36,500							
Range	Miles	1,135		1,135		NV		1,180		NV	

		LF VIII		HF VIII		HF IX		LF IX		X	
Span	Ft in.	36	10	40	2	36	10	32	2	NV	
Length	Ft in.	30	4	30	4	31	4	30	6	NV	
Height	Ft in.	NV		NV		11	5	11	5	NV	
Weight	Lb	7,767		7,767		7,500		7,500		8,159	
Speed	m.p.h.	404		416		416		404		416	
at	Ft	21,000		27,500		27,500		21,000		NV	
Ceiling	Ft	41,500		44,000		45,000		42,500		NV	
Range	Miles	NV		1,180		980		980		900	

		XI		XII		XIII		XIV		XVI	
Span	Ft in.	36	10	32	7	NV		36	10	32	8
Length	Ft in.	31	4	31	10	NV		32	8	31	4
Height	Ft in.	NV		NV		NV		12	8	12	7⅜
Weight	Lb	7,900		7,400		NV		8,500		7,500	
Speed	m.p.h.	422		393		400		448		405	
at	Ft	NV		18,000		NV		26,000		22,000	
Ceiling	Ft	NV		40,000		NV		44,500		40,500	
Range	Miles	2,000		493		700		850		980	

		XVIII		XIX		XX	
Span	Ft in.	36	10	36	10	36	10
Length	Ft in.	33	3¼	32	8	30	6
Height	Ft in.	NV		12	8	NV	
Weight	Lb	9,320		9,000		NV	
Speed	m.p.h.	442		460		NV	
at	Ft	NV		NV		NV	
Ceiling	Ft	41,000		43,000		NV	
Range	Miles	NV		1,550		NV	

		XXI		XXII		XXIV	
Span	Ft in.	36	11	36	11	36	11
Length	Ft ins	32	8	32	11	32	11
Height	Ft in.	NV		NV		NV	
Weight	Lb	9,200		9,900		9,900	
Speed	m.p.h.	454		454		454	
at	Ft	26,000		26,000		26,000	
Ceiling	Ft	43,500		43,500		NV	
Range	Miles	880		880		NV	

The Spitfire has become synonymous with the Battle of Britain. The perfect complement to the Hurricane, the Spitfire defeated the enemy in this most decisive air conflict of history, and one of the most momentous battles of all time. Designed by R. J. Mitchell, the Spitfire was the sole Allied fighter to be in production throughout the war. The prototype flew first on 5 March 1936, and its top speed of 349 m.p.h. placed it at once as the fastest fighter in the world. The Spitfire was an all-metal, low-wing cantilever monoplane with retractable landing gear, and the prototype was powered by one of the first Rolls Royce Merlin engines. The Spitfire I had a Merlin II or III engine and its two-blade wood fixed-pitch airscrew was later superseded by a three-blade variable pitch, duralumin airscrew. The fighter was armed with eight .303 machine guns, and subsequently with two 20 mm. cannon and four .303 machine guns.

The Spitfire joined the R.A.F. in 1938 and was in service with nine squadrons by September 1939. Spitfires shot down the first enemy aircraft over Britain since the First World War. The Spitfire II went into production powered by the Merlin XII engine of 1,175 h.p. Over 3,000 of the Spitfire I and II were made altogether. After the Battle of Britain, it was the Spitfire II that launched the 'Rhubarb' sweeps over Europe. The Spitfire IV met the requirement for a reconnaissance aeroplane of formidable speed. This was powered by the Merlin 45. It carried cameras and extra oxygen but no armament. The Spitfire V was one of the best-known marks, also powered by the 1,440 h.p. Merlin 46. Its extra assets included a clearer windscreen and special tropical equipment, as well as drop tanks. It operated from summer 1941 and was the first Spitfire to serve beyond Britain. But the main claim of the V was as the first-line machine of Fighter Command through 1941 and 1942. Much later, in 1943, the Spitfire V had its wings clipped, literally, as a low-level fighter, and provision was made for it to carry two 250 or one 500 lb bomb. The Spitfire VI with Merlin 47 featured a pressure cabin for high-level flying. The Spitfire VII had the Merlin 61 engine and, like the VI, had extended wingtips yielding a span of 40 ft 2 ins. It was another high-level design and the more powerful engine enabled it to exceed 400 m.p.h. for the first time. The Spitfire VIII was designed to take the Merlin 61 engine and its aim was to counter the formidable Focke Wulf FW 190 fighter, whose speed was greater than earlier Spitfires. The IX was an adaptation of the VC using the same engine, and production of the Spitfire IX exceeded 5,000 aircraft.

The Spitfire X and XI were both long-range photo reconnaissance versions, the latter capable of up to 2,000 miles. The XI was, in fact, the principal aircraft of Coastal Command's photo-reconnaissance unit from then on. The first version with the Rolls Royce Griffon III or IV engine was the Spitfire XII, used to counter the Focke Wulf's switch to the low-level offensive role. The major Griffon variant was the Spitfire XIV with its 2,050 h.p. Griffon 65 engine. This went into service in 1944 and was responsible for the destruction of more than 300 V.I. flying bombs – as well as being the first R.A.F. aircraft to shoot down a German jet Me 262. Its maximum performance was at high level. Other refinements included a propeller of five blades and sliding 'bubble hoods' with improved rear vision for the pilot. The Spitfire XVI was powered by the Packard-built Merlin 266 engine. This was flown with normal 36 ft 10 in wings and clipped wings and like many of the later marks, it could carry bombs. This was the last version to be made in a quantity exceeding 1,000. The final distinguished wartime Spitfire was the XIX photo-reconnaissance edition of the XIV. It had a ceiling altitude of 43,000 feet and a top speed of 460 m.p.h. – at least 100 m.p.h. faster than the original Spitfires. The Spitfire went up to Mk XXIV after the war, the very last one emerging in 1947. Total production over the decade of its manufacture topped 20,000. The Spitfire was probably the most famous fighter aircraft ever made.

Appendix II
The Battle of Britain
Day by Day

Date	Weather conditions	Targets and Activity	LOSSES Luftwaffe	RAF
July				
10	Cloudy, clearing	Channel convoy. *First dogfight of over 100 aircraft.*	13	6
11	Cloudy	East-coast shipping. Portland, Portsmouth.	20	4
12	Fog, then thundery	East- and south-coast shipping. Aberdeen, Portland. (Night) Bristol, S. Wales.	7	6
13	Fog, cloudy	Shipping off Dover and Portland. *HQ 10 Group opens at Box.*	7	1
14	Light cloud, clear	Shipping off Dover and Swanage.	2	4
15	Cloudy	Shipping off Norfolk coast.	3	1
16	Fog and cloud	Little activity. *Hitler directive (No. 16) formally orders invasion preparations.*	3	2
17	Light rain	Shipping off Dundee and Beachy Head.	2	1
18	Light rain	Shipping off south-east coasts. South-coast ports. Some French and British airfields waterlogged.	4	3
19	Clear, showers	Dover. Bad day for Defiants of 141 Sqdn. *Hitler's 'peace-offer' in Reichstag speech.*	2	8
20	Cloudy, clearing	Heavy raids on shipping at Dover and Lyme Bay. Me 110 appears as a fighter-bomber. (Night) Merseyside.	9	3
21	Clear, showers	Heavy raids on shipping in Channel and Straits.	9	6
22	Clear, few showers	Shipping off south coast. *British rejection of 'peace-offer'.*	1	0
23	Cloudy, rain	A few attacks on east-coast shipping.	3	0
24	Cloudy, rain	Convoys in Channel.	8	3
25	Fine	Very heavy attacks on Channel convoy in co-operation with E-boats. 11 of 21 ships sunk or badly damaged	18	7
26	Rain	South-coast shipping. *Channel convoys suspended in daylight hours.*	4	2
27	Clear, then stormy	Shipping. Two destroyers sunk and one damaged.	4	1
28	Fine	Shipping off Dover. South-coast ports. *Destroyers withdraw from Dover to Portsmouth.* Malan's 74 Sqdn in heavy combat, the CO focing Moelders into crash-landing.	18	5
29	Fine	Heavy attacks on Dover harbour and convoy: one destroyer sunk.	8	3
30	Cloud, light rain	Shipping off east coast. *Hitler instructs Goering to be ready for intensive operations at 12 hours notice.*	5	0
31	Fine	Dover balloon barrage. Shipping off south-east and south-west coasts.	5	3

Date	Weather conditions	Targets and Activity	LOSSES Luftwaffe	RAF
August				
1	Fine, haze	Shipping off south and east coasts. Norwich (aircraft factory). (Night) S. Wales, Midlands. *Hitler directive (No. 17) to Luftwaffe to 'overpower the English air force with all the forces at its command, in the shortest possible time'. Invasion preparations to be complete by 15 September.*	9	1
2	Fine, drizzle over sea	Shipping off south-east coasts. (Night) S. Wales, Midlands. *Goering's* Adlerangriff *directive to Luftwaffe.*	4	0
3	Cloudy, bright intervals	Shipping. (Night) S. Wales, Crewe, Liverpool.	4	0
4	Mainly fine	Little activity.	0	0
5	Fine	Shipping in Straits.	6	1
6	Cloudy, windy	Little activity. Shipping. *Goering orders* Adlertag *for 10 August.*	1	1
7	Cloudy	Convoy off east coast.	2	0
8	Cloudy, bright intervals	Heavy attacks on Channel convoy (the first westbound since 25 July) off Dover and Wight. Heaviest air fighting so far, involving 150+ aircraft. Ju 87s prove very vulnerable. (Night) Liverpool, Leeds, Bristol, Birmingham.	31	20
9	Cloud and rain	East-coast shipping. Dover balloons. Adlertag *postponed.*	5	4
10	Cloud and rain	Little activity.	0	0
11	Fine	Dover and Portland heavily attacked. Several senior Luftwaffe officers killed or captured. Convoys off east coast. (Night) Merseyside, Bristol Channel.	38	32
12	Fine	Several RAF airfields (Manston, Lympne, Hawkinge) and radar stations (Dover, Rye, Dunkirk, Ventnor) attacked in preparation for *Adlertag* next day.	31	22

During this preparatory phase of the Battle the Luftwaffe attacked shipping on most days and laid mines on most nights, but sank only 30,000 tons out of the nearly 5 million tons which passed round the coasts. It lost 286 aircraft as against Fighter Command's 148 (plus two at night). Except on five days, most raids were undertaken by small forces. The widespread raiding at night was mainly by very small numbers of aircraft.

Date	Weather conditions	Targets and Activity	LOSSES Luftwaffe	RAF
13	Fine	*Adlertag* postponement to afternoon causes confusion in Luftwaffe, which nevertheless flies almost 1,500 sorties in 24 hours. Attacks on Southampton, Portland, airfields (Detling, Andover, Eastchurch, Lympne). (Night) Castle Bromwich (aircraft factory).	45	13
14	Cloudy, bright intervals	Dover, airfields (Manston, Middle Wallop, Sealand).	19	8

Date	Weather conditions	Targets and Activity	LOSSES Luftwaffe	RAF
15	Fine	*Heaviest day's fighting so far, with* Luftflotte *5 joining in from Scandinavia at heavy cost to its bombers and* Me 110s. Many airfields damaged (Lympne, Hawkinge, Middle Wallop, West Malling, Eastchurch, Croydon, Martlesham, Driffield), but north of England never attacked in strength by day again. Fighter Command flies 974 sorties. *Germans more strongly escorted. Hitler confirms invasion preparations to be completed by 15 September.*	75	34
16	Fine	Heavy raids on airfields (in Kent, and at Gosport, Tangmere, Brize Norton). Ventnor radar station. Luftwaffe flies over 1,700 sorties. (Night) Home Counties, Bristol Channel, East Anglia.	45	21
17	Fine	Lympne, otherwise mysterious silence from Luftwaffe. *Shorter courses introduced for British fighter pilots.* (Night) Mersey, S. Wales, Midlands.	3	0
18	Fine at first	Heavy fighting in course of intensive bombing of airfields in south and south-east (Croydon, Gosport, Ford, Thorney Island). Portsmouth. Big damage at Kenley airfield and Poling radar station. No. 1 (Royal Canadian Air Force) Sqdn's first operations.	71	27
19	Cloudy	Southampton area, Pembroke docks. *Goering issues orders for renewed attacks on Fighter Command. He orders stronger escort to* Luftflotte *2's bombers, and transfers single-engined fighters for this purpose from* Luftflotte *3, which is to concentrate more on night bombing.* Ju 87s *to be conserved for the invasion and special tasks.*	6	3
20	Cloudy, windy over land, becoming rainy	Weather restricts German activities. Manston, Martlesham. Polish 302 Sqdn in action for first time, vengeful and effective. Churchill's 'Never . . . has so much been owed by so many to so few.'	7	2
21	Cloudy, rainy	Enemy operations mainly limited to fighter 'tip and run' raids. Airfields in East Anglia, south and south-west attacked lightly.	14	1
22	Cloudy	Convoys in Dover Straits. Manston. (Night) Aberdeen, Yorkshire, Hampshire, S. Wales, Bristol, Filton (airfield and Bristol Co.'s works).	3	5
23	Cloudy, showers	Minor activity. (Night) Bristol, S. Wales, Cardiff.	2	0
24	Fine	Violent increase in Luftwaffe activity. Ramsgate, Dover, Portsmouth, and airfields (Manston five times, Hornchurch, N. Weald). (Night) S. Wales, Birmingham (aircraft factory), north-east coast and *unintentional bombs on central London.*	38	22

Date	Weather conditions	Targets and Activity	LOSSES Luftwaffe	RAF
25	Fine, then cloudy	Driffield. Airfields in south-east, south and south-west (Warmwell), the bombers heavily escorted. (Night) *RAF bomb Berlin in retaliation for bombs on London.*	20	16
26	Cloudy, brighter later	*Fierce and effective raids on airfields (especially Debden) mark the period of Fighter Command's greatest strain.* Dover, Folkestone. Ineffective attacks on Hornchurch and Portsmouth. (Night) Coventry, Birmingham, Plymouth.	41	31
27	Cloudy, rain	Weather restricts enemy action. (Night) Widely scattered raids on airfields and industrial areas. *German army invasion plan settled.*	9	1
28	Fair over land, cloudy over sea	Airfields (Eastchurch, Rochford). Luftwaffe fighters in sweeps. After further heavy losses the Defiant fighter is pulled out of the daylight battle. (Night) *Much heavier night raiding begins* – c. 160 bombers against Merseyside, 180 elsewhere. In 600 sorties by night, *Luftflotte* 3 has lost only 7 aircraft.	30	20
29	Cloudy, clearing later	Some 700 Luftwaffe fighters in provocative sweeps to which RAF do not respond. The Chief of Kesselring's fighter organisation claims unlimited fighter superiority has been achieved. South and south-east airfields. (Night) Heavy raiding continues against Merseyside (176 sorties) and elsewhere (44 sorties).	17	9
30	Fine	Very heavy bombing of airfields (Lympne, Biggin Hill twice, Detling). Vauxhall works at Luton. (Night) Heavy bombing again on Merseyside.	36	26
31	Fine	Very heavy bombing of airfields (Detling, Eastchurch, Croydon, and sector stations Biggin Hill, Hornchurch twice, and Debden). Some close to unserviceability. Radar stations also attacked. (Night) Merseyside heavily, Midlands.	41	39

September

Date	Weather conditions	Targets and Activity	LOSSES Luftwaffe	RAF
1	Fine	Tilbury, Chatham. South-east airfields (Debden, and severe damage at Biggin Hill, Eastchurch, Detling). (Night) Bristol, S. Wales, Midlands, Merseyside.	14	15
2	Fine	Several airfields (including Biggin Hill, Lympne, Detling, Eastchurch three times, Hornchurch twice, Gravesend). Rochester (aircraft factory). (Night) Merseyside, Midlands, Manchester, Sheffield.	35	31
3	Fine	Airfields again (Manston, West Malling, much damage at North Weald) and	16	16

286

Date	Weather conditions	Targets and Activity	LOSSES	
			Luftwaffe	RAF

		heavy fighting. (Night) Merseyside, S. Wales, south-east England. *Hitler moves target date for invasion from 15 to 21 September. Decision to be taken ten days beforehand.*		
4	Fine	Airfields (Bradwell, Lympne, Eastchurch twice). Medway towns (aircraft factory at Rochester), Weybridge (aircraft factory). (Night) Liverpool, Bristol, south-east England. *Hitler publicly threatens invasion, also reprisals for British bombing of German towns.*	25	17
5	Fine	Biggin Hill yet again, and Detling. Thameshaven oiltanks set on fire (extinguished).	23	20
6	Fine	Airfields in south-east including Biggin Hill. Rochester and Weybridge (aircraft factories). A few Ju 87s employed again, and roughly handled, as were the Poles of 303 Sqdn. Heavy and accurate attack on oil targets at Thameshaven: fires not extinguished attract further attack during the night. Coastal Command's Photographic Reconnaissance Unit during the week has photographed steadily growing numbers of invasion craft in the Dutch, Belgian and French Channel ports, which from 5 September have come under attack from Bomber Command. *British order Invasion Alert No. 2 – attack probable within three days.*	35	23
		In the period from *Adlertag* on 13 August to 6 September, characterised by repeated attacks on the British airfields, the Luftwaffe has lost about 670 aircraft, Fighter Command 400. Fighter Command is holding its own, but is running down. The danger-points are that wastage of fighters is exceeding production, that a shortage of skilled pilots has developed, and that there has been much damage to the sector stations. Fortunately the Germans are about to switch to a different main objective.		
7	Fine	*The Luftwaffe switches to London,* granting relief to the airfields: the turning-point in the Battle. Some 1,000 enemy aircraft over and around the capital by day, followed by heavy night raid. Thameshaven and the London docks the main objective in both cases. *Code-word 'Cromwell' brings British forces to highest pitch of readiness and action stations.*	41	28
8	Fine	Lull by day. London bombed heavily by night. Dowding's 'Squadron	15	2

Date	Weather conditions	Targets and Activity	LOSSES Luftwaffe	RAF
9	Fine	Stabilization' scheme introduced. Thames Estuary, Southampton. Major attack with some 200 bombers on London frustrated by 11 and 12 Groups, jettisoned bombs damaging suburbs widely.	28	19
10	Cloudy, rain	Slight activity. (Night) London, S. Wales, Merseyside. Bomber Command raid on Eindhoven airfield knocks out ten He 111s. *Hitler postpones taking decision on the invasion until 14 September.*	4	1
11	Cloudy, then fine	Four airfields. London, Southampton, Portsmouth. (Night) London, Merseyside.	25	29
12	Rain	Slight activity. The German barge concentrations still growing. (Night) London, S. Wales, Midlands, Merseyside.	4	0
13	Showers, bright intervals	Small raids only on London – little damage. (Night) London. All forces of Bomber Command, day and night, attack invasion ports and continue during next fortnight.	4	1
14	Showers, bright intervals	South London and radar stations. (Night) London, S. Wales. *Hitler still pinning his faith on the Luftwaffe postpones invasion decision for three more days, i.e. until 17 September.* Earliest date for invasion would then be 27 September.	14	14
15	Fine	Largest ever German formations over London and south-east, in two big raids, but mainly broken up by the 24 Fighter Command squadrons operating on this day, since known as Battle of Britain Day. An undisputed victory. Attacks also on Portland and Southampton. (Night) London, Midlands.	60	26
16	Cloudy, rain	Slight activity, mainly in south-east and East Anglia. (Night) London, Midlands, Merseyside.	9	1
17	Cloudy, showers	Activity as for the previous day, few bombers but fighter sweeps. British bombers sink 84 barges at Dunkirk. (Night) London, Merseyside. *Hitler postpones invasion indefinitely,* but orders preparations to continue.	8	5
18	Showers	The few daylight bombers, some attacking oil targets in the Estuary, suffer badly, nine Ju 88s of III/KG77 being shot down in 2 or 3 minutes. (Night) London, Merseyside. *Germans begin to disperse invasion fleet to avoid further damage from bombing.*	19	12
19	Showers	Little daylight activity. (Night) London, Merseyside and routine minelaying.	0	0
20	Showers	Heavy fighter-sweep towards London leads to dogfights, the outcome	7	7

| Date | Weather conditions | Targets and Activity | LOSSES | |
			Luftwaffe	RAF
		favouring the Luftwaffe more than usual. (Night) London.		
21	Fine later	Fighter-sweeps in east Kent. (Night) London, Merseyside.	0	0
22	Fog, showers	Slight activity. (Night) London, Merseyside.	1	0
23	Fine	Sweeps towards London. (Night) London, Merseyside.	9	11
24	Fine	Tilbury, Southampton (Woolston Spitfire factory damaged by fighter-bombers). (Night) London, Merseyside.	11	4
25	Fine	Plymouth, Portland, Bristol (Filton). Further attack by heavily escorted bombers on aircraft factories. (Night) London, S. Wales, Lancashire.	13	4
26	Fine	Southampton. Woolston factory gutted but Spitfire production now well dispersed.	9	9
27	Fine	London, Bristol. Heavily escorted bomber raids on London and Filton largely frustrated, with big losses to Ju 88s and Kesselring's fighters. (Night) London, Midlands, Merseyside.	55	28
28	Fine	London, Solent. Scattered bomber raids massively escorted, with inevitable consequences. Hurricanes particularly suffering. (Night) London.	16	16
29	Fine	Some activity, reduced, in south-east and E. Anglia. Liverpool bombed in daylight from the west, but raid intercepted. (Night) London, Merseyside.	5	5
30	Fine	London, Westland factory at Yeovil (attack defeated). On this last day of mass daylight bomber raids the Luftwaffe reintroduces expensively discredited tactics and pays a heavy price in bombers and fighters for negligible damage. (Night) London.	48	20
October				
1	Fair	A new phase opens in which the Germans use their main bomber force almost entirely under cover of darkness. In daylight they send over only small numbers of fast Ju 88s together with Messerschmitt fighters at high altitude carrying bombs, protected by further fighters above. This activity occurs every day and proves extremely difficult to deal with, but strategically is of little benefit to the Germans. At night London is bombed heavily (by an average of 150 bombers) every night of the month except one 'Fighter-bomber sweeps' and 'London' are the entries to be understood for each date in this month.	6	4
2	Fine		10	1
3	Rain	Within the standard activity, a single Ju 88 hits the de Havilland factory at Hatfield.	9	1

Date	Weather conditions	Targets and Activity	LOSSES Luftwaffe	RAF
4	Fog, rain	At their meeting Hitler informs Mussolini that only the lack of five days of consecutively good weather has frustrated his invasion plans.	12	3
5	Showers, bright periods	West Malling and Detling airfields. Southampton bombed without opposition in the air.	13	8
6	Rain	Small raids penetrate to several airfields (Middle Wallop, Northolt, Biggin Hill).	6	1
7	Cloud, showers	Heavier raid by escorted Ju 88s on Westland factory at Yeovil. Little damage and 7 of the enemy shot down.	21	17
8	Fair	Attack on Rootes' works at Speke.	14	4
9	Cloud, rain	Airfields in the south-east.	9	3
10	Showers, bright intervals	Fighter-bombers in streams, great difficulty in intercepting.	4	4
11	Fair			
12	Fog, clearing	Biggin Hill, Kenley. *Hitler postpones invasion until – if then thought advisable – the spring of 1941.*	11	10
13	Fog, clearing		5	2
14	Rain	(Night) Heaviest raid on London thus far. Coventry also bombed.	4	0
15	Fair	For once, RAF fighters bounce high-flying Me 109s out of the sun, shooting down 4. (Night) Heavier still on London – 400+ bombers. Much damage and many railway termini out of action.	14	15
16	Cloudy	With the autumn weather, accident casualties on both sides from now on often exceed combat casualties.	13	1
17	Showery, bright intervals		15	3
18	Fog	Goering praises his fighter pilots for inflicting such terrible losses on Fighter Command, and his bomber pilots for having 'reduced the British plutocracy to fear and terror'.	15	4
19	Cloud		5	2
20	Cloud	High-flying fighter-bombers revert to mass attacks in place of streams.	14	4
21	Fog		6	0
22	Fog	Five German crashes lead to loss of several senior officers.	11	5
23	Cloudy	(Night) Glasgow as well as London.	3	1
24	Cloudy		8	4
25	Cloudy	Airfield at Montrose. (Night) Italians reluctantly allowed by the Germans to join in the bombing (Harwich), but with dismal results.	20	10
26	Cloudy, showers		10	4
27	Cloudy	Seven airfields attacked. Continuing fighter-bomber raids and individual tip-and-run bomber attacks force Fighter Command to fly over 1,000 sorties. That it can do so is proof of its continuing strength.	15	10
28	Cloudy		11	2
29	Fair	Portsmouth, Ramsgate, N. Weald. Tactical foresight leads to the shooting	19	7

Date	Weather conditions	Targets and Activity	LOSSES Luftwaffe	RAF
		down of 11 high-flying Me 109s in 6 minutes. The Italians reappear briefly by day with 15 bombers and 73 fighters, the CR42 biplanes causing more puzzlement than anxiety.		
30	Rain	Unsuccessful attempt to penetrate to London by day.	8	5
31	Rain	The great Battle fizzles out damply, the Germans having exhausted every tactical alternative after being deprived of their best chance of victory by the inept decision of their Supreme Command to attack London rather than continue with the direct offensive against Fighter Command and its ground installations.	0	0

Appendix III
Basic Information Concerning RAF Fighter Command and Luftwaffe Aircraft Involved in The Battle of Britain

British

Fighters:

	MAX. SPEED	CEILING IN FT	ARMAMENT
Hurricane I	316 mph @ 17,500 ft	32,000	8 × .303 mg
Spitfire I	355 mph @ 19,000 ft	34,000	8 × .303 mg
Defiant	304 mph @ 17,000 ft	30,000	4 × .303 mg
Blenheim IV	266 mph @ 11,000 ft	26,000	7 × .303 mg

German

Messerschmitt 109E	355 mph @ 18,000 ft	35,000	2 × 7.9 mm mg 2 × 20 mm cannon (variable)
Messerschmitt 110	345 mph @ 23,000 ft	33,000	6 × 7.9 mm mg 2 × 20 mm cannon

Bombers:

Junkers 87B	245 mph @ 15,000 ft	23,000	3 × 7.9 mm mg
Junkers 88	287 mph @ 14,000 ft	23,000	3 × 7.9 mm mg
Dornier 17	255 mph @ 21,000 ft	21,000	7 × 7.9 mm mg
(Dornier 215 slightly enhanced performance)			
Heinkel III	240 mph @ 14,000 ft	26,000	7 × 7.9 mm mg

Appendix IV
RAF Fighter Command Order of Battle 8 August 1940

HQ Bentley Priory, Stanmore
(Air Chief Marshal Sir Hugh Dowding)

NO. IO GROUP, BOX, WILTS.
(Air Vice-Marshal Sir Quintin Brand)

Squadron	Aircraft	Station
Pembrey Sector		
92	Spitfire	Pembrey
Filton Sector		
87	Hurricane	Exeter
213	Hurricane	Exeter
St Eval Sector		
234	Spitfire	St Eval
247 (one flight)	Gladiator	Roborough
Middle Wallop Sector		
238	Hurricane	Middle Wallop
609 (West Riding)	Spitfire	Middle Wallop
604 (County of Middlesex)	Blenheim	Middle Wallop
152	Spitfire	Warmwell

NO. II GROUP, UXBRIDGE
(Air Vice-Marshal K. R. Park)

Squadron	Aircraft	Station
Tangmere Sector		
43	Hurricane	Tangmere
601 (County of London)	Hurricane	Tangmere
145	Hurricane	Westhampnett
Kenley Sector		
615	Hurricane	Kenley
64	Spitfire	Kenley
111	Hurricane	Croydon
Biggin Hill Sector		
32	Hurricane	Biggin Hill
610 (County of Chester)	Spitfire	Biggin Hill
501 (County of Gloucester)	Hurricane	Gravesend
600 (City of London)	Blenheim	Manston
Hornchurch Sector		
54	Spitfire	Hornchurch
65	Spitfire	Hornchurch
74	Spitfire	Hornchurch
41	Spitfire	Hornchurch

Squadron	Aircraft	Station
	Northolt Sector	
1	Hurricane	Northolt
257	Hurricane	Northolt
	North Weald Sector	
151	Hurricane	North Weald
56	Hurricane	Rochford
25	Blenheim	Martlesham
	Debden Sector	
17	Hurricane	Debden
85	Hurricane	Martlesham

NO. 12 GROUP, WATNALL, NOTTS.
(Air Vice-Marshal T. L. Leigh-Mallory)

Squadron	Aircraft	Station
	Duxford Sector	
19	Spitfire	Duxford
	Coltishall Sector	
242	Hurricane	Coltishall
66	Spitfire	Coltishall
	Wittering Sector	
229	Hurricane	Wittering
266	Spitfire	Wittering
23	Blenheim	Colly Weston
	Digby Sector	
46	Hurricane	Digby
611 (West Lancashire)	Spitfire	Digby
29	Blenheim	Digby
	Kirton-in-Lindsey Sector	
222	Spitfire	Kirton-in-Lindsey
264	Defiant	Kirton-in-Lindsey and Ringway
	Church Fenton Sector	
73	Hurricane	Church Fenton
249	Hurricane	Church Fenton
616 (South Yorkshire)	Spitfire	Leconfield

NO. 13 GROUP, NEWCASTLE UPON TYNE
(Air Vice-Marshal R. E. Saul)

Squadron	Aircraft	Station
	Catterick Sector	
219	Blenheim	Catterick
	Usworth Sector	
607	Hurricane	Usworth
72	Spitfire	Acklington
79	Spitfire	Acklington
	Turnhouse Sector	
232 (one flight)	Hurricane	Turnhouse
253	Hurricane	Turnhouse
605 (County of Warwick)	Hurricane	Drem
141	Defiant	Prestwick

Squadron	Aircraft	Station
	Dyce Sector	
603 (City of Edinburgh)	Spitfire	Dyce and Montrose
	Wick Sector	
3	Hurricane	Wick
504 (County of Nottingham)	Hurricane	Castletown
232 (one flight)	Hurricane	Sumburgh
	Aldergrove Sector	
245	Hurricane	Aldergrove

Total   55½ squadrons (28 Hurricane, 19 Spitfire, 6 Blenheim [night], 2 Defiant, ½ Gladiator).

Appendix V
RAF Fighter Command Order of Battle 7 September 1940

HQ Bentley Priory, Stanmore
(Air Chief Marshal Sir Hugh Dowding)

NO. 10 GROUP, BOX, WILTS.
(Air Vice-Marshal Sir Quintin Brand)

Squadron	Aircraft	Station
	Pembrey Sector	
92	Spitfire	Pembrey
	Filton Sector	
87	Hurricane	Exeter and Bibury
213	Hurricane	Exeter
	St Eval Sector	
238	Hurricane	St Eval
247 (one flight)	Gladiator	Roborough
	Middle Wallop Sector	
234	Spitfire	Middle Wallop
609 (West Riding)	Spitfire	Middle Wallop
604 (County of Middlesex)	Blenheim	Middle Wallop
56	Hurricane	Boscombe Down
152	Spitfire	Warmwell

NO. 11 GROUP, UXBRIDGE
(Air Vice-Marshal K. R. Park)

Squadron	Aircraft	Station
	Tangmere Sector	
43	Hurricane	Tangmere
601 (County of London)	Hurricane	Tangmere
602 (City of Glasgow)	Spitfire	Westhampnett
	Kenley Sector	
66	Spitfire	Kenley
253	Hurricane	Kenley
72	Spitfire	Croydon
111	Hurricane	Croydon
	Biggin Hill Sector	
79	Spitfire	Biggin Hill
501 (County of Gloucester)	Hurricane	Gravesend

Squadron	Aircraft	Station
Hornchurch Sector		
222	Spitfire	Hornchurch
603 (City of Edinburgh)	Spitfire	Hornchurch
600 (City of London)	Blenheim	Hornchurch
41	Spitfire	Rochford
Northolt Sector		
1 (Royal Canadian Air Force)	Hurricane	Northolt
303 (Polish)	Hurricane	Northolt
504 (County of Nottingham)	Hurricane	Northolt
1	Hurricane	Heath Row
North Weald Sector		
249	Hurricane	North Weald
46	Hurricane	Stapleford Abbots
Debden Sector		
17	Hurricane	Debden
257	Hurricane	Martlesham and North Weald
25	Blenheim	Martlesham
73	Hurricane	Castle Camps

NO. 12 GROUP, WATNALL, NOTTS.
(Air Vice-Marshal T. L. Leigh-Mallory)

Squadron	Aircraft	Station
Duxford Sector		
19	Spitfire	Duxford
310 (Czechoslovak)	Hurricane	Duxford
Coltishall Sector		
242	Hurricane	Coltishall
616 (South Yorkshire)	Spitfire	Coltishall
266	Spitfire	Coltishall and Wittering
Wittering Sector		
23	Blenheim	Wittering
229	Hurricane	Wittering and Bircham Newton
Digby Sector		
151	Hurricane	Digby
611 (West Lancashire)	Spitfire	Digby
29	Blenheim	Digby
Kirton-in-Lindsey Sector		
74	Spitfire	Kirton-in-Lindsey
264	Defiant	Kirton-in-Lindsey
Church Fenton Sector		
85	Hurricane	Church Fenton
302 (Polish)	Hurricane	Church Fenton
64	Spitfire	Church Fenton and Ringway

NO. 13 GROUP, NEWCASTLE UPON TYNE
(Air Vice-Marshal R. E. Saul)

Squadron	Aircraft	Station
Catterick Sector		
54	Spitfire	Catterick

Squadron	Aircraft	Station
219	Blenheim	Catterick
	Usworth Sector	
607	Hurricane	Usworth
610 (County of Chester)	Spitfire	Acklington
32	Hurricane	Acklington
	Turnhouse Sector	
65	Spitfire	Turnhouse
141	Defiant	Turnhouse
605 (County of Warwick)	Hurricane	Drem
615	Hurricane	Prestwick
	Dyce Sector	
145	Hurricane	Dyce and Montrose
	Wick Sector	
3	Hurricane	Castletown
232 (one flight)	Hurricane	Sumburgh
	Aldergrove Sector	
245	Hurricane	Aldergrove

Total 59½ squadrons (31 Hurricane, 20 Spitfire, 6 Blenheim [night], 2 Defiant, ½ Gladiator).